Agro-industrial Labour in Kenya

Gerda Kuiper

Agro-industrial Labour in Kenya

Cut Flower Farms and Migrant Workers' Settlements

palgrave
macmillan

Gerda Kuiper
Global South Studies Centre
University of Cologne
Köln, Germany

ISBN 978-3-030-18045-4 ISBN 978-3-030-18046-1 (eBook)
https://doi.org/10.1007/978-3-030-18046-1

Cover illustration: Maram_shutterstock.com

This Palgrave Macmillan imprint is published by the registered company Springer Nature Switzerland AG.
The registered company address is: Gewerbestrasse 11, 6330 Cham, Switzerland

Acknowledgements

Although I have spent many hours alone behind my computer screen, writing this book has been far from a solitary process and I have to thank a number of people for their contributions and support.

First of all, I am grateful to everyone in Naivasha who helped me with this research and who spent time with me while I was there. Special thanks go out to my assistants and key informants (most of all to those whom I call Flora, Lucy, and Richard in this book) and to the management and employees of "Karibu Farm". I would not have been able to write this book without their cooperation and interest.

This book was originally written as a PhD thesis. I thank my PhD supervisor Michael Bollig for initiating the (sub)project of which this research formed a part and for his constructive comments over the past five years. In addition, I thank David Anderson, Dorothea Schulz, and participants in several colloquia and workshops in Cologne and Bonn for their comments on preliminary ideas and on draft chapters. My inclusion into another subproject led by Clemens Greiner and Patrick Sakdapolrak provided me with some extra time to finish this book while it also gave me the opportunity to look at my data from a new angle.

I thank the staff from project partners in Kenya, the British Institute in Eastern Africa and the National Museums of Kenya, for their assistance with cars and permits. I also thank Anne Wegner for proofreading parts of the original dissertation, Monika Feinen for making the maps, and Ken Ondoro for the initial assistance with statistical analysis.

I am grateful to both the "Ethnodocs" in Cologne and my fellow PhD students from the "RCR" research group for the supportive working environment they created. Most notably, I shared much of this journey (sometimes literally) with Hauke-Peter Vehrs, Marie Gravesen, Andreas Gemählich, Matian van Soest, Innocent Mwaka, Johanna Treidl, and Elsemi Olwage, which has been a great pleasure.

Last but not least I thank my husband Seif Chinowa for being extremely supportive throughout the whole project, and my son Amani Chinowa for his patience with his restless mother during the final stages of finishing this book.

Contents

Abbreviations

AEA	Agricultural Employers' Association
AR	Annual Report
CBA	Collective Bargaining Agreement
COTU	Central Organization of Trade Unions
DC	District Commissioner
DO	District Officer
HR	Human Resources
KES	Kenyan Shilling
KFC	Kenya Flower Council
KHRC	Kenya Human Rights Commission
KISIP	Kenya Informal Settlements Improvement Project
KNA	Kenya National Archives
KNBS	Kenya National Bureau of Statistics
KPAWU	Kenya Plantation & Agricultural Workers Union
LNGG	Lake Naivasha Growers' Group
LNRA	Lake Naivasha Riparian Association
LNROA	Lake Naivasha Riparian Owners' Association (previous name of the LNRA)
NGO	Non-Governmental Organization
PPE	Personal Protective Equipment
SACCO	Saving and Credit Co-operative

List of Figures

List of Tables

CHAPTER 1

Introduction

Lake Naivasha in Kenya is marked by the presence of an export-oriented cut flower industry. The shores of the lake are scattered with greenhouses and production fields, interspersed with densely populated settlements and a few farm compounds where the farm workers live. The main road—Moi Lake Road—is used intensively by trucks transporting the flowers to the airport in Nairobi and by staff buses bringing workers to the farms and back to the settlements. Bus stop shelters, boreholes, and clinics carry the names of sponsoring flower farms.

Despite the flower industry's distinct presence, Naivasha[1] is a varied place. The greenhouses are landmarks in the landscape, yet the flower farms occupy relatively little space. Perhaps surprisingly, considering the presence of this agro-industry, Naivasha is also a well-known environmental conservation area. The ecosystem of the lake is characterized by a high biodiversity, especially of birds and plants. Hell's Gate National Park and several private conservancies are located in the lake's vicinity. Partly because of these natural attractions, Naivasha has developed into a popular destination for both international and domestic tourists. In addition, it has become an important site for geothermal energy production since the 1980s (Becht, Odada, & Higgins, 2005). This modest use of space by the flower industry stands in contrast to other types of agro-industrial enterprises, where the fields dominate the landscape. Sydney Mintz, in his work on the sugar cane industry in the Caribbean, described how he felt himself "floating in a sea of cane". Cane occupied almost all space, except for the

G. Kuiper, *Agro-industrial Labour in Kenya*,
https://doi.org/10.1007/978-3-030-18046-1_1

road, villages, and an occasional barren field (1985, p. xviii). In comparison, Naivasha has a varied landscape and a varied economy. Despite the flower industry's dominant presence, there also remains space for wildlife, geothermal power plants, tourist hotels, fishermen, and pastoralists.[2]

Nevertheless, as Kioko (2012, p. 38) remarked, the main economic activities in the area all depend directly or indirectly on the lake's resources. It is therefore not surprising that the flower industry has attracted much scrutiny for possible damage caused to the environment. Labour conditions on the farms have also been questioned. The flower farms, primarily financed by foreign investors, provide ten thousands of jobs in this previously rural area. The industry has attracted scores of labour migrants from other regions in Kenya, who mostly have come to reside in one of the unplanned settlements along the Moi Lake Road. Naivasha therefore has an urban appearance, despite its reliance on an agro-industry, which is usually associated with rural areas. According to the most recent national population and housing census, the area had 376,243 inhabitants in 2009 (Kenya National Bureau of Statistics [KNBS], 2010). The population is also shifting, as migrant workers are moving in and out of Naivasha.

Whereas most research studies carried out in Naivasha have ignored these migrant workers, the numerous media reports and campaigns of non-governmental organizations (NGOs) on the flower industry have depicted the workers in a generalizing manner. Little attention has been paid to the workers' pasts or their future plans, or to their position outside the farms. The experiences of these migrant workers in the Naivasha settlements deserve more attention than they have received until now. Moreover, agro-industrial labour in general has received little attention in social scientific literature, especially when it comes to farms and plantations on the African continent. This ethnography addresses this lacuna and follows the migrant workers who look for a flower farm job from their arrival in Naivasha to their departure.

1.1 Lake Naivasha: A Contested Research Site

Lake Naivasha has been researched intensively and, as a result, much is known about its biophysical features. Becht et al. (2005), Mavuti and Harper (2006), and Harper, Morrison, Macharia, Mavuti, and Upton (2011) provide comprehensive introductions to the geological, ecological, and economic characteristics of Lake Naivasha and its surroundings. Lake Naivasha lies at an altitude of approximately 1890 metres above sea level and is situated in the semi-arid Eastern Rift Valley, about 100 kilometres north of the Kenyan capital, Nairobi. It is one of the few freshwater lakes in the Rift Valley and is fed by the rivers Malewa and Gilgil. As the lake is very shallow, its surface fluctuates tremendously whenever water levels change: "The water level can change several metres within a few months, causing a horizontal change of several kilometres" (Mavuti & Harper, 2006, p. 30). Soils developed on volcanic ashes and therefore do not retain water well, making frequent irrigation necessary for farming. This need for irrigation meant that large-scale cultivation did not take place in the area for a long time. Instead, the area was used for keeping livestock, first by Maasai pastoralists, and since the early twentieth century by colonial settlers. It was not until the 1960s that farmers started to use the lake water for irrigation for the production of vegetables, followed by the production of flowers.

There were several reasons for horticultural firms to choose Naivasha as a production site. One reason was the existing infrastructure and the relative proximity to an international airport. Also the presence of good and affordable labour made Naivasha attractive. At least as important were the availability of irrigation water and the favourable climatic conditions. The temperatures and light intensity associated with Naivasha's altitude are agreeable to the crop and therefore reduce production costs considerably when compared to production in Europe (Kazimierczuk, Kamau, Kinuthia, & Mukoko, 2018, p. 31; Whitaker & Kolavalli, 2006, p. 337).

The export of flowers from Kenya to (mainly) European markets has increased steadily ever since the industry started. Statistics from the Kenyan Horticultural Crop Directorate indicate a growth from a modest 3264 metric tons of exported flowers in 1973 to 120,221 metric tons in 2010. The most recent data over 2017 show that the industry continues to grow, as export volumes increased further to 159,961 metric tons. Kenya is therewith the largest flower-exporting country to the European markets (Kenya Flower Council [KFC], 2019; Mwembe, 1979). It is therefore not surprising that the industry figures in a World Bank report titled *Technology, Adaptation, and Exports. How Some Developing Countries Got It Right* (Whitaker & Kolavalli, 2006). At the same time, the industry has faced massive critique for possible environmental harm and exploitative labour conditions.

Numerous, mostly foreign, researchers have studied the ecological, biological, and hydrological state of the lake and the catchment area. This body of research has investigated how resilient Naivasha's ecological system is to major changes that have taken place. This includes the rise of the flower industry, with a concurring influx of migrant workers, but also the increase in tourism and the introduction of alien plant and animal species into the lake. Within these studies, people were initially either completely ignored or their presence and their economic activities were mainly seen as problematic and detrimental to the local environment (Becht & Harper, 2002; Mavuti & Harper, 2006). More recently, researchers have started to pay attention to the social aspects of ecological changes in Naivasha (see, for instance, Morrison, Upton, Pacini, Odhiambo-K'oyooh, & Harper, 2013). But also these researchers take the ecological state of the area as their starting point. Few studies have taken the major social transformations as a point of departure. Exceptions are a recent article by Lowthers (2018) and studies on the Kenyan flower industry in general (Dolan, 2007; Gibbon & Riisgaard, 2014; Kazimierczuk et al., 2018; Riisgaard & Gibbon, 2014). Additionally, I have been able to build on a handful of exploratory studies by master's students, carried out within the framework of the research group[3] of which my research formed a part (Kioko, 2012; an unpublished thesis by Hanna Kunas; Lang & Sakdapolrak, 2014; Lembcke, 2015).

Even though the Naivasha flower farms received remarkably little scholarly attention up till now, the industry caught the attention of critical journalists and of national and international NGOs. These activists examined possible environmental damage caused by the production of flowers and investigated the work and living conditions of the so-called general workers of the farms: the employees at the bottom of the farm hierarchy who do not have a specific job description. The activists have voiced their findings and concerns through numerous news items, reports, websites, and television broadcasts. The critical reports—succinctly summarized by Kazimierczuk et al. (2018, p. 5)—exposed the industry to negative media attention both in Kenya and in the main market, Europe. The main product of the industry—the rose—sparks the imagination, and NGO and media reports on the industry that appeared within Kenya carry expressive titles such as *Wilting in Bloom* (Kenya Human Rights Commission [KHRC], 2012) and "Naivasha's Withering Rose" (Opala, 2007). An example of international exposure is a former campaign by the large Dutch NGO Hivos, targeting the Dutch market. The campaign website (Hivos, n.d.) criticized the flower industry for long working hours, low payment, a lack of proper housing, job insecurity, the danger of chemicals to employees, and cases of sexual harassment. As asserted by Dolan (2007), the flower industry thus became a symbol for gross injustices within globalized capitalism.

Concerns about labour conditions in the industry have also brought forth a mass of NGO-commissioned research reports and social science studies. Numerous, often foreign, consultants and researchers have conducted quick surveys and more in-depth research within Kenyan flower farms. Studies appeared on ethical standards within these farms (Dolan, Opondo, & Smith, 2003), on labour rights (KHRC, 2012), and on the value chain of the flowers (Hale & Opondo, 2005). The main goal of those studies has usually been to evaluate the flower industry against certain international standards or labour laws. They usually do not pay attention to how workers themselves evaluate and value their work. In such reports, and especially in NGO campaigns based on them, workers are described in a stereotypical manner. They are typified as being unskilled, originating from rural areas in the western parts of Kenya, predominately female (moreover, mostly single mothers), and young. Although there is some truth in these descriptions, this book will show that they are too generalizing.

Hivos' online campaign (n.d.), for instance, edited out all the men employed by the flower industry and made sweeping statements about conditions in the industry:

> The campaign "Power of the Fair Trade Flower" tells the story of women in the African flower industry. Every year, billions of flowers are being shipped from Africa to our country. Flowers which are being cultivated and harvested by women. Often under bad conditions. Elementary labour rights are being violated, sexual harassment is rampant and exposure to pesticides harms the health of the workers. [My translation from Dutch]

But do such alarming descriptions do justice to the situation on the farms? When considering this example of selective representation of the industry's workers, it seems problematic that the discourses these campaigns have put forward have become hegemonic in consumer markets in Europe, despite all good intentions. It is also not surprising that the flower industry has attempted to counteract such discourses through the creation of its own lobbying organizations. Much is at stake for both farms and workers, and these different representations have real effects. An example is an increased influence of consumer standards that impact labour conditions within the farms.

The question what is happening on the farms in Naivasha as well as in the settlements where the flower farm workers live is clearly highly contested. I argue that, to attain a more nuanced understanding of the position of workers in Naivasha's agro-industry, this question deserves more scholarly attention than it has received until now.

1.2 Ethnographic Research in an Agro-Industrial Context

Naivasha is a dynamic, diverse, and by times contradictory place. Consequently my fieldwork days were also varied. I moved between different and sometimes even contrasting circumstances within short time spans and within a relatively confined geographical space. To give an impression of some of the eventful encounters I had, I here provide a description of one of the fieldwork days.

One morning in April 2015, my assistant Richard[4] and I met at my house in Naivasha Town, got on the car, and headed towards the northern part of the lake, where we went for an interview and a tour on a vegetable farm. The aim of this visit was to get an impression of the production process of vegetables, in order to be able to compare it to the processes on the flower farms. One of the farm managers, a Kenyan man, showed us around the fields and the packing and storage area. After this tour of the production site, Richard and I took a look at the workers' compound on the premises of the farm, which used to be a livestock ranch in previous times. It was only then that Richard told me that he was born there. His grandfather had worked on the ranch as a mechanic. However, he also told me that his mother, a civil servant working for a local government office in Naivasha Town, does not like to go back to this place, which she associates with poverty. Furthermore, in the eyes of Richard himself, the compound had become dilapidated compared to 20 years ago when he lived there as a small child. When we visited, we found mainly wattle-and-daub houses with thatched roofs (unlike the roofs of corrugated iron common in the unplanned settlements), plus a few brick buildings for management. The few functional buildings—such as the first shop in the area and the social hall where Richard's aunt had had her wedding reception years ago—seemed to be no longer in use, presumably because their functions have been taken over by newer facilities in Kasarani, the more recently established settlement next to the farm.

We left the farm by noon and headed for this settlement. We paid a visit to Richard's aunt and uncle, who were still living in Kasarani and who were running a small grocery store there. Most of the days that I visited this settlement, I would pass some time at their store. The shop was a quiet spot, from where I could observe the daily movements in the settlement. On this day, one of the customers of the grocery shop started to chat and asked me whether I already knew Jesus. This opened up a conversation, and when I told him about my research, he explained to me that he used to work on a flower farm himself. However, some years ago, he had made a career move and had become a pastor in one of the many Pentecostal churches in the area.

I had lunch at the house of Lucy, a friend whom I will introduce further in Section 3.1.2. We knew each other from my visits to "Karibu Farm",[5] the flower farm where she works as a supervisor. Lucy lives in a regular one-room brick apartment with her husband and two young children. Like most migrant workers, they are tenants in Naivasha. However, Lucy and her husband have managed to acquire a *shamba* (plot of land, used for cultivation) in the western part of Kenya. When I visited her on this day in April, she had just been travelling to her "home" the week before. She had planted maize on their plot and had visited her family on the way. She had not had a resting day since she had come back. She therefore was very tired and I did not stay long.

Later that afternoon I had an appointment with Oria Rocco. Rocco's parents were a French-Italian couple who came to the area during colonial times. Their daughter still lived on a remaining part of their estate, located not far from Kasarani, in a beautiful colonial house set in a green environment full of signs of wildlife. She told me about the changes in Naivasha since the flower industry emerged. However, she surprised me most already before I actually met her, when I was still in Kasarani and called her from there. I asked her at which time I should come, and she replied in a matter-of-fact way that I could come once I heard her husband leaving with his airplane. This sign of wealth stood in stark contrast to the modest environment of next-door Kasarani.

After this interview, Richard and I headed back to Naivasha Town. We gave a lift to another supervisor of Karibu Farm, Yvonne, who went to town for her day off the next day. This gave her the opportunity to see her children, who lived in Naivasha Town with her sister. During our 40-minute drive, Yvonne told us enthusiastically about the process of planting new seedlings in "her" greenhouse.

Thus, within one day, I met a range of people who lived and worked on the same few square kilometres and who in multiple ways related to each other but at the same time had very different positions in life. Days such as this one, including its extremes—where I moved between affluence and "abject poverty",[6] from green space and pristine wildlife to orderly greenhouses and vegetable fields and to cramped workers' housing—were common during my stay in Naivasha. These eventful days were interesting and exciting, but initially also confusing. How could I make sense of this complex, changing, and large agro-industrial area? And where could I position myself as a researcher?

1.2.1 Methodology

The variability of the area, in combination with the massive scale and the mobility of the residents, posed challenges in designing my research. My approach was rooted in the epistemological conviction that good ethnographic research is based on interactions and connections, developed over time, between the researcher and the researched (Fabian, 1971; Okely, 2012). But to whom could and should I make connections in such a large, urbanizing, agro-industrial area?

A possible way to narrow the research down would be to focus exclusively on the workplace: the flower farms themselves. This approach has been followed in much of the research on (agro-)industrial labour, for instance, by Burawoy (1979) in his classic monograph on industrial relations. In such an approach, a factory or farm is studied as an "integrated social system" (Holzberg & Giovannini, 1981, p. 328). However, I did not want to make an analytic distinction between "home" and "work". For one, workers' motivations and experiences are not constituted either at home or in the workplace but in both places. As Westwood (1984, p. 1) argued, "home and work are part of one world". Hann and Hart (2011, p. 152) likewise emphasized the interconnectedness between households, the workplace, and even regions of origin in their discussion of studies on mine workers on the Zambian Copperbelt: "it is always necessary to situate the formal workplace in a local context of households and family life, informal economy and community, as well as within the larger framework of relations between city and countryside."

Moreover, despite the high fences between farms and settlements, which at first sight indicated clear boundaries, I found the distinction between "work" and "home" to be fuzzy in Naivasha. Many migrant workers call their region of origin *nyumbani* ("home") and regard the whole of Naivasha as a "workplace", even their dwellings in the settlements where they reside. An exclusive focus on the flower farms as the place of work would not provide a comprehensive understanding of labour relations in Naivasha. Apart from a description of the farms, this book therefore also discusses the workers' settlements and even the connections to migrant workers' region of origin.

Previous social scientific and NGO-commissioned research on the Naivasha cut flower industry and the workers' settlements has been mainly based on formal interviews and focus group discussions, supplemented with secondary data (Dolan, 2007; Gibbon & Riisgaard, 2014; KHRC, 2012). Findings stemmed from standardized questionnaires, administered by researchers who would only meet the respondents once within their workplace, with permission of farm management. Occasionally, researchers have supplemented formal interviews with more intersubjective methods, such as transect walks (Lang & Sakdapolrak, 2014) and participant observation (Kioko, 2012). Partly taking inspiration from other studies on (agro-)industrial relations, I chose to apply an array of ethnographic methods, which allowed me to address processes both on the farms and in the settlements, and which provided opportunities to connect to people in diverse ways and in diverse places.

Ferguson (1999), in his monograph on (economic) crisis on the Zambian Copperbelt, aimed to develop appropriate tools to conduct anthropological research in an urban context where there is not a single "whole" to study. "I knew my informants in the way most urbanites know one another: some quite well, some only in passing, others in special-purpose relationships that gave me detailed knowledge of some areas of their lives and almost none of others" (Ferguson, 1999, p. 21). I recognized this lack of a single whole in the context of Naivasha, an ever-changing place, where most people do not stay their whole lifetime. Despite fluctuating lake levels and frequent changes in farm ownership, it is the lake and the farms that are the more constant features in Naivasha, not the people. According to Ferguson (1999, p. 21), the analytic object of study in such a fragmented urban context cannot be one space, one community, or one occupational category, but should be "a mode of conceptualizing, narrating, and experiencing socioeconomic change".

Unlike in Ferguson's case, there has not been a crisis in Naivasha. However, even the economic "boom" that Naivasha experienced has not been equally beneficial to all. Moreover, it also had its failures, such as farms going bankrupt or closing down. I therefore, like Ferguson, turned my attention towards the various ways in which different groups of Naivasha residents experience social, economic, and ecological changes and continuities. These narratives in their turn helped to understand migrant workers' position in Naivasha. With what expectations did migrant workers come to Naivasha, why did many choose to work on the farms, and how were these moves experienced by those who had arrived previously?

I applied a number of methods which helped me to systemize the research and to connect to a range of people. In order to gain broad insights into household and work characteristics of migrant labourers in Naivasha, I conducted an explorative survey among 176 residents of three locations. These locations were the workers' settlements Kasarani and Karagita, and the *kambi* (workers' compound)[7] of "Sharma Farm". Karagita, located along the Moi South Lake Road, is the most populous as well as the most notorious shantytown around Naivasha and has featured in newspaper articles about the flower industry (M. Mwangi, 2007). It is more easily accessible than Kasarani. The latter is a settlement with a more rural feel, located along the Moi North Lake Road, which was not yet tarmacked at the time I conducted the survey. Sharma Farm was a large-scale flower farm of which the ownership changed in 2007. The farm subsequently endured financial stress and was under receivership of two banks at the time I carried out the survey. Production completely came to a standstill at a later stage.

The repetitive visits to blocks of houses were helpful in familiarizing myself with the settlements and with the conditions on flower farm compounds. The survey thus functioned as a first step in making connections. Nevertheless, the survey as a method has been treated with suspicion by anthropologists. It is questionable how much information people are willing to share with a stranger. Moreover, a survey on its own shows individuals, not relationships, and shows just one moment in time. These limitations are especially poignant when studying the dynamic processes of labour migration (Moore & Vaughan, 1994; Okely, 2012; Ong, 1987; Ross & Weisner, 1977; Van Velsen, 1964). Thus, the numbers that result from the administration of a survey questionnaire can only be meaningfully interpreted with the help of observations that have been made over a longer time span, with attention for interactions (Hall, Scoones, & Tsikata, 2017; Wolf, 1992). I therefore interviewed 23 of the survey respondents at a later stage again, when I carried out interviews for one of the other methods I used. I also met again with several survey respondents during visits to farms.

Ethnographies on (agro-)industrial work are usually based on some form of (participant) observation. Many researchers—especially those who conducted research in their own society and therefore did not stand out among the workers—worked along for a period of time, sometimes as a regular labourer (Burawoy, 1979; Westwood, 1984) and sometimes more informally (Besky, 2014). Other researchers "hung around" in a factory or plantation for a substantial amount of time, observing what was going on without participating in the work (Freeman, 2000; Friedemann-Sánchez, 2009; Lee, 1998). I also spent time on flower farms and combined these two approaches. I paid one-off visits to five different farms. These visits lasted several hours and all included an interview with a manager and a farm tour. The tours allowed for observation, but they did not provide time for a more in-depth engagement with the actual work practices. I therefore visited one farm ("Karibu Farm") regularly over the course of several months. This rose-producing farm, which I here call "Karibu Farm", had around 600 employees at the time. It is immediately adjacent to Kasarani, where virtually all the employees live. Only some of the Kenyan managers and the Dutch general manager ("Jan") and his family live on the farm premises.

While the one-off farm visits were usually well orchestrated and always under the guidance of a high-ranked manager, I was allowed to move around on my own within Karibu Farm. I was "trained on the job" by supervisors in one of the greenhouses and in the packhouse, where the flowers are prepared for shipment. The supervisors explained all the work to me and let me try some of the tasks. I also attended meetings, conducted interviews, and had lunch in the farm canteen. These small attempts to working along and the "hanging around" gave me a good impression of work rhythms and processes and of labour relations.

I was warned beforehand by other researchers working on the flower industry that it would be difficult to get access to the farms, although it is deemed even more difficult for Kenyan researchers than for Europeans (M. Opondo, personal communication, February 26, 2014). Previous researchers have been forced to use "convenience sampling", as they could only include farms that were willing to cooperate in their research (Omosa, Kimani, & Njiru, 2006, p. 6). I found that most farms were open to receiving visitors, but access was always only allowed after making an appointment with the management. Moreover, there were a few farms (including the largest Naivasha flower farm with a large workers' compound) that denied access. It was therefore crucial to also employ other methods apart from on-farm (participant) observation and to approach workers in the settlements where they live.

I executed listing and piling exercises on the different types of jobs performed in the settlements and on the flower farms. Secondly, in order to recognize social structure in a place that seemed to be constantly fluctuating, I conducted two types of social network analysis, which is a classic method in studies on labour relations in industrial production

(Kapferer, 1969; Scott, 2013). I thus explored the relations between workers within one farm and between flower farm workers and their neighbours in the settlements. Thirdly, I conducted archival research and oral history interviews to understand how history had shaped workers' expectations of their stay in Naivasha. Finally, I conducted open-ended, semi-structured interviews with flower farm workers, their managers on the farms, their neighbours in the settlements with different occupations, in a few cases their relatives "back home" or their former colleagues who had left Naivasha again, and people who aimed or claimed to defend their cause such as NGOs, the trade union, and government officials.

In addition to these planned interviews, there were numerous encounters and moments for observation "in between" the more formal methods (Davies, 2008, p. 23). Walking through settlements, having lunch there, chatting with friends, teaching in a secondary school for one afternoon, giving rides to people along the way, and visiting church services were all occasions for learning. These unplanned moments filled my field diary. My "field" thus did not consist of one settlement or one farm, but was defined by my diverse encounters and repetitive contacts within the larger volatile context of Naivasha (Okely, 2012, p. 28).

1.2.2 My Position Within Social Hierarchies

I have lived in Naivasha intermittently between November 2013 and June 2016, for 13 months in total. Many researchers who work on the topic of (agro-)industrial labour stay where the workers live, mostly for part of their fieldwork (Bolt, 2016; Ong, 1987; Rutherford, 2001). I did not get permission to stay in a *kambi*. There are just a handful of farms with workers' compounds in Naivasha and none of these are very hospitable towards researchers. Although the receiving managers of Sharma Farm allowed me to conduct interviews for the survey on their premises, I always had to be accompanied by a welfare officer during these short visits. The management deemed it unsafe for me to spend time there alone, even during the day. It was thus impossible to get permission to stay there overnight.

Another possibility to stay where the workers live would have been to look for a one-room apartment in one of the workers' settlements outside the farms. I deliberated this possibility beforehand but in the end decided against it. It would be a conspicuous move for a foreign, relatively wealthy person like myself to go and live there, and I was simply unsure how people would interpret such a move and what consequences it would have for my research. In addition, I did not want to focus on one specific settlement. A final reason was that I did not stay in Naivasha alone. For the larger part of my fieldwork, I was accompanied by either my partner or fellow researchers. We rented an apartment together in a middle-class neighbourhood close to the centre of Naivasha Town. I visited the flower farms and workers' settlements around the lake from there on a daily basis.

Not only did I share a house with fellow researchers, we also collaborated extensively during the initial phases of fieldwork. I conducted the first interviews with farm managers and other stakeholders, together with geographers Andreas Gemählich and Vera Tolo, and we shared our notes and occasional interview recordings afterwards. In addition, Gemählich, who conducted research on the global value chain of the flowers, has provided me with transcripts from interviews that he conducted on his own. Wherever I make use of his interview transcripts, I mention this in a footnote.

My position as a researcher was initially shaped by this collaboration, which emphasized another feature which created a (psychological) distance to most of my interlocutors: my skin colour. I found there are surprisingly many people of European descent (*wazungu*) living around Naivasha. Some of them are members of families that have stayed there from colonial times and that have made Kenya their home. Others, for example, flower farm managers, have arrived more recently. Regardless of when they have arrived, most *wazungu* are well-off and live in fenced-off houses close to the lake or in a gated community. Even though some of them live close to the workers' settlements and even though most of them interact on a day-to-day basis with the migrant workers whom they employ in their homes or on their farms, there is an immense social distance.

My positionality in conducting research on the large-scale Naivasha cut flower farms as a young white woman from Europe can be compared and contrasted to Nungari Mwangi's positionality in her research on smallholder cut flower farmers in Kenya (2019). As a young Kikuyu woman, it was possible for Mwangi to engage with Kikuyu smallholder farmers, while it was easier for me to get access to large flower farms managed by Europeans than it is for Kenyan researchers. Whereas Kenyan researchers have experienced a lack of access to the industry, it was relatively easy for my European colleagues and myself to gain access to the large-scale flower farms. Yet, this was also a disadvantage. Whereas I appeared to be a natural ally of flower farm managers due to my skin colour, class position, and educational background, my primary aim was to engage with the migrant workers.

My interactions with farm workers and with other settlement residents were thus complicated by my status of *mzungu*. When visiting a farm, I was automatically identified as part of the management, which sometimes made workers fearful of talking to me. Interviewees in the settlements often assumed I was working for an NGO. They would therefore ask for material assistance or a job. Children approached me on the street in English and asked for or even demanded money or sweets. Being classified as an *mzungu* thus provided insights into class and race relations in Naivasha, but it was most of all an impediment to gaining people's trust. Many people, especially women, felt uneasy when meeting me for the first time. The other way around, I sometimes felt uncomfortable myself because my presence created expectations that I felt I could not fulfil.

My assistants were invaluable in the process of gaining trust. A few respondents only agreed to talk to me—an *mzungu*—after they had talked to my assistant. During my several stays I worked with five different assistants, three men and two women. They were all living in or close to Naivasha Town at the time, but had different ethnic, professional, and migration backgrounds. As Nungari Mwangi (2019, p. 23) pointed out, the (ethnic) position of assistants influences a researcher's access. I therefore chose to work with assistants from varying backgrounds, who connected to the flower industry in diverse ways. On most fieldwork days, one of them would come along to help me with establishing contacts, with driving, and with conducting interviews. These assistants were pleasant and resourceful companions. They provided me with many insights, through their own stories and opinions as well as through their interactions with others along the way.

My thorough knowledge of Swahili, acquired in Tanzania, was another important resource. Although a majority of the people in the area understand and speak (some) English, almost all of them are more comfortable with speaking Swahili or a mixture of Swahili and English. Swahili is also the "bridging" language in the area, the lingua franca. I therefore conducted most of the interviews in Swahili, although both foreign and Kenyan farm managers usually preferred to speak English, which is considered to be a more "professional" language (N. Mwangi, 2019, p. 22). My assistant Richard even urged me to speak English when introducing myself to the chiefs, local government officials, as he feared that they would not take me seriously if I would start speaking Swahili. In addition to English and Swahili, I could speak Dutch, my native tongue, to Dutch managers.[8] In a few cases interlocutors were more comfortable with speaking Kikuyu and Richard had to translate for me. These interviews were fortunately exceptions. As Fabian (1971, p. 33) asserted, knowledge is constituted through language, and therefore the possibility to communicate directly without the assistance of a translator greatly enhanced my learning process.

Furthermore, whereas my skin colour immediately classified me as wealthy, my language skills made me stand apart from other *wazungu*. Notably, the use of Swahili levels class and ethnic differences in the Kenyan context (N. Mwangi, 2019, p. 22). But most flower farm managers do not know any Swahili, which reinforces the already immense class-based differences between them and the general workers. People from European descent who have stayed in the area for a long time often are able to speak Swahili, but they do so in a specific manner, as they are used to speaking it only with servants or subordinates. They make use of what Abdulaziz (1982, p. 4) called "*Ki-Setla*": Swahili of settlers. My ease in speaking "everyday" Swahili created goodwill and made it much easier to connect to people, if only because I aroused their curiosity. This does not mean that communication always went fluently. The Swahili spoken in Kenya is slightly different from what I had learned in Tanzania, which occasionally hindered mutual understanding.[9] Nevertheless, I was able to communicate immediately with my interlocutors, which made forging connections and gaining trust much easier. As noted by Nungari Mwangi (2019, p. 21), being able to speak several languages enables a researcher to build rapport with different people.

In sum, the colour of my skin, my language skills, and my choice of assistants all shaped my connections in Naivasha. Also factors that I have not discussed here, such as my gender, level of education, and age, have played a role. A researcher's positionality has epistemological consequences (N. Mwangi, 2019). As stated by Hastrup (2004, p. 456):

> If in fieldwork the anthropologist gains knowledge by way of social relations, this relational aspect has a general bearing on the processes by which facts are established as (relevant) facts in the first place. The relation between the "knower" and the "object" of necessity bends back into the perception of the object itself and is cemented in writing.

My understanding and representation of migrant workers' experiences in dynamic and populous Naivasha have thus undeniably been shaped by my specific position there. My writing has furthermore been shaped by three strands of scholarly literature, which I discuss in the following section.

1.3 Theoretical Positioning

The themes of agro-industrial labour, the "production" of a (gendered) workforce for global firms, and translocal labour migration run through this book. What these three themes have in common is that they have been studied by anthropologists but also by scholars from a variety of disciplines—from ecology and agronomy to disciplines closer to my own, such as sociology, history, and geography. Thus, although my methodology and writing style are predominantly anthropological, this book has been informed theoretically by interdisciplinary debates. A critical engagement with theories related to global capitalism, agro-industry, gendered divisions of labour, and labour migration can bring to the fore some of the specificities of the flower industry in Naivasha and can shed light on how its labour arrangements came into being.

1.3.1 Agro-Industrial Labour

Anthropologists have paid remarkably little attention to the topic of wage labour in the agricultural sector (Hann & Hart, 2011, p. 149; Ortiz, 2002). Notably, only older editions of anthropological and sociological handbooks contain entries on agro-industry—if at all (see Giddens, 1989; Seymour-Smith, 1986). This lack of attention reflects the emphasis in anthropology on the peasantry and on small-scale agriculture, which has effectively relegated the topic of large-scale agricultural production to agronomists and economists. Ortiz (2002) attributes this neglect to the analytic divide between rural and urban studies, which resulted in two separate strands of literature on (small-scale) agriculture and on industry. Moreover, commercial agriculture on the African continent has received particularly little scholarly attention, due to other familiar analytic binaries. "Africa" is associated with "traditional" and "local" cultivation practices and not with "modern", "globalized" agro-industry (Ferguson, 1999; Piot, 1999).

The neglect among anthropologists of labour relations within large-scale agricultural firms is furthermore due to their use of a narrow, technological, and teleological definition of "agro-industry". According to the scarce anthropological literature on the topic, agro-industry's main characteristic is an increased mechanization of the production process. It "uses the products of industry in its own production process. Industrial agriculture is capital-intensive, substituting machinery and purchased inputs such as processed fertilizers for human or animal labor" (Barlett, 1989, p. 253).[10] Authors who follow such a technological definition take mechanized agriculture in the United States as the predominant example of agro-industry. They state that as far as this type of agriculture exists in less wealthy nations, it is mainly export-oriented. They furthermore critically appraise such agro-industries for exacerbating wealth differences between elites and peasants or between skilled and unskilled labour, and for being environmentally unsustainable (Barlett, 1989; Giddens, 1989; Seymour-Smith, 1986; Woodhouse, 2010).

The Kenyan flower industry is also burdened with this interpretation of agro-industry as unsustainable. Implicit in such conventional definitions of agro-industry is a teleological modernization narrative. "Modern" mechanized agriculture is perceived to be replacing or even ousting "traditional" small-scale peasantry. However, in the case of the Naivasha flower industry, large-scale rose production can potentially coexist (and does to some extent) with smallholder production of other types of flower. Cut flowers, and especially roses, are a difficult product for smallholder farmers because the production process requires large capital investments. Smallholders cannot provide the "squeaky-clean environment" (Little, 2014, p. 188) needed to produce the high-quality roses that conform to ever more stringent market demands. They cannot afford the increasingly technically sophisticated greenhouses and refrigerated storage facilities, nor can they afford to pay the royalties on types of flowers, such as roses, that are licenced by breeders. Smallholder farmers also lack connections to the export markets. Nevertheless, small-scale cut flower production does take place in Kenya, albeit on a modest scale. Smallholders account for 6% of Kenya's flower export. These smallholders do not operate around Naivasha but in other parts of the Rift Valley and the Central Highlands. In addition, they do not produce roses. They grow so-called fillers, several types of seasonal flowers that are used to fill up bouquets, which they sell on the auction, usually through export firms. They do not have the means to compete with large farms or to sell their flowers in large quantities to supermarkets (Kazimierczuk et al., 2018; N. Mwangi, n.d.; Whitaker & Kolavalli, 2006).

The narrative that juxtaposes agro-industrial production with small-scale production assumes that these are two alternative ways of producing the same product. However, in the case of the flower industry, large-scale farms produce different types of flowers than the smallholders do. Another underlying premise of the conventional definition of agro-industry is that it is less labour-intensive than "regular" commercial agriculture due to increased mechanization, and that it therefore provides less job and income opportunities for (unskilled) labour (Barlett, 1989, p. 253; Woodhouse,

2010, p. 442). When following this definition, the Naivasha flower farms do not seem to constitute an agro-industry. Although the sector is innovative and uses expensive input such as greenhouses and chemicals, it is not mechanized to an extent that less labour is needed. On the contrary, despite innovations in the production process, the process remains labour-intensive, as asserted by Staelens, Desiere, Louche, and D'Haese (2018) for the Ethiopian flower industry. I nevertheless maintain that the flower farms in Naivasha form an "agro-industry". I base this assertion on Sydney Mintz' definition of agro-industry, taken from his seminal work *Sweetness and Power* (1985).

Mintz showed the interdependencies between the Industrial Revolution and the emergence of a proletariat in England on the one hand and the development of a plantation economy, based on slave labour, in the Caribbean on the other. Through analysing these connections, he furthermore showed that the sugar production in the Caribbean was already industrial in nature even before the Industrial Revolution in England took off. A large part of the processing of the sugar cane took place on the plantations due to the perishable nature of the crop. The production process of refined sugar therefore required mechanization and an industrial division of labour. It is worthwhile to cite Mintz (1985, p. 51) at length when he explains why he typifies these plantations as "agro-industrial":

> Today we speak of "agro-industry", and the term usually implies heavy substitution of machinery for human labor, mass production on large holdings, intensive use of scientific methods and products (…) and the like. What made the early plantation system agro-industrial was the combination of agriculture and processing under one authority: *discipline* was probably its first essential feature. This was because neither mill nor field could be separately (independently) productive. Second was the organization of the labor force itself, part skilled, part unskilled, and organized in terms of the plantation's overall productive goals. To the extent possible, the labor force was composed of interchangeable units—much of the labor was homogeneous, in the eyes of the producers—characteristic of a lengthy middle period much later in the history of capitalism. Third, the system was time-conscious. This time-consciousness was dictated by the nature of the sugar cane and its processing requirements, but it permeated all phases of plantation life.

Cane workers in the Caribbean were not smallholder peasants. Instead, "[t]hey were wage earners who lived like factory workers, who worked in factories in the fields, and just about everything they needed and used they bought from stores" (Mintz, 1985, p. xxiii).

Industrial labour is thus defined by discipline, a segmentation of the labour force, and time consciousness, and not by the type of product or the level of mechanization involved. I argue that the "unskilled", repetitive, and standardized manual work on middle- to large-scale flower farms can be interpreted as industrial labour in this sense.[11] Furthermore, I propose to apply insights from anthropological and sociological literature on industrial labour relations in general on the analysis of labour relations on the Naivasha flower farms.

Holzberg and Giovannini (1981), in their review article on the anthropology of industrial relations, asserted that "industry" in general does not only include "operative forces" such as tools, machinery, and raw materials. They argue that it is the organization of relations *around* these objects that constitutes an industrial society. Those social arrangements have been the focus of anthropologists and sociologists studying industrial labour. This strand of literature has focussed on two main themes, which also are integral to Mintz' definition of agro-industry: work rhythm and labour control.

Interestingly, work rhythm and changing divisions of labour over time have also been prominent themes in studies on small-scale agriculture on the African continent (Heald, 1991; Moore & Vaughan, 1994). In the context of industrial work, the attention for rhythm follows from Thompson's distinction between "pre-industrial task-time" and "industrial clock-time". In his article titled "Time, Work-Discipline, and Industrial Capitalism" (1967), Thompson called attention to a historical shift in the sense of time in English society, from a task-oriented way of organizing work to work governed by abstract clock-time. This shift increased discipline over labour and also implied a more thorough break between "work" and "life". According to Thompson, this shift was caused by a process of mechanization, which called for an increased synchronization of labour.

Thompson's compelling analytical distinction has been attenuated by other authors. Ingold (1995, p. 7) has argued that task orientation—which he defined as "an orientation in which both work and time are intrinsic to the conduct of life itself, and cannot be separated or abstracted from it"—might be denied by modern technology but is nevertheless persisting in the experience of industrial work. Parry (2012, p. 159) has argued that not all types of machines ask for constant labour. Moreover, he pointed out that the need for a synchronization of labour is not exclusive for industrial production either, as it also exists in some types of peasant agriculture. Nevertheless, even though such a sharp break as defined by Thompson is no longer presupposed in current studies, the question whether and how (work) rhythms and conceptions of time change when people start working in an (agro-)industrial setting remains a central one (Parry, 2012).

The second set of anthropological questions relating to industrial labour was most prominently posed by Burawoy (1979): why do workers consent to do their work? How and why do workers either resist to or comply with management and firm policies? And how and where (i.e. in the production locality or also elsewhere) do employers attempt to control their employees (Parry, 2012, p. 147)?

Braverman (1998) described the effects of so-called scientific management, which entails an attempt to make labour control more effective by applying scientific insights. An example is the process of "de-skilling", in which tasks are deliberately fragmented. Thus, workers acquire no specific skills and their bargaining position is weakened. Workers become "interchangeable parts" in the production process (Braverman, 1998, p. 125). Anthropologists studying industrial labour have described workers' reactions to such attempts to control them; see, for instance, Ong's classic monograph *Spirits of Resistance and Capitalist Discipline* (1987). However, as argued by Kondo (1990), some of these studies have been too schematic, classifying workers' reactions as either resistance to or accommodation of management's control. As Wright (2006, p. 18) pointed out, resistance to certain hierarchies might unintentionally affirm others, for instance, gendered inequalities. Moreover, as asserted by Du Toit (1993, p. 331): "We should not equate anger with militancy—of even acceptance with false consciousness." We should also not assume a need for resistance by considering industrial work as necessarily more exploitative than other economic systems. As argued by Parry (2012, p. 159), it might well be that "for many neophyte proletarians in many parts of the world, the fields were never so happy nor the mills so dark and satanic".

But while moving away from stark dichotomies, the questions of labour control and workers' consent only gain in relevance, also within the context of agro-industrial labour. Strategies for labour control such as a process of "de-skilling" can be recognized in both industry and wage labour agriculture. Furthermore, workers in both settings react in diverse ways to those strategies. "The major contribution of anthropologists to the literature on labor control has been to highlight the connection between modes of control, contestation, and confrontation with social realities outside the workplace" (Ortiz, 2002, p. 409). In other words, a factory or farm should not be studied as a confined place. Instead, its organization of labour and hierarchies should be assessed within the historical context of the society in which it is located.

The importance of context for understanding industrial relations can be illustrated by comparing the Kenyan flower industry to the well-researched commercial farms in South Africa and Zimbabwe that produce for global markets (Addison, 2014a, 2014b; Bolt, 2013, 2016; Du Toit, 1993, 2004; Moyo, Rutherford, & Amanor-Wilks, 2000; Orton, Barrientos, & McClenaghan, 2001; Rutherford, 2001, 2014). These farms have been shaped by the history of apartheid and the traditional paternalistic system of labour control. African labourers usually lived on the farms, and their labour and living conditions were based on their personal relations to the farm owners. When the white-owned farms were no longer supported by the government after the abolishment of apartheid, the farms had to be made commercially more viable. Casual, off-farm labour became more important, as well as the recruitment of workers through brokers and African managers. Nevertheless, some aspects of the paternalistic system also persisted, such as the gendered division of labour, in which women are mostly employed for seasonal jobs (Addison, 2014a; Orton et al., 2001). Addison (2014b) has summarized a few trends within the resulting "hybrid" labour regimes: a more pronounced segmentation of the workforce, increasingly impersonal relations between management and workers, less provision of services such as free housing, and a more pronounced role for South African managers and supervisors in controlling casual migrant labour. Addison (2014b, p. 79) concluded that "the private or domestic authority of farmers has persisted, with diminished moral and social obligations towards workers and only minimal interference from the state".

As I discuss in this book, the Kenyan flower industry showed different trends, such as an increased prevalence of permanent contracts instead of a casualization of labour and formalization of recruitment practices instead of an increasing reliance on brokers. This diversity in labour conditions on export-oriented farms on the African continent indicate that the topic of agro-industrial labour deserves more attention than it has received until now.

1.3.2 *The Production of a (Gendered) Workforce*

Considering the general lack of attention for (agro-)industrial work in anthropology, there appeared over the past three decades a remarkably large number of ethnographies—written by both anthropologists and sociologists—on women working in global industries. This strand of literature started with explicitly feminist studies on female factory workers in Great Britain (Pollert, 1981; Westwood, 1984). These studies were followed by ethnographies on the *maquiladoras*, assembly-line manufacturing plants in a special export zone on the border between Mexico and the United States (Fernández-Kelly, 1983; Peña, 1997; Salzinger, 2003), and on similar global manufacturing companies located in Asian countries (Kim, 1997; Lee, 1998; Ong, 1987; Wolf, 1992). The Kenyan flower industry has been compared to these other industries that move across the globe and that employ women in unskilled positions. "Like its kin the maquiladora, for example, the flower industry depends on migrant women who face low wages, excessive working hours, job insecurity and embedded gender discrimination" (Dolan, 2007, p. 243). My assessment of women's position in the Naivasha flower industry is different, as I discuss in Chaps. 3 and 4. Nevertheless, the body of literature on women "along the global assembly line" does discuss relevant questions with regard to (gendered) labour relations.

Most ethnographies on women working in global factories relate to the two main themes which are also central to the general literature on industrial work: workers' consent, compliance, and resistance; and struggles over conceptualizations of time and timing of work. Economists Elson and Pearson (1984) noted that female workers are typically portrayed in global capitalism as being "naturally" docile and dexterous, which would make them especially suitable to perform unskilled labour. Elson and Pearson asserted that there is nothing natural about these characteristics and that they are socially produced. The sociologist Thomas (1985), for instance, showed how agro-industrial lettuce farms in the United States made use of distinguishing statuses that already existed in American society, such as gender but also citizenship, and transformed them into the organization's advantage. Others have developed this argument further and showed that docile female labour is produced differently in different cases (Freeman, 2000; Salzinger, 2003). These authors have argued that capital cannot simply tap into a reserve of labour but has to "produce" workers. This "production" of workers takes place both at the point of hiring and in daily routines on the work floor. Gender is an important factor in these processes. Lee (1998), for instance, described two factories of the same company within the same region where different mechanisms of labour control constructed different gendered identities and practices. As argued by Ong

(1987, p. 155), employers use "preexisting [*sic*] cultural constructions of inequality", such as skills, ethnicity, and gender, in their system of labour control. A similar argument has been made by Mills (2003, p. 43) in her article titled "Gender and Inequality in the Global Labor Force".

On the other hand, Freeman (2000) drew attention to workers' agency within these processes. She has argued that such differences among workers take on unpredictable forms and get recreated, within an historical context, by employers as well as by the workers themselves. Moreover, in her ethnography on the flower industry in Colombia, Friedemann-Sánchez (2009) has argued that employment in global industries might be empowering for individual women, even when these industries draw on women's generally disadvantaged position.

The "women-along-the-global-assembly-line" literature primarily discusses industrial labour within manufacturing companies, not agro-industry. Furthermore, few of these studies focus on an African context. Finally, many of these authors have followed a distinct feminist or Marxist tradition and perceived of management and (female) workers as two separate, antagonistic groups. I interpret labour relations differently. Following Kondo (1990), I do not perceive of workers (or managers) as a homogenous and closed group. Employees move in and out of farm work, and they can assume varying positions within farm hierarchies over time. In addition, there are also individuals who cannot be categorized as either worker or manager, for instance, supervisors. Nevertheless, despite my more fluid understanding of labour relations, questions on the organization of industrial labour that have been put forward by the above-mentioned authors have informed my approach. I do not aim to draw a literal comparison between the conditions on the Naivasha flower farms and the conditions in factories in Asian countries or in sweatshops along the border between Mexico and the United States. Instead, I take from this strand of literature its attention for the "production" of the workforce: how do firms attempt to recruit and control labour? Why do workers consent to this work? (How) did the Naivasha flower industry tap into an existing system of migrant wage labour, which hinges on "cultural factors" of inequality such as ethnicity, class, and gender (Ong, 1987; Tsing, 2009)? And how did workers themselves define these differences among themselves (Freeman, 2000)? Finally, I examine how gendered ideologies have shaped representations of the industry in the consumer markets in Europe and in policy circles in Kenya, and what impact such representations might have had.

1.3.3 Translocal Labour Migration in Kenya

Whereas the role of gender in the flower industry has received due attention, this is different for another outstanding characteristic of many flower farm workers and of some of their neighbours in the Naivasha settlements: their migratory background. Labour migration to cities, mines, and plantations on the African continent has been a popular anthropological object of study since colonial times (Cooper, 1992; Geschiere & Gugler, 1998; Gluckman, 1961; Moore & Vaughan, 1994; N. Nelson, 1992; Ross & Weisner, 1977).

Anthropologists and colonial officers alike initially perceived of labour migration as a threat to the "tribal" way of life and to "native" agricultural production (Moore & Vaughan, 1994, pp. 140–141). Ferguson (1999, pp. 123–128) described how the colonial Zambian government therefore stimulated retired mine workers to "go back to the land". Also in the Kenyan context, colonial officials intended labour migration to be a temporary move and expected migrant workers to return to their rural regions of origin (Oucho, 1996, p. 10). Labour migrants were thus perceived as temporary residents of urban centres or mine and plantation compounds, who ultimately remained rural dwellers.

Anthropologists subsequently proposed to study labour migration as a more permanent move. These scholars described a shift from circular migration via return migration to permanent migration. This approach thus had an evolutionary undertone (Moore & Vaughan, 1994; Ross & Weisner, 1977).

Finally, more recent studies have focussed on the connections *between* the city and the village, and on how these two geographical areas impact on each other. Oucho (1996, p. 69) stated in his study on labour migration among the Luo in Kenya: "The ambivalence of urban migrants, with one foot in the transient urban destination and another in the rural areas with which they identify as home, is a well-established phenomenon of African migration." Some scholars even argued to stop perceiving of "the urban" and "the rural" as two distinct entities. Ross and Weisner (1977) considered the city and the village to be part of one "social field", as the migrants they studied maintained close connections to their rural regions of origin in western Kenya while residing in Nairobi. "Visiting and various forms of exchange between the urban and the rural areas are frequent, migrants plan to leave the city when they no longer need a cash income, and rural and urban goals are hard to separate" (Ross & Weisner, 1977, p. 360).

Recently, geographers and anthropologists have started to make use of the concept of "translocality" to interpret the myriad connections between migrants' regions of origin and their places of work. As argued by McGarrigle and Ascensão (2017), migration is a process and not a completed act. In other words, emplacement does not necessarily imply permanent settlement. Migrant workers in Naivasha can therefore be characterized as "translocal": temporarily grounded in the place of work while ultimately—when looking over a longer time span—being on the move (Brickell & Datta, 2011; Greiner & Sakdapolrak, 2013). In this book, I use the concept of translocality and its emphasis on simultaneous connectivity and situated-ness to analyse the experiences of migrant workers on the flower farms in Naivasha. The concept furthermore has informed the overall structure of this book, which loosely reflects the migration process, from coming to Naivasha to leaving again.

1.4 Aims and Outline of the Study

This book provides a case study of labour relations within a global agro-industry on the African continent. I emphatically do not aim to evaluate labour conditions in the Naivasha flower industry against certain global standards, which has been done before (Dolan et al., 2003; KHRC, 2012; V. Nelson, Martin, & Ewert, 2007; Omosa et al., 2006). Instead, I examine how these labour conditions and the labour relations within the Naivasha flower industry came into being and how these have changed over the years. This includes an analysis of the accommodation of workers on on-farm compounds and, for the majority of the workers, in off-farm, unplanned settlements. I aim to put the migrant workers in Naivasha, who have not received much scholarly attention before and who have been pictured one-dimensionally in much of the relevant grey literature, at the centre of analysis.

In line with the approach of Mintz (1985) and Besky (2014), I investigate the connections between the ecological characteristics of the crop and the organization of labour within the farms. A description of the rhythm and temporalities of the work is integral to my theoretical understanding of agro-industry. I moreover explicitly address the temporal and spatial dimensions of labour migration. Inspired by Greiner and Sakdapolrak (2013) and other scholars working on the topic of translocality, I investigate the influence of the migratory background and the translocal connections of the workers on their position within the farms and in the settlements where they live.

Following Burawoy (1979) and other sociologists studying industrial labour, I ask how consent is "manufactured" and a labour force is being "produced". In other words, why do labour migrants come to Naivasha and agree to work in the farms? Following Ong (1987) and other researchers who wrote about women working along assembly lines around the world, I probe into the roles of "cultural factors" such as gender and ethnicity within the divisions of labour and hierarchies within the farms.

The outline of the book is as follows. Chapter 2 describes the gradual development of Naivasha as an agro-industrial hub. The chapter shows that the flower industry did not establish itself in an "empty" area. Naivasha is a place with a distinctive history of agricultural wage labour. This history has shaped the labour arrangements within the flower farms.

The next four chapters build the backbone of this book. These chapters follow the migrants who form the labour force of this "global" industry, from the decision to come to Naivasha to the point of leaving again, often many years or even decades later. This chronological description brings to the fore very individual choices and decisions, taken in Naivasha as well as in labour-sending regions and in the consumer markets in Europe, which together keep the flower industry going. Chapter 3, on arriving in Naivasha, shows how the flower industry depends on both existing patterns of labour migration in Kenya and aspirations of workers and landowners in Naivasha for the recruitment and accommodation of labour. Chapter 4 provides a description of the flower farms and of labour conditions, and shows how the industry has attempted to retain and control labour. Chapter 5 describes the workers' settlements in Naivasha, which were not planned for by the flower farms or the local government. It questions the presumed disorder of these settlements. Finally, Chap. 6 describes how migrants residing in Naivasha prepare for a future elsewhere and examines what happens once migrants decide to leave.

By providing a historical background and by following migrant workers from their arrival until their departure, I aim to show how labour arrangements and conditions within this agro-industry have come into being and how these have changed over the years. Moreover, I aim to provide a more nuanced understanding of the translocal workers' experiences with working on the flower farms and living in the Naivasha settlements.

Notes

1. Naivasha is the name of the lake as well as of the town located next to it. In this book, I use "Naivasha" to refer to the whole area surrounding the lake unless I specify otherwise.
2. See Kuiper (2017) for a visual representation of this diverse landscape.
3. The interdisciplinary research project *Resilience, Collapse and Reorganization of Social Ecological Systems of Africa's Savannahs*, funded by the Deutsche Forschungsgemeinschaft (DFG)—FOR1501.
4. Richard is not my assistant's real name. As I narrate personal details, I use pseudonyms in this book for all respondents and other people I worked with, with the exception of the respondents with whom I conducted oral history interviews.
5. Even though I cannot guarantee anonymity, I have chosen to replace the names of farms that I visited with pseudonyms. I have reasons similar to Orr's (1996, p. 6). Orr wrote about technicians of a well-known firm. He only mentioned the name of the company once: "I believe that very little of what I say is unique to Xerox, and I do not want to burden the observations with that identification." Likewise, my aim is not to write about one specific farm. I therefore use pseudonyms.
6. Paraphrased from M. Mwangi (2007).
7. Farm compounds are referred to as *kambi* in Swahili, which derives from the English word "camp". This terminology reflects that workers' compounds originally had consisted of makeshift accommodation.
8. Wherever I quote from interviews conducted in Swahili or Dutch in this book, I have translated the quote myself.
9. One of the first flower farm workers I interviewed—not a young man anymore—explained he had migrated to Naivasha together with his *bibi*. I was a bit surprised, as *bibi* in Tanzania means grandmother. Upon noticing my confusion, my assistant explained to me that Kenyans use the word *bibi* to refer to their wife.
10. Scholars writing on the topic tend to use the word "agribusiness" as a synonym for agro-industry; see Seymour-Smith (1986, p. 7) and Hann and Hart (2011, p. 149). In contrast, Barlett (1989, p. 267) uses the term "agribusiness" to refer to distinct companies that provide farms with agricultural inputs and services. I therefore only use the term "agro-industry" to describe the flower farms.
11. Friedemann-Sánchez (2009, p. 5) likewise argues that flower farms in Colombia form an agro-industry. However, she bases herself on yet another definition of agro-industry, or rather of industry in general. This definition emphasizes, in the words of Holzberg and Giovannini (1981, p. 323), "the mass production of standardized and interchangeable parts".

References

Abdulaziz, M. H. (1982). Patterns of language acquisition and use in Kenya: Rural-urban differences. *International Journal of the Sociology of Language, 1982*(34). https://doi.org/10.1515/ijsl.1982.34.95

Addison, L. (2014a). Delegated despotism: Frontiers of agrarian labour on a South African border farm. *Journal of Agrarian Change, 14*(2), 286–304. https://doi.org/10.1111/joac.12062

Addison, L. (2014b). The sexual economy, gender relations and narratives of infant death on a tomato farm in Northern South Africa. *Journal of Agrarian Change, 14*(1), 74–93. https://doi.org/10.1111/joac.12008

Barlett, P. F. (1989). Industrial agriculture. In S. Plattner (Ed.), *Economic anthropology* (pp. 253–291). Stanford, CA: Stanford University Press.

Becht, R., & Harper, D. M. (2002). Towards an understanding of human impact upon the hydrology of Lake Naivasha, Kenya. In *Lake Naivasha, Kenya* (pp. 1–11). Springer. Retrieved from http://link.springer.com/chapter/10.1007/978-94-017-2031-1_1

Becht, R., Odada, E. O., & Higgins, S. (2005). *Lake Naivasha. Experience and lessons learned brief.* Kosatsu: International Lake Environment Committee Foundation. Retrieved from https://worldlakes.org/uploads/17_Lake_Naivasha_27February2006.pdf

Besky, S. (2014). *The Darjeeling distinction: Labor and justice on fair trade tea plantations in India*. Berkeley: University of California Press.

Bolt, M. (2013). Producing permanence: Employment, domesticity and the flexible future on a South African border farm. *Economy and Society, 42*(2), 197–225. https://doi.org/10.1080/03085147.2012.733606

Bolt, M. (2016). Accidental neoliberalism and the performance of management: Hierarchies in export agriculture on the Zimbabwean-South African Border. *The Journal of Development Studies, 52*(4), 561–575. https://doi.org/10.1080/00220388.2015.1126252

Braverman, H. (1998). *Labor and monopoly capital: The degradation of work in the twentieth century* (25th Anniversary ed.). New York: Monthly Review Press.

Brickell, K., & Datta, A. (2011). Introduction: Translocal geographies. In K. Brickell & A. Datta (Eds.), *Translocal geographies: Space, places, connections* (pp. 3–22). Farnham: Ashgate.

Burawoy, M. (1979). *Manufacturing consent: Changes in the labor process under monopoly capitalism*. Chicago: University of Chicago Press.

Cooper, F. (1992). Colonizing time: Work rhythms and labour conflict in colonial Mombasa. In N. Dirks (Ed.), *Colonialism and culture*. Ann Arbor: University of Michigan Press.

Davies, C. A. (2008). *Reflexive ethnography: A guide to researching selves and others* (2nd ed.). London: Routledge.

Dolan, C. S. (2007). Market affections: Moral encounters with Kenyan fairtrade flowers. *Ethnos, 72*(2), 239–261. https://doi.org/10.1080/00141840701396573

Dolan, C. S., Opondo, M., & Smith, S. (2003). *Gender, rights and participation in the Kenya cut flower industry* (NRI Report No. 2768). Chatham, UK: NRI.

Du Toit, A. (1993). The micro-politics of paternalism: The discourses of management and resistance on South African fruit and wine farms. *Journal of Southern African Studies, 19*(2), 314–336.

Du Toit, A. (2004). 'Social exclusion' discourse and chronic poverty: A South African case study. *Development and Change, 35*(5), 987–1010.

Elson, D., & Pearson, R. (1984). The subordination of women and the internationalisation of factory production. In K. Young, C. Wolkowitz, & R. McCullagh (Eds.), *Of marriage and the market: Women's subordination internationally and its lessons* (2nd ed., pp. 18–40). London: Routledge and Kegan Paul.

Fabian, J. (1971). Language, history and anthropology. *Philosophy of the Social Sciences, 1*(1), 19–47.

Ferguson, J. (1999). *Expectations of modernity: Myths and meanings of urban life on the Zambian Copperbelt*. Berkeley: University of California Press.

Fernández-Kelly, M. (1983). *For we are sold, I and my people: Women and industry in Mexico's frontier*. Albany: State University of New York Press.

Freeman, C. (2000). *High tech and high heels in the global economy: Women, work, and pink collar identities in the Caribbean*. Durham: Duke University Press.

Friedemann-Sánchez, G. (2009). *Assembling flowers and cultivating homes: Labor and gender in Colombia* (1st Paperback ed.). Lanham, MD: Lexington Books.

Geschiere, P., & Gugler, J. (1998). Introduction: The urban-rural connection: Changing issues of belonging and identification. *Africa: Journal of the International African Institute, 68*(3), 309–319. https://doi.org/10.2307/1161251

Gibbon, P., & Riisgaard, L. (2014). A new system of labour management in African large-scale agriculture? *Journal of Agrarian Change, 14*(1), 94–128. https://doi.org/10.1111/joac.12043

Giddens, A. (1989). *Sociology* (1st ed.). Cambridge: Cambridge Polity Press.

Gluckman, M. (1961). Anthropological problems arising from the African industrial revolution. In A. Southall (Ed.), *Social change in modern Africa* (pp. 67–82). London: Oxford University Press.

Greiner, C., & Sakdapolrak, P. (2013). Translocality: Concepts, applications and emerging research perspectives. *Geography Compass, 7*(5), 373–384. https://doi.org/10.1111/gec3.12048

Hale, A., & Opondo, M. (2005). Humanising the cut flower chain: Confronting the realities of flower production for workers in Kenya. *Antipode, 37*, 301–323.

Hall, R., Scoones, I., & Tsikata, D. (2017). Plantations, outgrowers and commercial farming in Africa: Agricultural commercialisation and implications for agrarian change. *The Journal of Peasant Studies, 44*(3), 515–537. https://doi.org/10.1080/03066150.2016.1263187

Hann, C., & Hart, K. (2011). *Economic anthropology*. Cambridge: Polity Press.
Harper, D. M., Morrison, E. H., Macharia, M. M., Mavuti, K. M., & Upton, C. (2011). Lake Naivasha, Kenya: Ecology, society and future. *Freshwater Reviews, 4*(2), 89–114.
Hastrup, K. (2004). Getting it right: Knowledge and evidence in anthropology. *Anthropological Theory, 4*(4), 455–472. https://doi.org/10.1177/1463499604047921
Heald, S. (1991). Tobacco, time and the household economy in two Kenyan societies: The Teso and the Kuria. *Comparative Studies in Society and History, 33*(1), 130–157.
Hivos. (n.d.). Power of the fair trade flower. Retrieved January 24, 2014, from http://www.powerofthefairtradeflower.nl/
Holzberg, C. S., & Giovannini, M. J. (1981). Anthropology and industry: Reappraisal and new directions. *Annual Review of Anthropology, 10*, 317–360.
Ingold, T. (1995). Work, time and industry. *Time & Society, 4*(1), 5–28. https://doi.org/10.1177/0961463X95004001001
Kapferer, B. (1969). Norms and the manipulation of relationships in a work context. In J. Clyde Mitchell (Ed.), *Social networks in urban situations: Analyses of personal relationships in Central African townships* (pp. 181–244). Manchester: Manchester University Press.
Kazimierczuk, A., Kamau, P., Kinuthia, B., & Mukoko, C. (2018). *Never a rose without a prick: (Dutch) multinational companies and productive employment in the Kenyan flower sector* (ASC Working Paper No. 142). Leiden: African Studies Centre.
KFC. (2019). Industry statistics. Retrieved February 15, 2019, from http://kenyaflowercouncil.org/?page_id=94
KHRC. (2012). *Wilting in bloom: The irony of women labour rights in the cut-flower sector in Kenya*. Nairobi: KHRC.
Kim, S. (1997). *Class struggle or family struggle? The lives of women factory workers in South Korea*. Cambridge: Cambridge University Press.
Kioko, E. M. (2012). *Poverty and livelihood strategies at Lake Naivasha, Kenya: A case study of Kasarani Village*. Cologne: Cologne African Studies Centre.
KNBS. (2010). *Kenya population census 2009*. Nairobi: KNBS.
Kondo, D. K. (1990). *Crafting selves: Power, gender, and discourses of identity in a Japanese workplace*. Chicago: The University of Chicago Press.
Kuiper, G. (2017). Get on a boat! A photographic view from Lake Naivasha. Retrieved from http://voices.uni-koeln.de/2017-3/getonaboataphotographicviewfromlakenaivasha
Lang, B., & Sakdapolrak, P. (2014). Belonging and recognition after the post-election violence: A case study on labour migrants in Naivasha, Kenya. *Erdkunde, 68*(3), 185–196. https://doi.org/10.3112/erdkunde.2014.03.03

Lee, C. K. (1998). *Gender and the South China miracle: Two worlds of factory women*. Berkeley: University of California Press.

Lembcke, L. (2015). *Social-ecological change and migration in South-East Lake Naivasha*. Cologne: Cologne African Studies Centre.

Little, P. D. (2014). *Economic and political reform in Africa: Anthropological perspectives*. Bloomington: Indiana University Press.

Lowthers, M. (2018). On institutionalized sexual economies: Employment sex, transactional sex, and sex work in Kenya's cut flower industry. *Signs: Journal of Women in Culture and Society, 43*(2), 449–472. https://doi.org/10.1086/693767

Mavuti, K. M., & Harper, D. M. (2006). The ecological state of Lake Naivasha, Kenya, 2005: Turning 25 years research into an effective Ramsar monitoring programme. In E. Odada & D. O. Olago (Eds.), *Proceedings of the 11th World Lakes Conference* (Vol. 2, pp. 30–34). Retrieved from http://www.oceandocs.net/handle/1834/2127

McGarrigle, J., & Ascensão, E. (2017). Emplaced mobilities: Lisbon as a translocality in the migration journeys of Punjabi Sikhs to Europe. *Journal of Ethnic and Migration Studies, 48*, 1–20. https://doi.org/10.1080/1369183X.2017.1306436

Mills, M. B. (2003). Gender and inequality in the global labor force. *Annual Review of Anthropology, 32*(1), 41–62. https://doi.org/10.1146/annurev.anthro.32.061002.093107

Mintz, S. W. (1985). *Sweetness and power: The place of sugar in modern history*. New York: Viking.

Moore, H. L., & Vaughan, M. (1994). *Cutting down trees: Gender, nutrition, and agricultural change in the Northern Province of Zambia, 1890–1990*. Portsmouth, NH: Heinemann.

Morrison, E. H. J., Upton, C., Pacini, N., Odhiambo-K'oyooh, K., & Harper, D. M. (2013). Public perceptions of papyrus: Community appraisal of wetland ecosystem services at Lake Naivasha, Kenya. *Ecohydrology & Hydrobiology, 13*(2), 135–147. https://doi.org/10.1016/j.ecohyd.2013.03.008

Moyo, S., Rutherford, B., & Amanor-Wilks, D. (2000). Land reform & changing social relations for farm workers in Zimbabwe. *Review of African Political Economy, 27*(84), 181–202.

Mwangi, M. (2007, August 18). Naivasha Town: Where poverty and affluence live side-by-side. *Daily Nation*, p. 26.

Mwangi, N. (2019). 'Good that you are one of us': Positionality and reciprocity in conducting fieldwork in Kenya's flower industry. In L. Johnstone (Ed.), *The politics of conducting research in Africa* (pp. 13–33). Cham: Springer International Publishing.

Mwangi, N. (n.d.). Propertied proletarians? The Kenyan cut-flower industry. Retrieved December 4, 2018, from http://roape.net/2017/06/21/propertied-proletarians-kenyan-cut-flower-industry/

Mwembe, K. wa. (1979, August 19). Flower power! A fast blooming money-spinner for Kenyan economy. *Daily Nation*, p. 23.

Nelson, N. (1992). The women who have left and those who have stayed behind: Rural-urban migration in central and western Kenya. In S. Chant (Ed.), *Gender and migration in developing countries* (pp. 109–138). London: Belhaven Press.

Nelson, V., Martin, A., & Ewert, J. (2007). The impacts of codes of practice on worker livelihoods: Empirical evidence from the South African wine and Kenyan cut flower industries. *Journal of Corporate Citizenship, 28*, 61–72.

Okely, J. (2012). *Anthropological practice: Fieldwork and the ethnographic method*. London: Berg.

Omosa, M., Kimani, M., & Njiru, R. (2006). The social impact of codes of practice in the cut flower industry in Kenya. Natural Resources Institute and DFID. Retrieved from http://projects.nri.org/nret/final_kenya_main_report.pdf

Ong, A. (1987). *Spirits of resistance and capitalist discipline: Factory women in Malaysia*. Albany: State University of New York Press.

Opala, K. (2007, April 2). Naivasha's withering rose: Flower companies threaten to move to Ethiopia as workers and council protest. *Daily Nation*, pp. 4–5.

Orr, J. E. (1996). *Talking about machines: An ethnography of a modern job*. Ithaca, NY: ILR Press.

Ortiz, S. (2002). Laboring in the factories and in the fields. *Annual Review of Anthropology, 31*(1), 395–417. https://doi.org/10.1146/annurev.anthro.31.031902.161108

Orton, L., Barrientos, S., & McClenaghan, S. (2001). Paternalism and gender in South African fruit employment. *Women's Studies International Forum, 24*(3–4), 469–478. https://doi.org/10.1016/S0277-5395(01)00166-2

Oucho, J. O. (1996). *Urban migrants and rural development in Kenya*. Nairobi: Nairobi University Press.

Parry, J. P. (2012). Industrial work. In J. G. Carrier (Ed.), *A handbook of economic anthropology* (2nd ed., pp. 145–165). Cheltenham: Edward Elgar Publishing.

Peña, D. G. (1997). *The terror of the machine: Technology, work, gender, and ecology on the U.S.-Mexico Border*. Austin: University of Texas.

Piot, C. (1999). *Remotely global: Village modernity in West Africa*. Chicago: The University of Chicago Press.

Pollert, A. (1981). *Girls, wives, factory lives*. London: The Macmillan Press Ltd.

Riisgaard, L., & Gibbon, P. (2014). Labour management on contemporary Kenyan cut flower farms: Foundations of an industrial-civic compromise. *Journal of Agrarian Change, 14*(2), 260–285. https://doi.org/10.1111/joac.12064

Ross, M. H., & Weisner, T. S. (1977). The rural-urban migrant network in Kenya: Some general implications. *American Ethnologist, 4*(2), 359–375. https://doi.org/10.1525/ae.1977.4.2.02a00090

Rutherford, B. (2001). *Working on the margins: Black workers, white farmers in postcolonial Zimbabwe*. London: Zed Books.

Rutherford, B. (2014). Organization and (de)mobilization of farmworkers in Zimbabwe: Reflections on trade unions, NGOs and political parties. *Journal of Agrarian Change, 14*(2), 214–239. https://doi.org/10.1111/joac.12065

Salzinger, L. (2003). *Genders in production: Making workers in Mexico's global factories*. Berkeley: University of California Press.

Scott, J. (2013a). *Social network analysis* (3rd ed.). London: SAGE.

Seymour-Smith, C. (1986). *Macmillan dictionary of anthropology* (Paperback ed.). London: The Macmillan Press Ltd.

Staelens, L., Desiere, S., Louche, C., & D'Haese, M. (2018). Predicting job satisfaction and workers' intentions to leave at the bottom of the high value agricultural chain: Evidence from the Ethiopian cut flower industry. *The International Journal of Human Resource Management, 29*(9), 1609–1635. https://doi.org/10.1080/09585192.2016.1253032

Thomas, R. J. (1985). *Citizenship, gender, and work: Social organization of industrial agriculture*. Berkeley: University of California Press.

Thompson, E. P. (1967). Time, work-discipline, and industrial capitalism. *Past & Present, 38*, 56–97.

Tsing, A. (2009). Supply chains and the human condition. *Rethinking Marxism, 21*(2), 148–176. https://doi.org/10.1080/08935690902743088

Van Velsen, J. (1964). *The politics of kinship*. Manchester: Manchester University Press.

Westwood, S. (1984). *All day every day: Factory and family in the making of women's lives*. London: Pluto Press.

Whitaker, M., & Kolavalli, S. (2006). Floriculture in Kenya. In V. Chandra (Ed.), *Technology, adaptation, and exports: How some developing countries got it right* (pp. 335–367). Washington, DC: The World Bank.

Wolf, D. L. (1992). *Factory daughters: Gender, household dynamics and rural industrialization in Java*. Berkeley: University of California Press.

Woodhouse, P. (2010). Beyond industrial agriculture? Some questions about farm size, productivity and sustainability. *Journal of Agrarian Change, 10*(3), 437–453.

Wright, M. W. (2006). *Disposable women and other myths of global capitalism*. New York: Routledge.

CHAPTER 2

Naivasha's History: From Livestock to Flowers

The establishment of the flower industry around Naivasha has been portrayed as a violent and sudden rupture with an idyllic natural past. The farms themselves have been depicted as a brutal industrial force destroying the lake and its social and ecological surroundings. Consider the following quote from a biography on Joan Root, an environmentalist who lived in Naivasha at the time the industry established itself:

> Over the preceding two decades, peaceful, pastoral Lake Naivasha had been invaded by armies of flower growers who created some of the biggest flower farms in the world. These farms covered the lakeshore with huge plastic hothouses, inhibited the natural migration of wildlife, and attracted a desperate tide of hundreds of thousands of impoverished migrant workers, resulting in slums, squalor, crime and, some insisted, ecological apocalypse. (Seal, 2011, p. xiv)

A Kenyan lady of European descent, whose family has owned a ranch at North Lake[1] since colonial times, stated that life in Naivasha has changed 180 degrees since the flower industry arrived (O. Rocco, interview on April 25, 2015). There appeared newspaper articles with alarming titles such as "Scramble for land spells doom" and "The tragedy that is Lake Naivasha" (Hunter, 2009; Ngesa & Mwangi, 2005).

According to the national census, Naivasha's population increased from 95,339 inhabitants in 1979 to 376,243 inhabitants in 2009 (KNBS, 1981, 2010).[2] These exploding population numbers indicate that major shifts

G. Kuiper, *Agro-industrial Labour in Kenya*,
https://doi.org/10.1007/978-3-030-18046-1_2

have taken place around Lake Naivasha, and perhaps increasingly so in the last decades. But was the flower industry really an overriding external force that "took over" the area, or did it tap into and adapt to historically shaped local circumstances? This chapter aims to provide a varied perspective on Naivasha's rich and complex history of agricultural wage labour, along with major social and environmental changes that took place around the lake over the course of a century.

The chapter is based on an analysis of material from the Kenya National Archives (KNA), the provincial KNA deposit for the Rift Valley Province based in Nakuru,[3] and the digitalized newspaper archive of the Nation Media Group. I furthermore accessed court case proceedings and government announcements online.[4] I supplemented this archival material by conducting oral history interviews with a range of individuals who have stayed in Naivasha for a long period of time, such as some of the first inhabitants of the settlements Karagita and Kasarani, (former) flower farm employees, and Kenyans of European descent.

The chapter provides a chronological discussion of the continuities and discontinuities between the ranches of colonial settlers before independence, a few of which remain until today; African-owned cooperative farms after independence, which were subdivided later on and transformed into workers' settlements; and the mostly foreign-owned, export-oriented vegetable and flower farms that were established in the 1970s and began to flourish in the 1990s and early 2000s. The chapter starts out at a time when Lake Naivasha was not yet associated with fish and flowers but with wildlife and livestock.

2.1 Colonial Period: Settlers and Squatters

One of the first written accounts of the Lake Naivasha area was provided by the explorer Joseph Thomson in a book that was published in 1887. Swahili and Arab trade caravans had passed Naivasha before but Thomson was one of the first Europeans to arrive at the lake. In his descriptions of the landscape, he painted an idyllic picture: "Our way at first lay across the grassy plain which lies to the north of the lake, and we were amused and delighted by the way in which the numerous herds of zebra played and frisked in the pure enjoyment of life and utterly unconscious of danger, within forty yards of us" (1887, p. 189). And: "The bosom of the lake itself was one moving mass of ducks, with ibises, pelicans and other aquatic birds" (1887, p. 187). These and later descriptions of the pristine environment led colonialists to conclude that there were "no natural African tenants" in Naivasha[5] and that it was an area where they could settle freely. Karen Blixen, the author of the famous book *Out of Africa*, once wrote in a letter: "It is absolutely delightful here. I think that Naivasha is a paradise on earth, with the water and the mountains around the lake, and the air is so lovely here and it is so peaceful without any people and so much game" (Oberlé, 1990).

These descriptions of pre-colonial Naivasha as a natural paradise untouched by humans do not acknowledge that the savannah around the lake was more or less permanently inhabited by pastoralist Maasai who were roaming the area. Thomson (1887, p. 188) described his meetings with Maasai warriors. The name "Naivasha" is even believed to derive from a Maa expression, *E-Nai'posha*, which could be translated as "rough waters". Furthermore, apart from the nomadic Maasai who used Naivasha as a grazing area for their livestock, Kikuyu traders were also present at the lake (Chege, Tarus, & Nyakwaka, 2015; Kioko, 2016).

In any case, as elsewhere in East Africa, social and ecological arrangements around the lake changed drastically with the colonization of the area by the British around 1900. Naivasha eventually became part of what was unofficially known as the "White Highlands": an area of approximately three million hectare reserved for European settler farmers (Morgan, 1963, p. 146; Odingo, 1971, p. xix).

Not only Naivasha but all of the Highlands—officially known as the "Scheduled Areas"—were perceived of as being uninhabited previously: "the country in question is either utterly uninhabited for miles and miles or at most its inhabitants are wandering hunters who have no settled home, or whose fixed habitation is the lands outside the healthy area" (Special Commissioner Sir Harry Johnston in 1901, as cited in Morgan, 1963, p. 140). Truly, some of the land in the Scheduled Areas had before been left unused, as these spaces functioned as a buffer zone between rivalling pastoralist groups. But apart from these fallow zones, and contrary to the Commissioner's statement, large parts of the White Highlands had been in use by Africans before. Due to uncertain rainfall, the area was unattractive for African agriculturalists, who did not have the aids such as bore-holes that European farmers used later on. But although the land was not used for cultivation, much of it served as grazing grounds for pastoralist groups, predominantly the Maasai. However, the colonialists did not consider the pastoralists to be permanent inhabitants because of their nomadic lifestyle. It was also convenient to conclude that the land in use by the pastoralists was unoccupied, as it opened up legal opportunities to take over the pastoralist areas. The Land Ordinance, created by the colonial government in 1902, contained a provision that postulated that land occupied by Africans could not be sold or leased out. Hence, the only way in which the colonial government could freely give out land to settlers was by determining that there were no permanent African occupants on a certain piece of land. Colonial officers concluded for most of the White Highlands, including Naivasha, that there were no permanent occupants. Apart from this legal possibility to take over the land, the colonialists also did not need to use much force to expel the Maasai. At the time that the first Europeans arrived, around the turn of the twentieth century, the Maasai as a group were weakened and had been diminished considerably in numbers due to civil war between rival Maasai factions, diseases such as smallpox and cattle plague, and drought.[6] They agreed to be relocated to two designated reserves in 1904. In this way, the area around Naivasha indeed was made void of permanent African occupants. The way was open for Europeans to move in (Bradshaw, 1990, p. 5; Chege et al., 2015; Morgan, 1963; Odingo, 1971, p. 28).

Hence, the Maasai were swiftly replaced by new inhabitants. The railway connecting the coastal town of Mombasa with the hinterland had reached Lake Naivasha in 1900. This railway was constructed with the help of migrant labourers from India. Those Indians who remained in East Africa after the construction work was over, turned to small trade, as it was forbidden for them to own land outside townships. A few Indians started to run shops at the new Naivasha station in Naivasha, which they rented from a former railway official, and a trading settlement was established. Next to these few residents of Asian origin, an increasing number of pioneering European settler farmers moved to the area around the lake. There were 86 occupied plots in Naivasha District by 1920, which had increased to 125 by 1930. The European-owned farms were extremely expansive—also when compared to other parts of the White Highlands—with an average size of over 2000 hectare in 1960 (Chege et al., 2015; Clayton & Savage, 1974, p. 14; S. Higgins, flower farm owner at South Lake, interview on February 10, 2015; Odingo, 1971, pp. 34, 45; Sorrenson, 1967, p. 16).

The European farmers were attracted to the idyllic surroundings of the lake. They were also encouraged by the colonial government to settle there. After having invested heavily in the construction of the railway, the colonial government entreated on white farmers—Brits, but also Boers from South Africa and Italians—to settle in East Africa, in order to make the colony economically productive and to ensure that the efforts of building the railway would pay off. The settlers were initially given freeholds to a limited portion of land on which they could build a homestead. In addition they were given leases of 99 years, which in some cases were even converted to leases of 999 years, for large tracts of land meant for production. After 1902 it became explicitly prohibited for non-Europeans to own or even to manage land in the Scheduled Areas. This prohibition was reinforced after official boundaries for these areas were set in 1939. Africans were removed to "reserves" which were separated by, what was then called, tribe. The creation of the reserves institutionalized the importance of ethnicity in the allocation of land by the central state, a feature that enhanced the formation of ethnic communities and that continues to have political, social, and economic consequences until the present time (Berman & Lonsdale, 1992, pp. 34–39; Boone, 2012, p. 78; Bradshaw, 1990, p. 5; Cohen & Atieno Odhiambo, 1989, p. 39; Kanyinga, 2009, pp. 327–328; Kioko, 2016, p. 94; Morgan, 1963; Odingo, 1971, pp. 28–30; Ominde, 1968, pp. 52–55; Sorrenson, 1967, pp. 15, 184).

Land in some of the reserves was scarce and of poor quality. In addition, the production of cash crops such as coffee became prohibited in certain areas to avoid competition for the settler farmers (Sorrenson, 1967, p. 41). Many Africans had little choice but to come to what were now European areas to temporarily work for the settlers, who were considered to be the economic backbone of the colony. "Capitalist production and authority over Africans became inextricably mixed" (Berman & Lonsdale, 1992, p. 36). This link between production and government was also reflected in the strict labour regulations during the first decades of settler colonialism. The legislation provided little protection to the workers, as its main goal was to provide the settlers with abundant cheap labour. Moreover, the approach of the colonial government was firmly rooted in racist attitudes towards the "natives". The Africans were portrayed as being reluctant to work, or as children who should be disciplined. They had to be "civilized" through wage labour. Legislation was therefore geared towards controlling the African workers, not towards protecting them. One example of this oppressive legislation is the infamous *Kipande* system, which was introduced in 1916. All African males who were over 15 years of age had to carry an identity certificate (*kipande*) that contained fingerprints and a record of employment. The system effectively meant that if a labourer left his employment without the signature of the employer, he could not get a job anywhere else anymore. Moreover, he could even be prosecuted for desertion and be convicted to flogging or imprisonment. In addition, the display of previously earned wages made it difficult to negotiate for better wages when changing jobs. The *Kipande* system is just one example of the many ways in which Africans were informally and formally coerced into poorly paid wage labour. Labour was also mobilized through conscript labour as well as through more informal pressure, such as the obligation to pay taxes and the prohibition on cultivating export crops in native reserves (D. M. Anderson, 2000; Berman & Lonsdale, 1992, pp. 101–122; Clayton & Savage, 1974; Cooper, 1996, p. 44; Kanogo, 1987, p. 1; Kanyinga, 2009, p. 327; Sorrenson, 1967, p. 47; Spencer, 1980). Settlers furthermore actively facilitated labour migration by sending trucks to the reserves to fetch prospective labourers (Kioko, 2016, p. 96). As stated by Cooper (1996, p. 45): "Thus British labor policy evolved in a complex spatial structure: small islands of wage labor, dependent on the poverty, induced or otherwise, of surrounding areas."

Naivasha soon turned into such a "small island of wage labour" and became an important area for employment, even though Naivasha settlers opted for agricultural activities that were not labour-intensive. They primarily chose to grow crops that they already knew from their countries of origin. Settlers in the higher-altitude areas towards the east of Naivasha, in the Kinangop, practiced mixed farming and produced cereals such as wheat, barley, and oats. Pyrethrum—a type of chrysanthemum that does not serve ornamental purposes but is used to create biological insecticides—was the most valuable crop that was cultivated there. The semi-arid climate at Lake Naivasha was less favourable for (non-irrigated) cultivation. Settlers there turned to ranching instead. Their main activity was to keep livestock such as cattle and sheep. They also produced fodder crops such as lucerne. The lake shores were used to cultivate Irish potatoes, which needed irrigation. Sisal was the only plantation crop grown in the area in the colonial period (the assistant chief of Olkaria Sublocation, interview on June 9, 2016; Casida, 1980, p. 190; LNROA, 1993, p. 50; Odingo, 1971; Ominde, 1968, pp. 56–58; O. Rocco, 2015).[7]

The ranch-owners in Naivasha employed casual and seasonal labour but they also heavily relied on labour provided by so-called squatters. "The term 'squatter', which originated in South Africa, denoted an African permitted to reside on a European farmer's land, on the condition that he worked for the European owner for a specified period. In return for his services, the African was entitled to use some of the settler's land for the purposes of cultivation and grazing" (Kanogo, 1987, p. 10).

The decision to employ squatters was related to a lack of capital among the settler farmers, a problem that was not recognized at the time. The colonial state chiefly depended on a few large-scale settlers and Kenya became, in Berman and Lonsdale's words (1992, p. 88), a "big man's country". However, as it turned out, these "big men" did not fulfil the expectations because they did not have sufficient capital to put their large tracts of land to use. They also did not use the land in the most effective way, as they mostly opted for practices that they were familiar with and not for agricultural activities that fitted best to the climate in their new environment. In short, the settlers could not put all their land to use with only temporary labour and had to accept the more or less permanent presence of Africans in the White Highlands. "By 1928 it was estimated that almost twenty per cent of the European farm area in the highlands was occupied by resident labourers and their stock" (Sorrenson, 1967, pp. 35–36). In this way, more of the land was put to productive use. The squatter system was also an effective way of retaining employees. It made labour not only cheaper but also more reliable, as the squatters could bring their family and keep their own livestock. However, the disadvantages of this system also surfaced. For the squatters, the main disadvantage was the strong dependency on a single patron or employer. They could end up in precarious situations if a farm was sold or if their employer passed away. There were also risks involved for the settlers. In some cases squatters were competing with the settlers with their produce. In other cases the livestock brought by the squatters came with diseases that affected the settlers' livestock. In addition, the squatters felt they were developing tenant's rights. This is not surprising when considering that landlessness in previous times was solved by clearing virgin land. From their own perspective, the squatters were therefore colonists in their own right, as they helped developing the land. Competition over land between settlers and squatters was also reported by the District Commissioner (DC) of Naivasha in 1917 (Berman & Lonsdale, 1992, p. 109). The government reacted by installing new legislation that limited the rights of the squatters, especially with regard to land use and the keeping of livestock. For instance, "[i]n 1946, the Naivasha District Council imposed a limit of fifteen sheep and reduced the cultivation area to one acre for each wife, with a maximum of two acres" (Sorrenson, 1967, p. 81). The number of days a squatter was legally required to work for the farmer was also increased from 180 to 270 days per year, even though wages stayed the same. Such restrictions culled the space for squatters to pursue their economic aspirations, made their position increasingly precarious, and eventually destroyed their autonomy (D. M. Anderson, 2000, p. 465; Berman & Lonsdale, 1992;

Clayton & Savage, 1974, pp. 128–129; Cooper, 1996, p. 47; Kanogo, 1987; Kanyinga, 2009, p. 328; Sorrenson, 1967).

Alongside these attempts to limit squatters' rights, the colonial government took on an increasingly ambivalent and diffuse role with regard to labour issues. On the one hand, the government aimed to facilitate profitable agricultural production in the colony. On the other hand, it tried to forestall excesses and to guarantee a minimum amount of protection for African labourers. There were regular differences of opinion between the several departments and offices within the government, especially between the administrators based in Nairobi and those in London. Initially, labour issues were primarily left to the settler farmers. The government only employed labour officers on a local level. There were no general minimum wages. Instead, the minimum wage depended on the industry and the locality, which left room to manoeuvre for the employers. Finally, there were no central pension schemes or other social benefits. However, the administration in Nairobi was increasingly influenced by industrial relation practices in Great Britain. In 1940, a central labour department was established for the colony. This department stimulated the formation of trade unions, which were successful in ameliorating labour conditions (Berman & Lonsdale, 1992, pp. 101–122; Clayton & Savage, 1974).

The General Agricultural Workers Union also opened an office in Naivasha and the local branch had 3000 members in 1960.[8] Some local government officials and individual settler farmers opposed this formal system of wage labour. Other farmers were more adaptive to these changes. They had managed to become more profitable through commercialization and mechanization after the Second World War. They therefore depended less on squatters and could pay higher wages. In 1955, wages in Naivasha were among the highest in Kenya (Clayton & Savage, 1974, p. 358).

The colonial government also started to consider the question how the labour force could be sustained, for instance, by the improvement of housing, all under the framework of "development" (Clayton & Savage, 1974, p. 297; Cooper, 1996, p. 207). The local government of Naivasha had a community development officer in the 1950s. This European officer coordinated adult literacy classes on the farms and a community centre and a football league in Naivasha Town. However, this "progressive and expansive" welfare programme curiously enough was mainly paid for by the profit of three beer halls—and therefore was effectively paid for by the workers themselves.[9]

A majority of the Africans who came to Naivasha during the colonial period were Kikuyu who originated from the Central Province, where land was most scarce (Kanogo, 1987, p. 14; Sorrenson, 1967, p. 35).[10] The importance of the Kikuyu for the ranches in Naivasha became especially apparent after 100,000 Kikuyu from all over the country were forcibly removed to the Central Province during the Mau Mau Rebellion in the early 1950s, in order to prohibit this violent resistance movement from spreading. After this "repatriation" of the Kikuyu, settlers in Naivasha complained about a shortage of (good) labour. Consequently, some Kikuyu squatters were brought back after the Rebellion was quelled (Clayton & Savage, 1974, p. 353; Kanogo, 1987, p. 138; Sorrenson, 1967, p. 99).[11] Hence, the establishment of the settler farms changed the population in the area: "Maasailand was being turned inside out, as African cultivators, the majority of them Kikuyu as they had been expropriated a lot, now invaded the choicest areas of the pastoral plain, under the protection of its new overlords" (Berman & Lonsdale, 1992, p. 90).

Although towards independence the Kikuyu had replaced the Maasai as the dominant group in the area, and were also considered by the government to be the main group of Africans living there,[12] other ethnic groups were also present. For example, with the start of the Mau Mau Rebellion, 1400 special farm guards, all non-Kikuyu, became employed in Naivasha (Clayton & Savage, 1974, p. 359). A few years later, in 1958, it was reported that both the Luo Union and the Abaluhya Association were active in Naivasha District, and that relations between all tribes and communities in the area were "cordial".[13]

Migration patterns differed per ethnic group and were partly linked to access to land and to the labour situation in the regions of origin (see for a comparison Moore and Vaughan (1994, pp. 143–144) on labour migration in colonial Zambia). Due to the shortage of land in Central Province, Kikuyu often came as squatters and took their families and livestock with them. They sometimes even held ceremonies, such as marriages and circumcisions, in the White Highlands and severed ties to the reserve. Members of other groups were usually "target workers", who worked only for a short period of time to earn money for a specific goal, or "career workers", who stayed away from their region of origin for many years. However short or long they stayed, most of these labourers stayed in close contact to their region of origin (Cohen & Atieno Odhiambo, 1989, p. 111; Kanogo, 1987). Migration patterns were also shaped by the housing situation on the farms. Whereas squatters could build their own house in a designated area of the farm on which they were working, contract labourers were housed in standardized lines of wattle-and-daub huts, often of poor quality (Kanogo, 1987, p. 19).[14] The result of these diverse patterns of labour migration was an ethnically mixed population by the time Kenya became independent. Even though the number of Kikuyu was not as high anymore as before the Mau Mau Rebellion,[15] the census of 1962 still counted 12,446 Kikuyu living in Naivasha ward, in a total population of 18,437. Furthermore, there were 1227 Luhya, 1180 Maasai, 737 Luo, and only 304 Europeans staying in this supposedly European area (Ministry of Economic Planning and Development, 1965).

As argued by Clayton and Savage (1974), the work on the farms shaped interethnic relations in the Highlands. A division of labour in which certain ethnic groups were assigned certain tasks gave ethnicity a meaning it had not had before. However, interethnic encounters on the farms also assisted in the creation of Kenya as a nation and in the spreading of Swahili as a shared language. The relation between the European settlers and the Africans was also determined by the context of wage labour: members of these two groups usually knew each other only "in the relationship of employee of employer" or, in Swahili terms, in the relationship between *bwana* (master) and *mfanyakazi* (the person who does the work) (Clayton & Savage, 1974, p. xiv).

The division of labour on the Naivasha farms was also gendered. Before the Second World War, it mainly were men who came to the European areas to work. These men received a so-called bachelor's wage, which only sufficed to support the worker himself (D. M. Anderson, 2000, p. 479; Cooper, 1996, p. 327; Sorrenson, 1967, p. 43). However, squatters who moved to Naivasha more or less permanently could bring their family along. The women and children initially took care of the squatters' plots and livestock. When the squatters' rights to property became severely restricted in later years, women and children were seasonally employed to execute the delicate job of picking pyrethrum. This labour was at some point even more sought after by the farmers than the labour of adult men, as pyrethrum was considered to be a "money-spinner", the more so since women and children could be paid lower wages than men (Casida, 1980, p. 190; Clayton & Savage, 1974, p. 129; Kanogo, 1987, p. 48; Odingo, 1971, p. 110).[16] The 1962 Annual Report (AR) of Naivasha mentions that even "unattached" (i.e. unmarried) women came to work as pickers.[17] In addition, a cereal and vegetable canning factory ("Pambora") in Naivasha Town provided employment to around 200 people, mainly women, in the early 1960s.[18] In general, it was not uncommon for women to be (seasonally) employed in the agricultural sector during the colonial period (Clayton & Savage, 1974, p. 151; Cooper, 1996, p. 463). Female employment in agriculture was thus by no means something that was introduced in Naivasha by the flower industry.

In sum, Naivasha and the wider Highlands had undergone a profound transformation by the end of the colonial era. Before the turn of the twentieth century, there were relatively few people living in the area and the land had been in use as grazing fields for livestock. After the colonization of East Africa, the land tenure system changed completely. The European settlers who leased the land confiscated by the government kept livestock as well but they also started cultivation in the area. Moreover, they brought in labourers to work on their farms, and their employment practices shaped ethnic and gender relations in the area. According to Morgan (1963), over 580,000 Africans were living in the Scheduled Areas by the late 1940s. "Although termed the White Highlands, it will be noted that they were occupied by over 200 Africans to every European" (Morgan, 1963, p. 153).

2.2 After Independence: "A Farming Town with Steady Growth"[19]

With independence approaching in the 1950s, and even more so after the Mau Mau Rebellion, British landowners in Kenya started to become nervous about their own future (Kanyinga, 2009, p. 328). Naivasha farmers wondered whether they would be allowed to retain their land. And would they be able to keep their farms running? Due to these fears, agricultural development in the area came to a standstill.[20] The lack of investment by settler farmers aggravated the already existing problem of unemployment in the country. Around the time of independence, population pressure in the reserves had caused people to flock to Nairobi and Mombasa, in search of work that was not there. Unplanned shantytowns emerged in those urban areas. But also rural production areas such as Naivasha received more job seekers than there were jobs available. The unsuccessful job seekers there in practice often ended up squatting on farms, with or without permission of the owner, even though the system of squatting had officially come to an end in 1963. The emergence of these various informal modes of residence indicated that landlessness, combined with unemployment, was a pressing problem that had to be addressed (Clayton & Savage, 1974, p. 363; Cooper, 1996, p. 360).

A first step was taken in 1960, when the provision that non-Europeans could not own land in the Scheduled Areas was removed from legislation. The colonial government initiated settlement and land purchase schemes to redistribute land, a policy that was pursued further after Kenya had gained independence. However, the main aim was to secure economic stability and to protect the agrarian economy, not to provide land to all landless African people. Consequently, and unlike what settlers had feared, the land redistribution did not take the form of forcing European settlers to leave without any form of compensation. To protect the economy, land policies were geared towards a gradual transition in the ownership of land over the course of a few decades. And although land tenure systems in some other parts of the Highlands changed drastically, the situation in Naivasha initially remained largely unaltered. This ranching area was not considered to be suitable for large-scale resettlement schemes as they were implemented in other parts of the Highlands, nor did individual wealthy African or Asian investors show much interest (Chambers, 1969, pp. 15–39; Kanyinga, 2009, p. 329; Morgan, 1963, p. 153; Odingo, 1971, pp. 187–192). A few European settlers whose farms were being mismanaged in the eyes of the government were forced to sell their estates (Odingo, 1971, p. 192).[21] But most settlers in Naivasha were able to retain their land. Loldia Estate at North Lake could, for example, renew its land grant for 942 years in 1963, against a new annual rent.[22]

Loldia Estate had been established as one of the first settler farms at Lake Naivasha in the first decade of the twentieth century and remains in the hands of the same family until today. This family, the Hopcrafts, continues to keep livestock on their 7000-acre estate (Chege et al., 2015, p. 156). In addition, they currently run a tourist lodge, and parts of the estate are leased out to vegetable farming companies, as the assistant manager of one of these companies explained. Other remaining colonial families also have started to put their estates to use for other purposes than ranching, such as tourism and conservation activities (S. Higgins, 2015; O. Rocco, 2015). Moreover, most European settlers in Naivasha started to sell (parts or all of) their land in the late 1960s. The practice of ranching thus slowly disappeared at Lake Naivasha in the decades after Kenya gained independence.

The land sold by the settlers was in some cases taken over by land-buying cooperatives or companies, consisting of a group of Africans who often belonged to a single ethnic group.[23] These transfers accelerated the population growth in the area in the 1970s and 1980s, as most of the cooperative members moved to the farms, together with their relatives.[24] Next to these groups of buyers, there were also individual buyers, including a few Kenyans of Asian origin, who took over complete estates or plots immediately adjacent to the lake. These rich individuals were usually based outside Naivasha.[25] Sales took place on the basis of the "willing-buyer, willing-seller" principle. The government reserved the largest plots of land in Kenya for those with the most capital, as it was expected that these rich farmers would be able to produce export products that could bring in foreign currency. This policy of favouring the economic elite in the long term exacerbated class differences. The more so because these African large-scale farmers were often members of the upcoming political elite. It were these politicians-cum-businessmen (the new "big men") who generally profited the most from these land policies. The redistribution programme thus made land ownership a central political issue in Kenya (Bradshaw, 1990; Kanyinga, 2009; Odingo, 1971, p. 192).

The land policies not only intensified wealth disparities but also made ethnicity more significant. When selling land, the government favoured members of those groups that could form a threat to settler farms if they would lose out on land, for instance, land-poor Kikuyu peasantry. In addition, former European estates were often allocated to those who had lived as labourers or squatters on these farms before—again in majority Kikuyu. This pragmatic approach on the one hand led to a smooth transition of land without much violence towards European farmers. At the same time, it antagonized ethnic relationships in the former Highlands, between groups that had lived there before the Europeans came, such as the Kalenjin and Maasai, and the new landowners after independence (Kanogo, 1987, p. 173; Kanyinga, 2009). At the time that the new land policies were being implemented, Morgan (1963, p. 153) remarked:

> It is most noticeable, however, that the only tribe which used any significant proportion of this land before the Europeans, the Masai, are taking no part in the present take-over. The effect of the European settlement will have been to settle these areas with cultivating peoples who formerly would not have entered the area for fear of the Masai or other pastoral tribes.

The long-term consequences were profound. "The settler farms became primary sites of intense competition between and among different land purchase groups, a majority of which were distinguished by their ethnic or class composition" (Kanyinga, 2009, p. 332). There have been simmering and occasionally violent conflicts between farmers and pastoralists in the hinterland of Lake Naivasha after former European-owned farms were sold to farming cooperatives. Kioko and Bollig (2015) wrote about the violent conflicts in Ng'ati farm in Maiella in 1993,[26] while cases of cattle theft in the cooperative farm Mirera signified a conflict between Kikuyu farmers and Maasai pastoralists ("Herdsmen Invade", 1995).[27]

The land-buying cooperatives did not only clash with other economic and ethnic groups over access to the land; internal relations were also often strained (Kioko, 2016, pp. 279–281; Odingo, 1971, p. 212).[28] Also in the Naivasha area, there were regular complaints about mismanagement by cooperative leaders, which led to distrust and disputes among the members.[29] Another problem was the tendency to subdivide the large farms and to give out individual plots to the cooperative members.[30] The central government favoured large-scale agriculture with its potential to produce export products and was not pleased with this development (Bradshaw, 1990, p. 11). The local government in Naivasha therefore attempted to discourage cooperatives from subdividing and warned that this practice increased unemployment in the area.[31] These appeals by the government were ultimately unsuccessful: most cooperative farms eventually were subdivided. To make matters worse, in many cases, company or cooperative directors did not actually give out the title deeds after a subdivision was announced. Subsequent conflicts could persist for decades and were a constant nuisance in the area. Some of the workers' settlements that developed on these cooperative farms have been heavily affected by these conflicts.[32] As late as 1998, local leaders were informed "that wrangles amongst directors of land companies and cooperatives are so prevalent and widespread throughout the division that no meanful [*sic*] development is taking place. This is because no financial credit can be given without title deeds."[33]

Governmental reports from the period after independence showed that Naivasha's economy—with little development taking place on the cooperative farms—continued to rely heavily on ranching activities. Initially, little innovation took place in the agricultural sector. The new African owners, whether cooperatives or individuals, also kept livestock and cultivated the same crops as the settler farms had done, such as barley and potatoes.[34] Naivasha's future position as an agro-industrial hub was yet unimaginable in 1978, when a government development plan stated: "The low potential zone of Naivasha, Bahati and Njoro divisions are mainly used for ranching purposes."[35] Nevertheless, and although the flower industry only established itself in the 1970s and 1980s, vegetable farming under irrigation was already introduced on a modest scale in the 1960s. Interestingly enough, not only new African and Asian owners but also remaining European settlers (such as the above-mentioned Rocco family) experimented with horticulture and thus created some new job opportunities in the area. This sector slowly expanded and produced French beans, asparagus, strawberries, onions, capsicum, beans, and tomatoes, for both the domestic market and the export market (English, Jaffee, & Okello, 2006; O. Rocco, 2015).[36]

In the 1970s, most of the job vacancies reported to the labour office in Naivasha were in the agricultural sector. Annual reports from the period show that job seekers were generally unskilled and that unemployment was a problem. On the other hand, there were regular complaints about job seekers turning down vacancies on farms and plantations: agricultural wage labour seemed to be unpopular.[37]

Apart from this dislike of farm work, labour relations in the time after independence were relatively harmonious. In contrast to the rough and by times violent colonial history of labour relations, the remaining European farmers gained a reputation of treating their workers relatively well. A report from 1973 stated: "It was interesting to note that European employers in this area were paying correct wages during the year while Asian and African employers underpaid their people."[38] As was the case during colonial times, the farm owners took it upon themselves to take care of the welfare of the workers, with little interference from the government. It was, for instance, reported in 1987 that the "Technical Public Health Assistant was also asked to pay frequent visits in the farm villages to see that the people were properly cared for. Farm owners and farm managers were positively amused to these visits."[39]

Nevertheless, labour issues such as the level of wages and the amount of working hours were not completely left to the employers' discretion. The industrial relations system in Kenya had taken further shape around independence and the main players were a federation of major expatriate firms, trade unions, and the Labour Department (Clayton & Savage, 1974, p. xxii). In 1963, several sectorial unions formed a federation called Kenya Plantation & Agricultural Workers Union, abbreviated to KPAWU (Clayton & Savage, 1974, p. 417). KPAWU soon became the major trade union in agricultural Naivasha and successfully negotiated with the Agricultural Employers Association about conditions on the farms.[40]

As Naivasha continued to attract a modest number of job seekers in this period, the population in the area became more diversified. It was, for instance, reported that an increasing number of immigrants from western

Kenya came to the wider Nakuru area—of which Naivasha forms a part—to look for work.[41] The general increase in population in Naivasha Division was around 5% per year in the 1980s. Population growth accelerated when new employment opportunities arose, also outside the agricultural sector, such as in a newly opened national prison and in the geothermal energy sector (Becht, Odada, & Higgins, 2005, p. 282).[42] The opening of Hell's Gate National Park in 1984 gave a boost to the tourism sector (Kiaye, 1986).

The establishment of the National Park was not advantageous for everyone: it created a conflict over land between the local government and the Maasai community that formerly had lived there.[43] Whereas this particular dispute resembled earlier contestations over resources in the area, other new environmental conflicts around Naivasha in the 1970s and 1980s mostly did not revolve around access to land. They centred on the lake and the lake water, and were related to the increase in economic activity and in human population in the area. An important and vocal group in these conflicts was a group of foreigners who had only purchased their plots of land immediately adjacent to Lake Naivasha after Kenya had become independent. These new inhabitants had no intention of farming. They simply were attracted to the natural environment of the lake and wanted to reside there. Among these new landowners at Lake Naivasha were famous and outspoken conservationists such as Joy and George Adamson and film-makers Joan and Allan Root. Their presence made Lake Naivasha more well-known outside Kenya, especially when they started to receive illustrious guests, for example, Jacky Kennedy Onassis in 1974 (Seal, 2011, p. 74). When from the 1970s onwards economic development in Naivasha started to take off, these new inhabitants saw the "natural" paradise they had been attracted to change before their eyes: more and more farms and other industries started to make direct use of the lake water. These farms used chemicals that were running off into the lake. In addition, the human population in the area increased rapidly. At this point, also nature-loving members of the remaining colonial families started to be concerned about the future of the lake and became involved in conservationist activities (Becht et al., 2005, p. 278; O. Rocco, 2015; Seal, 2011, p. 47).

In short, more and more people were attracted to the area: a new group of Europeans because of the natural environment, wealthy Kenyans because of possibilities to invest, and less well-off Kenyans because of the possibilities to acquire a small plot through a land-buying cooperative or to find a job in one of the farms or new industries. Next to a few remaining colonial families, these were the major interest groups in the area around the time that the first flower farms were established.

2.3 Blooming Business: The Establishment of the Cut Flower Industry

Pyrethrum flowers were the only flowers grown on an industrial scale in Kenya during the colonial period and the first years after independence. Nevertheless, the idea of growing cut flowers for ornamental purposes was not entirely new. Already in 1949, a colonial government official wondered whether it would not be possible to produce cut flowers of good quality in Kenya:

> If suitable arrangements could be made for their collection from such places as the Kinangop, Molo and the higher areas around Njoro, first class blooms of many varieties of Lilies, Roses, Gladioli and Chrysanthemums equal to those of hot-house standard produced in the United Kingdom, could be obtained.[44]

The officer also mentioned that there were already a few smallholders around Nairobi who produced cut flowers at the time. The first mentioning of cut flower production around Naivasha dates back to 1961, when it was reported that 15 acres of land in the "European areas" in Naivasha were used to grow flowers.[45] A report from the Ministry of Agriculture showed that in Kenya as a whole, production of flowers rapidly increased from 8290 kilograms in 1965–1966 to 58,200 kilograms in 1969–1970. The Ministry expected more growth in this sector because of the favourable climate in Kenya and because of a new agreement with the European Economic Community on the duty-free entry of certain products into Europe. The Ministry at that time already explicitly recognized the potential of flower growing, next to other horticultural production, for providing employment in Kenya.[46] A few years later, production indeed had increased tremendously, to 1,096,468 kilograms of flowers in 1973. These flowers were mainly exported to West Germany and the United Kingdom.[47]

The first flower farm in Naivasha was DCK ("Dansk Chrysantemum Kulter").[48] The company, owned by a Danish investor called Jan Bonde Nielsen, already had farms in Machakos and Nairobi before it took over the estate of the former sisal plantation located at the murram road along the southern shores of Lake Naivasha in the early 1970s. It started to produce seasonal flowers such as carnations and statices there. The company had been invited by the Kenyan Minister of Agriculture to start up a horticultural business in the country and was given exclusive rights to cultivate certain types of flowers for a period of eight years. Other reasons for the company to come to Kenya were the good climate, the availability of labour, the existing regular flights to the markets in Europe, and the political stability in the country. The company was financially supported by the Danish government through an "Industrialization Fund" and was successful in providing employment. The Naivasha farm had 3000 employees by 1975 (assistant chief of Olkaria Sublocation, 2016; English et al., 2006, pp. 139–140; S. Higgins, 2015; "Improve Working Conditions", 1974; Mwembe, 1979; O. Rocco, 2015; Whitaker & Kolavalli, 2006, pp. 341–342).[49] However, the company collapsed in that same year due to financial mismanagement:

> In the late sixties, documents show that DCK entered into an agreement with the Government of Kenya to grow chrysanthemum to be exported to Western Europe and the company rapidly started acquiring real estate and land in the country. In 1974, the DCK group consisted of companies operating in Switzerland, Germany, England and Denmark and in Kenya. The group employed thousands of workers. The growth was mainly funded by English, German and Swiss banks. DCK collapsed in 1975 with debts running to 100 million Danish kroners, which was largely unsecured loans and the management was blamed for the unexplained losses and accused of irresponsibility by a Danish task force that investigated the collapse. (Munene, 2013)

After the financial collapse, the DCK farm in Naivasha was taken over by a neighbouring farm, Sulmac. Sulmac became part of the multinational Brooke Bond Liebig in 1978. At the time of this second takeover, the farm was growing around 50 varieties of carnations on 120 hectares of land. The farm continued to expand afterwards: the number of employees had doubled to 6000 by 1986 ("Company Being Purchased", 1978; English et al., 2006, p. 140; Mwembe, 1979).[50]

Sulmac soon received competition from Oserian, another pioneering farm. Oserian, unlike DCK, has retained its original name until the present and continues to (partly) be in the hands of the founding family. The founder, a Dutch man called Hans Zwager, upon arrival in Kenya first started a company in chemicals and fertilizers for horticultural production called Kleenway Chemicals. In 1967, the family bought the estate *Oserian* in Naivasha, which covered 5000 acres of land. The estate also includes a colonial, oriental-style house with a turbulent past called Djinn Palace, which has become the residence of the Zwager family. The previous owners[51] had hardly utilized the land belonging to the estate except for some ranching activities, as the soil was considered to be unsuitable for cultivation. Nevertheless, Zwager decided to try vegetable farming under irrigation. He was successful and the products were both exported and sold to local processing companies. Yet

Zwager was not satisfied with the profits that were being made. Oserian therefore shifted to the large-scale production of seasonal flowers such as statices and carnations in 1982, which proved to be more profitable. Later on—allegedly as the first farm in Naivasha—the firm also started to grow roses. Oserian had 2000 employees by 1986 (English et al., 2006, p. 140; Hayes, 1997, pp. 347–352; S. Higgins, 2015; Seal, 2011, pp. 123–125; M. Wachira, 2011).[52]

After DCK/Sulmac and Oserian became successful, more flower farms were established in Naivasha. These smaller farms also mainly produced carnations, although chrysanthemums, statices, and roses were cultivated too. The production areas were concentrated at South Lake. The less accessible area at North Lake initially continued to be in use for pasture and for the production of lucerne and maize. Vegetable production also spread in this period (Kiaye, 1986; LNROA, 1993, p. 51; Oberlé, 1990).

The flower farms that were established early on were owned either by foreigners (mainly Dutch) or by Kenyans of European or Indian descent (Kazimierczuk, Kamau, Kinuthia, & Mukoko, 2018, p. 6; N. Mwangi, 2019, p. 19). They were the ones who recognized the profitability of the industry: "the first farms made a fortune" (S. Higgins, 2015). Not all of these pioneers were farmers by profession. The founders of Oserian and DCK were financial investors who were looking for a niche market and for ways to make large profits. The financial downfall of DCK moreover shows that these profits were not always made in wholly clandestine ways.[53] In later years, flower farmers from Europe followed the business to Kenya after production in their home countries became less profitable. Nevertheless, the industry also continued to attract foreign venture investors. There were echoes of the demise of DCK in the recent case of the Indian-owned Sharma Farm. This farm went bankrupt, allegedly likewise due to financial mismanagement and tax evasion.

The industry also attracted an increasing number of local investors, often in joint ventures with foreigners (Kazimierczuk et al., 2018, p. 8). Bradshaw (1990) analysed the link between agriculture, class, and the state in Kenya. The government did not assist smallholders but opted to subsidize large-scale agriculture, which was in the hands of "politicians-cum-businessmen". Bradshaw concluded that the agricultural sector in Kenya was mainly benefiting a small, urban-based elite that was linked to the Kenyan government. Initially it seemed that the flower industry would follow a similar path. There was a heated discussion in parliament about the special favours that DCK had received from the Kenyan government

(Republic of Kenya, 1973, pp. 568–570). Apparently the Minister of Agriculture who had given these concessions, Bruce McKenzie, acquired a considerable amount of shares himself in the same company. Nevertheless, this controversial case turned out to be an exception. There has been relatively little interference in the flower industry by the Kenyan political elite afterwards.[54]

Apart from this limited private involvement by politicians, the Kenyan government officially has not played an active role in the development of the flower industry anymore after the initial support to DCK. Following global trends, there was a move towards less regulation and less taxation in the 1980s and 1990s (Little, 2014). The Minister of Agriculture decades later even named the lack of government involvement as the main reason for the success of the industry, as did a report of the World Bank that praised the reduced control by the Kenyan government over, for instance, air freight rates (English et al., 2006, p. 141; "Govt Absence", 1999; Whitaker & Kolavalli, 2006, pp. 352–353). The local government in Naivasha has also not been actively involved in the flower industry that developed there. Whereas ranches were regularly monitored for livestock diseases[55] and whereas quota were set for the production of pyrethrum,[56] the topic of the rapidly growing flower industry was for a long time remarkably absent in the minutes of meetings of the local agricultural committee.[57]

It thus took some time before the potential of the cut flower industry was generally recognized. A newspaper article from 1972 reported that there were fears that the newly introduced cut flower chrysanthemum might bring viruses that could harm the pyrethrum industry (G. Wachira, 1972). As late as 1978, and despite the presence of the large cut flower farm DCK/Sulmac, an Annual Report mentioned pyrethrum as the only industrial crop grown around Naivasha.[58] However, by the mid-1990s, the expanding cut flower industry had started to outshine the once so significant pyrethrum industry.[59]

Due to the growth of the flower industry, labour migration to Naivasha started to take place on an accelerated pace. Most of the flower farms did not consider it their task to accommodate their workers. They paid out a housing allowance instead. The local government of Naivasha was also not prepared to accommodate the increasing number of migrants while it was used to the colonial arrangement in which agricultural employers took care of their workers themselves. The result was a lack of affordable housing in the area. Owners of small plots in the area seized their chance and started to build makeshift housing on their plots to rent out (S. Higgins, 2015). Many of these small-scale landowners were Kikuyu who had acquired their land some years earlier through their participation in land-buying companies or cooperatives. Letters from the archives show that landowners initially were not inclined to sell their land or to construct and rent out houses. They either preferred using their land for agricultural purposes[60] or considered their plot in Naivasha to be family land that should not be sold. One man tried to prevent his father from selling their plot on the cooperative farm Kihoto, which later turned into a workers' settlement. He wrote to the DC of Naivasha: "You know it is better to be dead than landless."[61] However, when rents and land prices increased sharply with the arrival of ever more migrant workers, many owners decided to either sell their plot or construct rental housing on it. But whereas housing was thus provided by private landowners, infrastructure such as sewerage and water supply was not taken care of (Becht et al., 2005, p. 278).

The farms provided certain facilities for their workers, just as the ranches had done before. They paid for medical care for employees or opened up farm dispensaries.[62] Some farms also facilitated schools, for instance, Maua ("Flowers") Primary School in DCK and Oserian Primary School ("Public Tasks", 1987).[63] Next to these on-farm facilities, the companies also sent representatives to meetings of local government committees that discussed the development of the workers' settlements.[64] But the lack of infrastructure was not sufficiently addressed, which led to the regular outbreak of water-borne diseases, such as bilharzia in the settlement at Sulmac/DCK in 1980 and typhoid, again in Sulmac, in 1991. Even in the few farms that did have a workers' compound, conditions were not always optimal and infectious diseases such as dysentery could spread easily ("Dysentery 'Controlled'", 1998, "Jabs Campaign", 1991).[65]

The poor living conditions of the migrant workers initially received little public attention, as did the labour conditions on the flower farms. Pictures that appeared in the *Daily Nation* in 1979 show packhouse workers without any protective clothing, which was not questioned in the accompanying article (Mwembe, 1979). Nevertheless, the union KPAWU remained active in Naivasha and signed agreements on wages and labour conditions with some of the early flower farms. An agreement between KPAWU and DCK, signed in 1971, for instance, determined that working hours should not exceed 46 hours per week. The agreement also included a paid annual leave of 18 days and an unpaid maternity leave of three months.[66] In 1998, the local KPAWU branch was even named after the two largest flower farms: Sulmac/Oserian Branch (instead of Naivasha Branch).[67] But not all flower farms were unionized. The KPAWU secretary-general Francis Atwoli complained in the same year that only 24 out of the estimated 100 Naivasha flower farms allowed their employees to become a member of the union ("Union Appeals to Govt", 1998).

Industrial disputes within flower farms in this period mostly revolved around low wages and threats of job loss. There were, for instance, disputes and (threats of) illegal strikes in the DCK/Sulmac farm after the takeover in 1976 and again in 1985 and 1996 ("4,000 Watisha Kugoma", 1985; Mwathi & Njuguna, 1996).[68] Relations within the union itself have not always been smooth either. In 1981, 3056 employees of Sulmac went on strike against a rise in the union contribution.[69] There were also conflicts between the union representatives within specific farms and the KPAWU branch office. The representatives within Sulmac, for instance, requested to elect a new branch office in 1997 because the branch secretary in their opinion did not properly assist the employees.[70] In short, although a system of industrial relations has been in place ever since the flower industry started, this did not prohibit the occurrence of occasional disputes.

Similar to the lack of public concern for labour conditions, the possible environmental damage caused by flower farming also received little attention in the early years. There was some awareness that the pesticides used by the flower farmers could be harmful when running off into the lake, but the government initially took no action.[71] The use of water was likewise not regulated. When the first flower farms started, there were no charges yet for the use of lake water. However, there started to grow a consciousness that water users could or should pay for this resource. A local government plan from 1986 stated:

> The lake water should be used on a commercial base by the farmers who irrigate their land for growing crops for sale. At the moment it is supplied for free. Some experts have expressed fear that the irrigation also interferes very much with the level of the water and that to control it, farmers should be charged, otherwise in the long run the lake will dry up completely as years go by. This may not sound true but at least such comments need a serious consideration and attention.[72]

Only around the year 2000, the existing legislation on water use and environmental issues, which stemmed from the colonial period and was not designed to manage the effects of agro-industrial production, was replaced by laws that were more fitting to the new situation (Becht et al., 2005, p. 279).

Not only legislation changed. Pressure on the farms to implement more environmental-friendly practices built up from several sides. The informal group of landowner-environmentalists, consisting of both members of colonial families and nature-lovers who had acquired land after Kenya gained independence, became more vocal. Their public expressions created the image of Naivasha as a natural sanctuary under siege. This powerful narrative started to gain traction in national and international media, especially after the flower industry was established. However, most of these conservationist efforts and their outcry about the deteriorating state of the lake were based on the contemporary situation. They did not (explicitly) recognize that the natural habitat around Naivasha had already slowly but steadily started to change many decades ago, with the arrival of the first European settlers.

One salient example is fish: the doom scenario of a lake deplete of fish because of massive fish poaching was successful in mobilizing protests and actions (Seal, 2011). Not all activists recognized that this scenario for the future actually pictured the state of the lake in the past, in the period before the European settlers had arrived. The presence of fish in the lake was not a "natural" given: the explorer Thomson only describes hippopotami and ducks in the lake, no remarkable fish (1887, p. 193). Worthington and Worthington wrote a few decades later: "Previous to 1925 there were no fish in that lake except *Haplochilichtys antinorii*, a minnow-like fish of no value to anyone. In that year, however, Mr. R.E. Dent, Fish Warden in Kenya, introduced *Tilapia nigra* (…) and after three years this fish had multiplied so enormously that great numbers could be netted anywhere along the lake shores" (1933, p. 174). Thus, previous to the arrival of the European settlers, there had been no indigenous large fish species in Lake Naivasha, presumably because the lake had almost dried up earlier in the nineteenth century. The settlers, and later on also the government, introduced tilapia, bass, crayfish, and common carp to the lake, with the goals of attracting rich sport fishers and of enabling a diversified fishing industry. Flourishing tourist businesses and increasing land prices at the lake in the early 1930s showed the early successes of these introductions. However, the introduction of alien species also markedly altered the complete ecological system and the chemical composition of the lake. It had a strong, and for some species even devastating, impact on the indigenous flora and fauna in and around the lake (Becht et al., 2005, p. 287; Mavuti & Harper, 2006, p. 32; Worthington & Worthington, 1933, pp. 174–176).

Paradoxically, it was precisely these introduced (and not indigenous) species that later became the subject of a pervasive environmental conflict in Naivasha. When net fishing was introduced in 1959, the fishing industry was valued for its economic value and potential (LNROA, 1993, p. 38).[73] However, from the 1970s onwards, the poaching of fish has posed a constant challenge, as there were always more people who wanted to fish than there were fish to catch and licences to give out.[74] It was now feared that the lake might be emptied of fish and the government installed yearly temporary fishing bans. Poaching continued to be the source of, by times violent, conflicts around the lake (Becht et al., 2005, p. 292; Seal, 2011, p. 159). Consequently, overfishing and fish poaching have gained a lot of attention. At a stakeholders' meeting in November 2014, an officer of the Fisheries Department blamed the high number of unlicensed fishermen on the attraction of job seekers by the flower industry. However, fish poaching already became a problem in the area years before the flower industry came up. Moreover, the *introduction* of fish might have done more damage to the ecosystem of the lake than the later issue of overfishing has done (Mavuti & Harper, 2006, p. 32).

Another problem blamed on the flower industry declining lake levels. However, and without denying that the irrigation by flower farms affects the lake, fluctuating lake levels are also a natural phenomenon. Stoof-Leichsenring, Junginger, Olaka, Tiedemann, and Trauth (2011, p. 363) describe extensive droughts and resulting extremely low water levels in the nineteenth century. The lake is very shallow and small changes in water levels therefore have large effects on the surface area (Mavuti & Harper, 2006, p. 30). Fluctuating lake levels have therefore already been a concern ever since farms were established at the lake shores. Around the years of independence, the lake was frequently flooding. These floods led to a loss of land for riparian landowners and damaged crops.[75] In the 1970s the situation changed and lake levels started to decline rapidly. Since then, the role of horticultural and later on floricultural farms has been continuously discussed whenever the lake levels are receding.[76]

Moreover, existing environmental issues such as the fluctuating lake levels also became more poignant with the increase in economic activity around the lake. As a result of these growing concerns, Lake Naivasha became a protected Ramsar Wetland Site under the international Ramsar Convention in 1995, which called for the development of an inclusive management plan for the lake. The statutory custodian of the Kenyan Ramsar Sites is the Kenya Wildlife Service, but the stakeholders were primarily united through the efforts of the Lake Naivasha Riparian Association (LNRA). This organization had taken the initiative for the Ramsar application. LNRA (originally called Lake Naivasha Riparian Owners' Association, abbreviated to LNROA) is an organization of riparian landowners founded in 1929. The original objective of the organization was to prevent land and boundary conflicts between owners of land adjacent to the lake. However, the organization increasingly presented itself as the steward of the riparian land and of the lake's ecological system. It set internal regulations for its members, such as a prohibition on cultivation and construction on the riparian land, and it organized research and educational activities. The LNRA and their Ramsar application played an important role in the emerging conservationist agenda surrounding Lake Naivasha (Harper, Morrison, Macharia, Mavuti, & Upton, 2011, p. 99; S. Wanjala, research officer of the LNRA, interview on November 24, 2014).[77]

Whereas conflicts over pollution and the use of lake water related immediately to the production of flowers, other environmental contestations were related to the human population that the flower farms had attracted, such as fish poaching and human-wildlife conflicts. Despite the increase in the human population, there continued to be plenty of wildlife around Naivasha. Even at the time of my fieldwork, wild animals such as giraffes and warthogs could be regularly spotted along the Moi Lake Road and even on the premises of flower farms that were on riparian land. During visits to Karibu Farm, I saw a monkey sneaking into a greenhouse and a group of zebras striding through an open field of roses. These animals sometimes damaged crops of both smallholders and large-scale farmers. Moreover, animals such as buffaloes and hippopotami can be outright dangerous to people. In 2010, a member of the colonial Hopcraft family of Loldia Estate was killed by a buffalo. On the other hand, the people also formed a threat to the animals: there was an increase in the poaching of wildlife. Also through other economic, partly illegal, activities such as the cutting down of trees and the watering of livestock at the lake, the increase in the human population had a large impact on the flora and fauna in the area (Becht et al., 2005, p. 278; "Flower Farm Owner", 2010; S. Higgins, 2015).[78]

The assistant chief of Olkaria Sublocation at South Lake explained that the area along the (then) murram South Lake Road, where he was born, had been "plain wilderness", where wildlife roamed around freely until the 1970s. However, because of human-wildlife conflicts and an increasing feeling of insecurity, flower farms and other riparian landowners started to fence off their land. Some, including several flower farms, even turned part of their land into a private conservancy.[79] Previously, there had been 16 corridors to the lake that were open to the public and that could be used by both wild animals and livestock. This number went down to five, due to the erection of fences (Becht et al., 2005; Lembcke, 2015). This lack of access was aggravated when some owners also made it impossible to pass their land via the lakeshore. Some even built permanent constructions on the riparian land, including greenhouses for flower production, even though they were officially not allowed to do so. Stakeholder groups such as the LNRA denounced the building of infrastructure, yet they at the same time supported restrictions on public access because of conservation purposes. The fencing severely hampered the economic activities of fishermen living in the settlements and of Maasai pastoralists, who had started to move back into the area to water their animals at the lake during the dry season (Ngesa & Mwangi, 2005; S. Wanjala, 2014).

In sum, life around Lake Naivasha had changed markedly after the first flower farms were established in the 1970s and the industry started to expand in the 1980s. This new situation caused tensions and conflicts over resources. These developments intensified towards the 2000s, when the Naivasha flower industry matured but also started to receive some serious critical attention.

2.4 Naivasha in the 21st Century: Paradise Lost?

In the late 1990s, the floriculture industry in Kenya started to grow at an accelerated pace (English et al., 2006). By 2002, the industry was so firmly established that a government report stated: "The expansive flower and vegetable farms most of which are under beautifully constructed greenhouses are synonymous with Naivasha."[80] The expansion of production fields, greenhouses, and residential areas is clearly visible on two satellite pictures from Naivasha, taken in 1995 and 2015; see Figs. 2.1 and 2.2.

The Naivasha flower industry has been characterized by quite some continuity. Many of the flower farms mentioned in a report from 2003 still existed during fieldwork in 2014 and 2015.[81] Nevertheless, changes in ownership—which also implies a change in name of the farm—were common. Just as the first flower farms had taken over the land and infrastructure of earlier European settler and cooperative farms, later investors in the flower industry took over already established flower farms. Whereas there had been quite a number of middle-sized companies in the early years, many of these farms merged or were incorporated by a multinational company. The result was that the core of the industry later on was formed by

Fig. 2.1 Satellite image of Naivasha in 1995 (Landsat imagery courtesy of NASA Goddard Space Flight Center and US Geological Survey)

just a handful of, mainly foreign-owned, large-scale farms, employing thousands of workers each. This process is exemplified by the history of the first flower farm DCK. DCK subsequently became part of Sulmac, Brooke Bond Liebig, the Commonwealth Development Cooperation (CDC),[82] Homegrown/Flamingo Holdings, and Finlays, one of the largest horticultural firms in the world. These regular transfers increased job insecurity because employees could never be certain that the new owner would re-hire them. The transfers could also lead to the termination of certain facilities provided by the previous owner. For instance, the takeover of Sulmac by Homegrown in 2002 led to the collapse of the farm's Saving and Credit Co-operative (SACCO). However, despite these changes in ownership that brought about some insecurity, the farms themselves remained. Moreover, they continued to expand and they provided ever more permanent employment throughout the 1990s and 2000s ("1,300 Flower Farm Employees", 2002; assistant chief of Olkaria Sublocation, 2016; S. Higgins, 2015;

Fig. 2.2 Satellite image of Naivasha in 2015, showing the location of the workers' settlements: 1. Kihoto; 2. Karagita; 3. DCK; 4. Kwa Muhia; 5. Kamere; 6. Kongoni; 7. Kasarani; 8. KCC (Landsat imagery courtesy of NASA Goddard Space Flight Center and US Geological Survey; numbers of the settlements added by the author)

Lembcke, 2015, p. 12; Riungu, 2005; Julius Wanjala, long-serving employee of Sharma Farm, interview on February 5, 2015).[83]

From around the year 2005, growth numbers became more modest because of increasing competition from the neighbouring country Ethiopia, where employees could be paid lower wages. Some farms moved there, while others used the option to move to put pressure on the government and the trade union. These farms warned to not make too high demands with regard to wages, taxes, labour conditions, or environmental measures

(Opala, 2007; Redfern, 2006). However, doom scenarios of a collapsing flower industry in Kenya due to the competition from Ethiopia have not materialized as yet. As explained by several managers, an important reason for this is the quality of the labour force in Kenya, which outweighs the disadvantage of having to pay higher wages.

Despite the overall continuity, the flower industry still underwent transformations with regard to the production process, labour relations, and environmental practices. These shifts were partly caused by a shift in the type of flowers that were grown. "By the mid-1990s, roses made up about 50 percent of total flower exports. By 2000, they constituted 70 percent of exports" (Whitaker & Kolavalli, 2006, p. 343). The farms thus gradually shifted from the production of carnations and summer flowers, which are grown outside or in wooden greenhouses, to the cultivation of roses, which is mostly done in large polythene greenhouses (Whitaker & Kolavalli, 2006, p. 344). This shift is also discernible in Naivasha, where by the year 2002, a larger surface was used to produce roses (569 hectares) than other types of flowers (555 hectares).[84] Data over the year 2013 on 17 Naivasha farms, provided by the lobby organization KFC (Kenya Flower Council), show that these farms used 420 hectares for the production of roses while they used 235 hectares for other flowers and ornamental plants. The shift to production in greenhouses is also clearly visible when comparing Fig. 2.1 to Fig. 2.2, which show Naivasha in 1995 and 2015 respectively.

The shift to rose production also had consequences for labour conditions on the farms, due to the characteristics of the crop. For instance, roses are a more permanent crop than most other flowers. A newspaper article on Sulmac from 1979 described that it takes six months for a carnation plant to flower for the first time, after which it can produce for another six months (Mwembe, 1979). In contrast to that, I was taught during my visits to Karibu Farm that rose plants are able to produce flowers for five or more years. Hence, the shift to roses created permanent employment opportunities instead of the seasonal jobs that had been common previously. In addition, the shift induced changes in the division of labour and the planning of the work, as the closed environment of polythene greenhouses requires stricter procedures for spraying pesticides than cultivation outside or in wooden greenhouses (Gibbon & Riisgaard, 2014, p. 112).

Another change was the adoption of more sophisticated production technologies. One of the farms I visited in 2014, which had only been established a few months before, had an assembly line in the packhouse.

It also had automatized the transport of flowers from the greenhouse to the packhouse through a small railway, an innovation that originally was developed on South American banana plantations. But most technical innovations were not meant to replace human labour through mechanization. As explained by Whitaker and Kolavalli (2006, p. 338), flowers need to be harvested by hand to ensure the quality of the product. Instead, innovations in the industry were geared towards creating better growing conditions for the flowers or towards more environmental-friendly production processes. The polythene greenhouses were improved by introducing computer-controlled regulation of the climate (temperature and humidity) and by automatizing irrigation and fertilization ("fertigation") systems. When it comes to the environment, farms invested in better irrigation techniques, biological pest control (***dudutech***[85]), or the creation of dams for recycling water and wetlands for the treatment of waste water. Other farms made investments in renewable energy by constructing their own geothermal or solar energy plants. One farm even opened a biogas plant fuelled by the crop waste it produced (Becht et al., 2005, p. 291; David, 2015; "Govt Absence", 1999; Riungu, 2007).[86]

Apart from these processes in Naivasha itself, the global value chain of the flowers also started to change around the year 2000. As Karibu Farm's general manager Jan explained, this relates to the type of roses that are grown in Naivasha. Whereas farms in higher-altitude areas such as around Mount Kenya can produce high-value flowers with large heads, climatic conditions in Naivasha favour the production of roses with intermediately sized heads. The "premium quality" flowers produced in other regions continued to be sold exclusively to florists via the auction located in the Netherlands, but a second value chain developed for intermediate flowers. These are increasingly sold via so-called direct sales to supermarket chains in several European countries (Whitaker & Kolavalli, 2006, p. 344).[87] These supermarkets are more vulnerable to the disapproval of consumers than of florists. Together with the increased scrutiny by NGOs, this shift in the global value chain has prompted two recent trends within the Kenyan flower industry, namely increased unionization and "standardization".

Whereas the trade union KPAWU has been present since the flower industry established itself, an increasing number of farms became unionized in the early 2000s. The farms started to adhere to the Collective Bargaining Agreement (CBA) signed biannually between the trade union KPAWU and the Agricultural Employers' Association (AEA). It sometimes were the workers themselves who pressed for this step. The Naivasha

District labour office reported on several strikes in the year 2003 within farms where employees demanded a shift from payment according to the Agricultural Wages Order (containing particularly low wages) to payment according to the CBA. But the increasing importance of the union was also related to the process of "standardization". In response to the mounting criticism on labour conditions and on possible environmental damage by the farms, parties within the industry itself developed certification schemes. These schemes typically contain a standard with environmental and labour-related regulations. Farms can only sell certified flowers when they adhere to these regulations. The participating farms are regularly audited (Omosa, Kimani, & Njiru, 2006). As a farm manager specifically in charge of the implementation of the Fairtrade standard explained, these are costly procedures, involving a lot of paper work. Nevertheless, over the past two decades, an increasing number of farms have applied for these certificates because they secure the farms' access to markets. And since some standards, such as those from the KFC and Fairtrade, require certified farms to allow their workers to join the union, standardization has reinforced the process of unionization (Riisgaard & Gibbon, 2014, p. 280).

The reputation of the flower industry has improved to some extent in recent years because of these two processes (Dolan, 2007; KHRC, 2012). The industry nevertheless continued to be questioned for the possible environmental damage it causes. The flower growers initially feared negative publicity and they established lobby groups such as the KFC and the Lake Naivasha Growers Group (LNGG). However, the flower farms also started to realize that being environment-friendly is an asset in the European market. Moreover, it is in their immediate interest to take environmental measures, as they depend on the lake water. For instance, when a drought hit Naivasha in 2000, the flower farms could not fall back on some of their irrigation systems because of electricity shortages, which affected their production. However, although the industry acknowledged there was a need for regulation, it tried to retain control over the regulation processes. It, for instance, lobbied for standardization to avoid stricter legislation. The LNGG have since the early 2000s worked together with the LNRA, other stakeholders, and environmental researchers in practical projects. These included the drafting of a Lake Naivasha Management Plan and the establishment of the "private-public-people initiative for sustainability", Imarisha Naivasha, an organization meant to coordinate the activities of stakeholders such as the flower industry, scientists, community groups, NGOs, and several local government offices (Becht et al., 2005; Harper et al., 2011; Mavuti & Harper, 2006; Omondi, 2010; S. Wanjala, 2014).[88]

A final development in the early 2000s was that the government undertook some attempts to regulate the flower industry. On a national level, labour legislation was revised in 2007 and again in 2012. Together with the new Kenyan constitution of 2010, the new provisions—at least on paper—strengthened the position of workers. However, there continued to be a lack of enforcement, as the Ministry of Labour was understaffed (KHRC, 2012). The local government in Naivasha, which initially had left the care for the flower farm workers' welfare to the farms, also slowly became more involved. It, for instance, started to organize adult literacy classes in the flower farms, just as it had done in the 1950s in the settler ranches.[89] And in early 2007, the town council tried to force the flower farms to pay local taxes. The council claimed its services were overstretched due to the large numbers of migrants attracted by the farms. The industry resisted fiercely and claimed it was protected by national law against paying those taxes.[90] The town council and the industry came to an agreement only later that year, when the council dropped the plan for taxing the farms and instead requested the flower farms for immediate donations, which it received. This less confrontational approach proved to be successful. In 2009, the LNGG agreed to pay annual taxes to pay for the use of infrastructure provided by the government ("Council Seals", 2009; M. Mwangi, 2007; Omondi, 2007; Opala, 2007).

Farms have developed in diverse ways within the framework of these larger trends of scaling up, "standardization", and increased cooperation with other stakeholders. These developments also had diverse implications on the farms' workers. The employees of Sharma Farm were severely affected by a change of ownership, as explained in several interviews with (former) employees of the farm and with the assistant chief of Olkaria Sublocation. Sharma was established in the late 1980s by a Dutch investor. It was an exceptional farm in the sense that it from the start only cultivated roses and no other flowers. The farm expanded quickly: it had several thousands of employees by 1996, in which year it also opened its own primary school. In 2002, the farm became unionized and it started to provide free transport to and from work for employees who did not live in the farm's *kambi*. Sharma by that time also had its own company hospital and was known for its good labour conditions, such as a high rate of permanent contracts. It had become one of the largest and most successful farms in Naivasha. The situation changed markedly after 2007, when the Dutch owner decided to start up a new farm in Ethiopia and sold Sharma to an Indian investor. The new owner allegedly did not make any investments in the production process, which started to show after a few years. Ripped polythene of the greenhouses was, for instance, not repaired. A former employee sneered that the only thing the new owner had done was to change the position of certain doors in the office buildings in line with religious prescriptions. Next to this obvious lack of investment, there were rumours about money laundry and tax evasion. From 2010 onwards, the farm was in serious financial trouble, until salaries were not being paid out for several months. The employees went on strike and production almost came to a standstill. Subsequently, the number of employees went down from about 6000 to 2000 employees, as some of them were laid off and others decided to leave themselves when they did not receive their salaries. The farm also did not pay its suppliers, who then stopped the deliveries, which further hampered production. Workers' welfare was also affected, as the workers' camp was cut off of electricity and the company hospital closed down. In 2014, the farm was declared bankrupt and the banks that had lent money to the Indian owner appointed receivers to manage the farm. After the receivers had taken over, the farm managed to get production back on track, until the ongoing court cases completely blocked the farm from producing in spring 2016. All remaining employees were rendered jobless. Moreover, those staying on the compound were uncertain about their living arrangements there. Especially those workers whose households had fully depended on the salaries from Sharma Farm were hit hard.

In contrast to Sharma Farm, another farm that features prominently in this book, Karibu Farm, illustrates the general stability of the industry. Karibu Farm was founded after independence—under a different name than the current one—by a British farmer. It specialized in fruits and vegetables. When the owner retired before or in 1979 and left Kenya, he sold the farm to a Kikuyu man, who continued with vegetable production and also started to cultivate roses around the year 1995 (D. Gitahi, landowner in Kasarani and retired farm manager, interview on January 22, 2015). In 2001, the farm was bought by the current owner, a Dutch family company. Several long-term farm employees mentioned that the farm under the new Dutch owners initially also cultivated seasonal flowers such as hypericum. However, eventually indoor rose production became the main activity. The new owners constructed greenhouses but otherwise continued to make use of the existing structures such as offices, managers' housing, and the packhouse. The farm's employees reside in the neighbouring settlement Kasarani. The farm has continuously expanded its number of greenhouses over the years and has become Fairtrade-certified in 2014, thus following general trends in the flower industry of scaling up and standardization.

Like Karibu Farm, many of the early founded flower farms were established on tracts of land with freeholds or long-running leases, previously occupied by ranches.[91] These early farms were not much affected by the steep increases in land prices around Naivasha in the 2000s.[92] Some of the more recently opened farms started up at hitherto undeveloped or underdeveloped plots, located at some kilometres from the lake. Reasons that flower farm managers gave for moving away from the lake are the decision of the government to stop giving out new permits to abstract lake water, the possibility to own land there instead of leasing, and the frequent social unrest along the Moi Lake Road. Getting access to land is complicated, also for the flower farms: two farms, located close to the settlements Kihoto and Karagita respectively, became caught up in land disputes. These farms were ordered to demolish (some of) their greenhouses after it was claimed that these had been constructed on land that was not legally theirs (*Geoffrey Muhoro v Lake Flowers Limited*, 2011; Kariuki, 2015).

There are two main roads in Naivasha that shaped its economy and that gained importance with the establishment of the flower industry. The first is the highway from Mombasa to Kampala that passes Naivasha. This road is heavily used by trucks, which has made Naivasha into a transit town and a popular stopover for truck drivers. This creates economic opportunities but also causes certain social problems, such as a relatively high prevalence of HIV/AIDS (Happ, 2016, p. 70). The highway is also crucial for the flower industry, as it is used to transport the flowers to the airport. The second important road in the area is the only road going around the lake, Moi Lake Road. It for a long time was in a bad state. The south-eastern part of the road, stretching from Naivasha Town up to the high-end Lake Naivasha Hotel opposite of Karagita, was tarmacked early on to accommodate tourism. However, it was not well-maintained. It had a lot of potholes and even complete stretches where no tarmac was left. The farms consequently were not well connected and there were continuous complaints about the state of the road. The following example comes from a letter sent to the *Daily Nation* at the time of President Moi (Cosmos, 1981):

> The "road" referred to is the South Lake Road, if this rocky, sandy dust-blown track can be called a road. Beyond the tarmacked portion one enters a stretch of the most nerve-wracking car-wrecking and dangerous "highway" in Kenya. To name this appalling "road" after our revered President is shameful.[93]

Only in the late 1980s, after the opening of Hell's Gate National Park, the government finally extended the tarmac up to Kongoni on the south-western lake shores. But although the South Lake Road recently has been in a good condition, maintenance of the road has mostly been paid for and organized by the flower farmers and other private stakeholders such as the geothermal power plant and hotels around the lake ("Farmers Group Demands", 2005; S. Higgins, 2015; "Rural Road", 1986; Oberlé, 1990).[94] Furthermore, the North Lake Road—the stretch between Kongoni on the south-western side of the Lake and the Nairobi-Nakuru Highway at the north-eastern side—was not tarmacked for a long time. It was not until 2015 that a stretch, connecting the gated community Greenpark with the highway, was tarmacked. Being the only main route leading around the lake to Naivasha Town and further away, flower farms depended on the Moi Lake Road for transporting their produce to the airport. For this reason, blocking this road proved to be an effective way of protesting. During my stay in Naivasha, both the unpaid employees of Sharma Farm and inhabitants of Karagita whose public corridor to the lake had been shut down once blocked the road, using for example burning tyres, as a way to invigorate their protests.

Apart from such incidental protests, there was a widespread perception among both private landowners and the local government that crime in general was on the rise after the flower farms had attracted all these migrants who came to live in unplanned settlements (Ombuor, 1996; O. Rocco, 2015).[95] A few of the larger farms, especially the ones that were established early on, provided housing and other facilities to their workers and their families. These farms appeared to be a town on their own, with schools and hospitals, and in some cases even with a private team of fire fighters or a professional football team ("100 Families Homeless", 2009; Okeyo, 2013). Nevertheless, it was estimated in 2007 that only one out of every four workers was housed by the flower farms (Opala, 2007). In fact a decreasing number of farms provide accommodation to the workers (Riisgaard & Gibbon, 2014, p. 109). Happ (2016) listed six flower farms with compounds in his overview of the Naivasha flower farms. Workers of the other farms have to look for rental housing themselves in the settlements that have sprung up around the lake (see Fig. 2.2). These settlements are perceived to be crime-ridden. In a special meeting in 2005, where security issues at South Lake were discussed, it was stated that criminals "reside in those slums as houses and life is very cheap. Also it is very easy for them to intermingle with the crowd as no one is concerned with what others are doing." The perceived causes for the "crime wave" were unemployment, carelessness on the side of landowners when it comes to who their tenants are, illicit brew, pool tables, and distrust towards officers.[96] Yet, the scale might have changed, but *chang'aa* (illicit brew) was already sold at a large scale in settlements such as Karagita in the 1970s. Furthermore, there continuously have been cases of theft and armed robbery since at least the 1960s, especially at North Lake ("Chotara Orders Demolition", 1984, "Police Rout", 1962).[97] Nevertheless, foreign farm managers and Kenyans of European descent living around the lake started to feel ever more threatened in the mid-2000s, after several Europeans were killed. This feeling of insecurity intensified when also farms became the target for violent robberies, especially around pay day (Njuguna, 2006; "Police Shoot", 2005; Seal, 2011, p. 180).

However, in early 2008, it became clear that not only wealthy landowners and farm managers were targets of violence but also the migrant workers residing in the settlements. In the aftermath of the elections in Kenya in late 2007, diverse militant youth groups enticed violence throughout the country with the support of political leaders. This violence—an expression of ethnic and class tensions rooted in historically shaped land relations in the former White Highlands—also erupted in Naivasha. Ethnicity, class, and ownership of land had become intertwined due to both the colonial invention of tribal reserves and land policies after independence (Boone, 2012; Kanyinga, 2009). Furthermore, as argued by Anderson and Lochery (2008, p. 339), more recent political discourses on ethnic territories (*majimboism*) have drawn attention away from class differences and have emphasized ethnic struggles over land. In Naivasha, where thousands of people live together as tenants in crowded settlements whereas large tracts of private land are fenced off, the land issue has become poignant. But also here, the issue has primarily been interpreted in ethnic and not in class terms.

The violence that took place in Naivasha in early 2008 was preceded by rumours that Luo tenants would no longer pay rent if "their" presidential candidate would be elected. These rumours created tensions between plot owners and tenants, especially after plot owners started to evict tenants out of fear for the looting of their property. These tensions eventually culminated in violence, which took the form of retaliation for atrocities committed against Kikuyu in other parts of the country, who had been displaced to Naivasha. Enticed by members of the *Mungiki* gang, some Kikuyu aimed to take revenge by attacking Luo, Luhya, and Kalenjin residents. They claimed

Naivasha to be "their" territory. In the last days of January 2008, an estimated 48 people were killed and an unknown number of houses were set on fire. The violence did not take place all around the lake. Especially the settlement Karagita and certain neighbourhoods in Naivasha Town were badly affected. Furthermore, the flower farms were not directly implicated in the violence. Some migrants even took refuge on farm premises. However, thousands of others fled from Naivasha. A flower farm worker who lived in Kasarani at the time explained that she and other members of targeted ethnic groups were even collected by government buses to be transported to their supposed "homes" in western Kenya. The situation caused a sudden shortage of labour, especially for the farms that did not provide housing. Nevertheless, the flower industry was little affected in the long run. Production was soon back on track when some of the workers who had fled started to return after the calm was restored. Yet, although daily production processes were resumed, some workers had left never to return again. Moreover, the violence has left its traces in neighbour relations within the Naivasha workers' settlements (D. Anderson & Lochery, 2008, pp. 338–339; Kanyinga, 2009, p. 340; Lang & Sakdapolrak, 2014; Mbogo, 2008; M. Mwangi 2008; Okanga, 2008; Republic of Kenya, 2008, pp. 113–128; "Waajiriwa Watoroka", 2008).

2.5 Conclusion: Naivasha's Past and Present

At the beginning of the twentieth century, Naivasha transformed from a pristine "paradise", containing wildlife and green pastures for scattered Maasai herds, to a colonized area with large stretches of under-utilized ranch land for European settlers. Another hundred years later, livestock as the main product of the area was replaced by flowers that were grown on an industrial scale.

Although this reorganization of the area was profound, it was a gradual process that took place over the course of more than a hundred years. Furthermore, many of the major shifts cannot be wholly ascribed to the establishment of the flower industry alone. These environmental and social changes were already initiated in the colonial era and in the first decades after independence. Harper et al. (2011, pp. 93–96) found that some of the most sweeping and devastating ecological changes in and around the lake have been induced by the introduction of several alien species into the ecosystem by European settlers and, after independence, by the government. In addition, agricultural activities by settler farmers in the catchment area caused major changes in the chemical composition and sediment accumulation rate of the lake (Stoof-Leichsenring et al., p. 365).

The arrival of European settlers in the area also brought about major social shifts. This chapter described how Kenyans were turned into labourers and squatters in the colonial era, through means that—as Meagher, Mann, and Bolt (2016) have pointed out—were common across the African continent, such as imposing taxes and prohibiting Africans from producing cash crops. This chapter furthermore described the arrival of small-scale landowners in the 1960s and 1970s. The long presence of colonial labourers and of African landowners in the area is mostly not discussed in accounts on how Lake Naivasha has changed. Becht et al. (2005, p. 278), for example, stated: “Before the horticultural developments, the population was comprised mainly of people born along the lake shores, or who were attracted by its peace and beauty.” These authors claimed that the people who have lived in Naivasha “all or most their lives” were afraid that the “paradise might get lost”. Articles such as this one, which have been influential in international debates on the state of the lake and its surroundings, contain echoes of the colonial image of Naivasha as an area void of people before the arrival of the white settlers. They provide a partial and elitist view on the changes in Naivasha’s social-ecological system.

Also the experiences of labour migrants who arrived in the area more recently have been largely ignored in hegemonic representations of Naivasha’s past and present. Some descriptions, especially those about the environmental effects of the flower industry, contain gross generalizations about the migrant workers. A flagrant example is the description by the biographer of the environmentalist Joan Root: “Here was a migration as wild and savage as the wildebeest migration Joan and Alan had filmed. This time it was massive numbers of people, hundreds of thousands of hungry, desperate, out-of-work men and women” (Seal, 2011, p. 127). Such accounts dehumanize the migrant labourers. In addition, these accounts do not recognize that the flower farms that established themselves in the 1970s arrived in an area with a long history of agricultural wage labour. Instead of erasing this earlier history, the flower farms became an additional, influential actor in a “wealth of coexisting variation” (Ferguson, 1999, p. 80).

The image of Naivasha as a “natural paradise” under threat of agro-industry nevertheless has become a powerful narrative that resonates globally. As argued by Appadurai (2013, p. 287), the production of a locality is an active, constant, collective, and imaginative process. Moreover, the production of "Naivasha" also is a contested process. Interpretations of Naivasha as a "natural paradise", as an agro-industrial hub, and as Kikuyu "territory" are competing with each other. Yet, migrant workers and their understanding of Naivasha as a place have been little represented in public discourse and in scholarly literature on the area. As argued by Cohen and Atieno Odhiambo (1989, pp. 29–30), history can be "material of power". Hegemonic historical interpretations of Naivasha have, for instance, enhanced the control over land of some while justifying the lack of access to land for migrant workers. In this chapter I have challenged some of these narratives by describing Naivasha's rich history as a place of agricultural wage labour. I have attempted to do justice to the diverse and changing meanings of Naivasha as a place to diverse groups of residents by putting the development of the flower industry in a larger historical context.

Notes

1. The areas along the Moi North Lake Road and Moi South Lake Road are commonly known as "North Lake" and "South Lake" respectively. I also use these terms in this book to refer to those areas.
2. Note that administrative boundaries also shifted and that Kenya as a whole experienced a large increase in population in this period. Nevertheless, the census showed that whereas the total Kenyan population had more than doubled in 2009 as compared to 1979, the population in Naivasha had quadrupled.
3. Officially the eight provinces of Kenya do not exist anymore as administrative units. They have been replaced by counties (see Cheeseman, Lynch, and Willis (2016) on the administrative restructuring process). However, they have not lost all their significance: the province names are still used in names of institutions such as the archives and also in everyday conversations. To confirm to common usage I therefore still refer to these provinces in this book.
4. All court cases cited in this book have been accessed via the database on the website of Kenya Law: http://www.kenyalaw.org/caselaw/ (accessed February 12, 2019). The *Kenya Gazette* has an online archive, which can be accessed via http://books.google.co.ke/books/about/Kenya_Gazette.html?id=SiZddRcP0BcC (accessed February 12, 2019).
5. The expression "no natural African tenants" derives from an interview that I conducted in 2015, which indicates the tenacity of colonial representations of Naivasha's pre-colonial situation.
6. The Kikuyu had faced similar predicaments. The diminished population numbers after these crises were another reason why large parts of the White

Highlands were seemingly unoccupied at the time of European settlement (Odingo, 1971, p. 28; Sorrenson, 1967, pp. 16–18).

7. Kenya National Archive (KNA), AN/42/35/10, Annual Report (AR) of the District Agricultural Officer South Kinangop Covering Naivasha Agricultural Committee District (Except Olkalou) 1961; KNA, DC/NKU/5/1, "Applications for Conscript Labour, Nakuru & Naivasha," 1942–1943.
8. KNA, DC/Nais/1/1/1/68, AR of the Labour Office of Naivasha District, 1960.
9. KNA, DC/UG/2/1/18/2, "Newsletter of the Ministry of Community Development and Rehabilitation," July, 1957.
10. The origins and consequences of the land shortage among the Kikuyu in the Central Province have been described by Sorrenson (1967).
11. KNA, DC/Nais/1/1/1/15, AR Naivasha Division 1953: 7.
12. See KNA, AR Naivasha 1961 and 1962, where "the African population in Naivasha" is equated with "the Kikuyu".
13. KNA, DC/Nais/1/1/1/52, AR Naivasha District 1958.
14. KNA, DC/Nais/1/1/1/52, AR Naivasha District 1958: 16; KNA, DC/Nais/1/1/1/63, AR Labour Officer Naivasha, 1959.
15. According to Kanogo (1987, p. 127), there were 22,136 registered Kikuyu squatters in Naivasha in 1945.
16. KNA, DC/Nais/1/1/1/63, "Annual Report".
17. KNA, AR Naivasha 1962.
18. Kenya National Archive, Provincial Deposit Nakuru (KNA Nakuru), GU/9/1/64, The District Officer (DO) of Naivasha to the Town Planning Department, Nairobi, "Naivasha Town Population Structure and Scope for Development," November 4, 1966.
19. Title derived from a newspaper article (Kiaye, 1986).
20. KNA, AN/42/74/32, Quarterly Report of the Naivasha District Agricultural Committee Area, September 30, 1962.
21. In Naivasha, the farms of Mrs. LG Lee (with a size of 2438 acres) and Mr. Arthur Williams (3249 acres) were supposed to produce wheat, oats, pyrethrum, dairy, and sheep. However, they were unsuccessful and were forcibly sold to New Karati Farmers Coop Society in 1970 (KNA, AN/22/19/8, The Area Manager to the Executive Officer of the Provincial Agricultural Board, "Mismanaged Farms—Nakuru, Kericho & Nandi districts," August 18, 1967; KNA, AN/22/19/144, P Wambani to the Executive Officer of the Nakuru District Agricultural Committee, "LR No. 8752—Mrs LG Lee—Naivasha," March 20, 1970; KNA, AN/22/19/145, P Wambani, to the Executive Officer of the Nakuru District Agricultural Committee, "LR No 8756—Arthure E Bedward Williams and Daphine G Bedward Hurt—Naivasha," March 20, 1970.)

22. *Kenya Gazette*, Notice No. 2,483, January 1, 1964.
23. Nakuru District, of which Naivasha formed a part, had 57 land-buying cooperatives in 1973 (KNA Nakuru, GU/9/1/104, The Provincial Planning Officer Rift Valley Province to all members of the Nakuru District Development Committee, "District Development Plan 1974–1978," August 16, 1973). Kanyinga (2009, pp. 332–336) described this process of resettlement through land-buying groups as it took place in other parts of the Rift Valley.
24. KNA Nakuru, GU/9/1/96, The DO Naivasha to the DC Nakuru, "Organisation of the District," January 29, 1971; KNA Nakuru, GU/9/1/188, Naivasha Town Council, "Local Authority Development Program," March, 1986.
25. See KNA, AN/22/16, Nakuru District Agricultural Committee, "African and Asian Large-Scale Farmers in the Rift Valley," 1966–1970.
26. Described from the perspective of the Maasai in: KNA Nakuru, GU/3/9/106, The Maasai Elders Community, Naivasha to the Provincial Commissioner Rift Valley Province, Nakuru, "Land Dispute (LR No 8398/1&2)," July 3, 1993.
27. KNA Nakuru, GU/10/5/53, AR for the year 1999 by the Area Chief H.K.O. Narangaik, Hell's Gate Location.
28. With the exception of Marie Gravesen's unpublished dissertation titled *Negotiating Access to Land in a Contested Environment: Opposing Claims and Land Use Fragmentation in Western Laikipia, Kenya*, I am not aware of any elaborate scholarly work on the prevalent conflicts within land-buying companies in Kenya. This is remarkable, considering the impact on individual livelihoods and the political salience of such conflicts.
29. This problem was mentioned in: KNA Nakuru, GU/1/5/41, S.B. Anunda, District Agricultural Officer Nakuru, to the DC, Nakuru, "District Development Plan," June 6, 1978. See for one of many examples that I encountered in the archives: KNA, TR/1/104/86, J.K. Mukamba, Hon Secretary of the North Karati Society, Naivasha, to the District Co-operative Officer in Nakuru, "Help," August 13, 1971.
30. Described in: KNA Nakuru, GU/1/5/41, "District Development Plan." Examples are the subdivisions of the land of Highland Modern and New Karati Farmers, which were approved of on the same day (see: KNA Nakuru, GU/3/25, Minutes of the Naivasha Land Control Board, January 12, 1984).
31. KNA Nakuru, ANN/1/1/21, The Divisional Agricultural Office, "Minutes of the Second Meeting of Naivasha Division Farmers Leaders Conference," March 26, 1977; KNA Nakuru, GU/9/1/104, "District Development Plan 1974–1978."
32. The conflict over a plot in Karagita, discussed in Sect. 5.2.1, provides an example here.

33. KNA Nakuru, GU/1/9/100, Minutes of the Naivasha Divisional Leaders' meeting, October 19, 1998.
34. See a report on former European farms taken over by cooperatives: KNA Nakuru, ANN/1/1/25, The Divisional Agricultural Office, "Minutes of the Joint Naivasha/Gilgil/Elementaita ASC Meeting," July 11, 1977.
35. KNA Nakuru, GU/1/5/41, "District Development Plan."
36. KNA Nakuru, GU/9/1/104, "District Development Plan 1974–1978"; AR Nakuru 1980, 1982.
37. KNA AR Naivasha 1973, 1976; KNA AR Nakuru 1978, 1980.
38. KNA AR Naivasha 1973.
39. KNA Nakuru, GU/1/7/34, Minutes of the Ndabibi Sublocational Development Committee, 15 April 1987.
40. KNA AR Naivasha 1977.
41. KNA AR Nakuru 1980.
42. KNA Nakuru, GU/9/1/188, "Local Authority."
43. KNA Nakuru, GU/3/36/41, The Maasai Elders Hell's Gate Location, Naivasha, to the Land Adjudication Officer, Nakuru Head Office, "Land Dispute Regarding LRN 74771," November 2, 1998.
44. KNA, TR/14/8, The Officer Administering the Government of Kenya to the Secretary of State for the Colonies, "O. 687 Saving," May 13, 1949.
45. KNA, AN/42/35/10, "AR 1961."
46. KNA, BV/64/50, Ministry of Agriculture, "Horticultural Development in Kenya. Synopsis of Horticulture Working Party Draft Report and Recommendations for Government Action," June, 1970.
47. KNA, TR/8/148/82, Horticultural Cooperative Union, "HCU Fresh Supermarket," 1974.
48. I do not use pseudonyms for the early farms as the descriptions reflect public knowledge.
49. *Kenya Gazette*, Notice No. 1,312, April 26, 1974; KNA Nakuru, GU/3/33/18, P.F. Alubbe, DO Naivasha, to the Manager, D.C.K., Naivasha, "DCK Trading Centre," June 27, 1975.
50. KNA Nakuru, GU/9/1/188, "Local Authority."
51. Among whom was Lord Erroll, who was a prominent member of the Happy Valley Set, a group of settlers infamous for their decadent lifestyle (Hayes, 1997).
52. *Kenya Gazette,* Notice No. 2,005, May 26, 1967; KNA Nakuru, GU/9/1/188, "Local Authority".
53. It is telling that the Danish founder of DCK has been caught up in several other financial scandals in Kenya afterwards (see Munene, 2013).
54. I do not mean to imply that Kenyan politicians have not been involved in the flower industry at all, but at least such connections are usually not publicly known. One of my assistants asserted that President Uhuru

Kenyatta owned shares in a recently founded, large-scale Naivasha flower farm that we visited. I could not verify his claim. However, it is not unlikely, since Kazimierczuk et al. (2018, p. 11) list six flower farms (of which none is located in Naivasha) that were (partly) owned by high-ranking politicians and civil servants, including former president Moi.

55. See, out of many examples of lists with affected farms, *Kenya Gazette*, Notice No. 1,579, May 30, 1969.
56. See KNA, AN/42/74/19, Naivasha District Agricultural Committee Area, "Quarterly Report," June 30, 1962.
57. See, for example, KNA Nakuru, GU/7/1/37, "Naivasha Agricultural Committee."
58. KNA AR Nakuru 1978.
59. Dolan, Opondo, and Smith (2003, p. 14) and Whitaker and Kolavalli (2006, p. 336) provide estimates of the value and volume of the continuously increasing export of cut flowers from Kenya in the 1990s. The production of pyrethrum by smallholders, on the other hand, continuously declined due to a malfunctioning centralized marketing system (see 'Ailing Pyrethrum Sector', 2014).
60. KNA Nakuru, EA/2/22/115, H.T. Matiru, Nairobi, to the Chairman of the Land Control Board, Nakuru, "Application for Subdivision," February 3, 1993.
61. KNA Nakuru, GU/3/26/212, Muniu Mbugua, Naivasha, to the DC Naivasha, no subject, July 25, 1989.
62. For instance, the Sulmac Farm dispensary, see KNA Nakuru, GU/1/6/23, Meeting of the Maiella Locational Development Committee, November 9, 1982.
63. KNA Nakuru, GU/3/33/64, DH Gray, Director of Sulmac Company Ltd., to the DO Naivasha, "Commercial Centre on Sulmac Land," January 28, 1991.
64. See KNA Nakuru, GU/1/5/61, Minutes of the Naivasha Locational Development Committee, November 30, 1978; KNA Nakuru, GU/1/7/34, "Ndabibi."
65. KNA Nakuru, GU/1/5/102, Minutes of the Naivasha Divisional Development Committee, February 4, 1980.
66. *Kenya Gazette*, Notice No. 1,312, April 26, 1974.
67. *Kenya Gazette*, Notice No. 7,174, December 18, 1998.
68. AR Naivasha 1976.
69. AR Naivasha 1981.
70. KNA Nakuru, GU/8/1/110, KPAWU Sulmac Co. LTD, Naivasha, to the DO Naivasha, "Branch Election Permit at Deb Pri. School Sports Ground," August 1, 1997.
71. KNA Nakuru, GU/1/7/59, "1988–1993 Draft Plan."

72. KNA Nakuru, GU/9/1/188, "Local Authority."
73. KNA Nakuru, GU/9/1/64, "Naivasha Town Population Structure."
74. KNA AR 1973 Naivasha; KNA AR 1975 Nakuru; KNA Nakuru, GU/9/1/188, "Local Authority."
75. KNA, DC/Nais/1/1/1/52, "AR 1958"; KNA, AN/42/35/10, "AR 1961."
76. See, for example, KNA Nakuru, GU/1/7/59, Z.O. Gori, District Fisheries Officer, Naivasha Station, to the District Development Officer, Nakuru, "1988–1993 Draft Plan," April 18, 1988.
77. KNA Nakuru, GU/1/9/9, Minutes of the Nakuru District Environment Management Committee, February 9, 1995.
78. KNA Nakuru, GU/7/1/153, Minutes of the Naivasha Subdistrict Agricultural Committee, November 11, 1993.
79. Oserian established its own conservancy on the estate (Hayes, 1997, p. 370). Sulmac donated a 2.7-hectare piece of (their leasehold) land to the Kenya Wildlife Service in 1998 (KNA Nakuru, EA/2/16/81, G. Ireri, for the Commissioner of Lands, to the Chairman of Nakuru Land Control Board, the Clerk of the County Council of Naivasha, the District Land Officer Nakuru and the Director of Surveys in Nairobi, "The Land Control Act (Cap 302)", August 14, 1998).
80. KNA Nakuru, 15/1/Vol. 1, AR of the District Labour Officer Naivasha, 2002.
81. KNA Nakuru, 15/1/Vol. 1, AR of the District Labour Officer Naivasha, 2003. Examples of farms are Shalimar, Longonot, Oserian, Panda, Wildfire, Maridadi, and Plantation Plants.
82. CDC was a developmental bank of the British government. It is not the only developmental aid that was invested in the Naivasha flower industry. Another example is funding by the German developmental bank DEG ('Flower Firm to Get', 2006). More recently, the Dutch government also invested five million euros in the Kenyan flower industry. However, this funding was mainly channelled to businesses in the supply chain and not to the flower farms themselves (Kazimierczuk et al., 2018, p. 40).
83. KNA Nakuru, GU/10/4/71, AR of the Co-operative Officer Naivasha Subdistrict, 2002.
84. KNA Nakuru, 15/1/Vol. 1, AR of the Agricultural Officer Naivasha, 2003.
85. *Mdudu* is Swahili for insect.
86. *Kenya Gazette*, Notice No. 2,674, April 8, 2004.
87. This shift and its implications are discussed in detail in Andreas Gemählich's dissertation (in preparation) with the preliminary title "Reorganising Global Agro-industries. Market Dynamics and the Cut Flower Industry at Lake Naivasha/Kenya".
88. KNA Nakuru, 15/1/Vol. 1, AR of the Coordinator for Agriculture and Livestock, Naivasha Division, 2000; interview by Andreas Gemählich with

the chief executive officer of KFC, October 17, 2014; observations during an Imarisha stakeholders' meeting in Naivasha, November 26, 2014.

89. KNA Nakuru, 15/1/Vol. 1, AR of the Department of Adult Education, Naivasha Division, 2003.
90. Notably, Friedemann-Sánchez (2009, p. 53) described a similar disagreement in the Colombian flower industry: much to the chagrin of the local authorities, the industry was exempted from taxes, even though it made use of the infrastructure maintained by the local government.
91. Examples are DCK and Oserian (KNA Nakuru, GU/3/33/18, "DCK Trading Centre"; Hayes, 1997, p. 339).
92. "For years an eighth of an acre in Villa View, Naivasha's first gated community, was priced at Sh100,000. Today, one pays as much as Sh1.8 million for that same piece of land" (Okeyo, 2014).
93. The writer refers to a name change during the rule of President Moi, when the road received the official name Moi Lake Road.
94. KNA Nakuru, GU/9/1/188, "Local Authority".
95. KNA Nakuru, 15/1/Vol. 1, AR of the Probation Office, Naivasha Division, 1999.
96. KNA Nakuru, GU/10/5/201, Minutes of a security meeting in Olkaria Sublocation, August 5, 2005.
97. KNA Nakuru, GU/1/7/34, "Ndabibi".

References

100 families homeless after fire guts houses. (2009, March 16). *Daily Nation*, p. 9.

1,300 flower farm employees sacked. (2002, August 17). *Daily Nation*, p. 3.

4,000 watisha kugoma Naivasha [2,000 threaten to strike in Naivasha]. (1985, March 18). *Taifa Leo*, p. 8.

Ailing pyrethrum sector gets Sh300m to revive business. (2014, May 2). *Daily Nation*. Retrieved from https://www.nation.co.ke/business/Ailing-pyrethrum-sector-gets-Sh300m/996-2301788-1d5yx5z/index.html

Anderson, D. (2000). Master and servant in colonial Kenya. *Journal of African History, 41*, 459–485.

Anderson, D., & Lochery, E. (2008). Violence and exodus in Kenya's Rift Valley, 2008: Predictable and preventable? *Journal of Eastern African Studies, 2*(2), 328–343. https://doi.org/10.1080/17531050802095536

Appadurai, A. (2013). *The future as cultural fact: Essays on the global condition*. London: Verso.

Becht, R., Odada, E. O., & Higgins, S. (2005). *Lake Naivasha. Experience and lessons learned brief.* Kosatsu: International Lake Environment Committee Foundation. Retrieved from https://worldlakes.org/uploads/17_Lake_Naivasha_27February2006.pdf

Berman, B., & Lonsdale, J. (1992). *Unhappy valley: Conflict in Kenya & Africa* (Vol. 1). Oxford: James Currey.
Boone, C. (2012). Land conflict and distributive politics in Kenya. *African Studies Review, 55*(1), 75–103. https://doi.org/10.1353/arw.2012.0010
Bradshaw, Y. W. (1990). Perpetuating underdevelopment in Kenya: The link between agriculture, class, and state. *African Studies Review, 33*(1), 1–28.
Casida, J. E. (1980). Pyrethrum flowers and pyrethroid insecticides. *Environmental Health Perspectives, 23*, 189–202.
Chambers, R. (1969). *Settlement schemes in tropical Africa*. London: Routledge and Kegan Paul.
Cheeseman, N., Lynch, G., & Willis, J. (2016). Decentralisation in Kenya: The governance of governors. *The Journal of Modern African Studies, 54*(1), 1–35. https://doi.org/10.1017/S0022278X1500097X
Chege, R. W., Tarus, I., & Nyakwaka, D. (2015). Lake Naivasha. The Maasai and the British in the making of Naivasha Town, 1850–1911. *Journal of International Academic Research for Multidisciplinarity, 3*(1), 142–162.
Chotara orders demolition of '*chang'aa* houses'. (1984, November 28). *Daily Nation*, p. 8.
Clayton, A., & Savage, D. C. (1974). *Government and labour in Kenya 1895–1963*. London: Frank Cass.
Cohen, D. W., & Atieno Odhiambo, E. S. (1989). *Siaya: The historical anthropology of an African landscape*. London: James Currey.
Company being purchased. (1978, October, 1). *Daily Nation*, p. 26.
Cooper, F. (1996). *Decolonization and African society: The labor question in French and British Africa*. Cambridge: Cambridge University Press.
Cosmos. (1981, February 12). This road is a shame. *Daily Nation*, p. 7.
Council seals Sh30m deal with flower farmers. (2009, October 23). *Daily Nation*, p. 33.
David, H. (2015, February 4). Biogas firm to supply national grid with 2MW of power. *Business Daily*, p. 4.
Dolan, C. S. (2007). Market affections: Moral encounters with Kenyan fairtrade flowers. *Ethnos, 72*(2), 239–261. https://doi.org/10.1080/00141840701396573
Dolan, C. S., Opondo, M., & Smith, S. (2003). *Gender, rights and participation in the Kenya cut flower industry* (NRI Report No. 2768). Chatham, UK: NRI.
Dysentery 'controlled'. (1998, July 28). *Daily Nation*, p. 4.
English, P., Jaffee, S., & Okello, J. (2006). Exporting out of Africa: The Kenyan horticulture success story. In L. Fox & R. Liebenthal (Eds.), *Attacking Africa's poverty. Experience from the ground* (pp. 117–148). Washington, DC: The World Bank.
Farmers group demands better roads. (2005, September 17). *Daily Nation*, p. 17.

Ferguson, J. (1999). *Expectations of modernity: Myths and meanings of urban life on the Zambian Copperbelt*. Berkeley: University of California Press.
Flower farm owner gored to death by buffalo. (2010, November 25). *Daily Nation*, p. 39.
Flower firm to gets Sh7m funding. (2006, June 4). *Daily Nation*, p. 15.
Friedemann-Sánchez, G. (2009). *Assembling flowers and cultivating homes: Labor and gender in Colombia* (1st Paperback ed.). Lanham, MD: Lexington Books.
Geoffrey Muhoro v Lake Flowers Limited (High Court of Kenya at Nakuru) (2011). Retrieved from http://kenyalaw.org/caselaw/cases/view/75475
Gibbon, P., & Riisgaard, L. (2014). A new system of labour management in African large-scale agriculture? *Journal of Agrarian Change, 14*(1), 94–128. https://doi.org/10.1111/joac.12043
Govt absence spurs growth. (1999, June 14). *Daily Nation*, p. 14.
Happ, J. (2016). *Auswirkungen der Fairtrade-Zertifizierung auf den afrikanischen Blumenanbau. Das Beispiel Naivasha, Kenia [Effects of Fairtrade-certification on the African flower production: The example of Naivasha, Kenya]* (Vol. 4). Norderstedt: Books on Demand.
Harper, D. M., Morrison, E. H., Macharia, M. M., Mavuti, K. M., & Upton, C. (2011). Lake Naivasha, Kenya: Ecology, society and future. *Freshwater Reviews, 4*(2), 89–114.
Hayes, C. (1997). *Oserian: Place of peace: A century of the Kenya story*. Nairobi: Rima Publications.
Herdsmen invade Naivasha farm land. (1995, December 30). *Daily Nation*, p. 2.
Hunter, N. (2009, October 5). The tragedy that is Lake Naivasha. *Business Daily*, p. 15.
Improve working conditions in farm industry. (1974, February 13). *Daily Nation*, p. 4.
Jabs campaign. (1991, July 6). *Daily Nation*, p. 5.
Kanogo, T. (1987). *Squatters and the roots of Mau Mau*. London: James Currey.
Kanyinga, K. (2009). The legacy of the white highlands: Land rights, ethnicity and the post-2007 election violence in Kenya. *Journal of Contemporary African Studies, 27*(3), 325–344. https://doi.org/10.1080/02589000903154834
Kariuki, J. (2015, May 17). Land fraud costs flower company Sh200m venture. *Daily Nation*, p. 35.
Kazimierczuk, A., Kamau, P., Kinuthia, B., & Mukoko, C. (2018). *Never a rose without a prick: (Dutch) multinational companies and productive employment in the Kenyan flower sector* (ASC Working Paper No. 142). Leiden: African Studies Centre.
KHRC. (2012). *Wilting in bloom: The irony of women labour rights in the cut-flower sector in Kenya*. Nairobi: KHRC.
Kiaye, G. (1986, August 5). A farming town with steady growth. *Daily Nation*, p. 16.

Kioko, E. M. (2016). *Turning conflict into coexistence: Cross-cutting ties and institutions in the agro-pastoral borderlands of Lake Naivasha Basin, Kenya*. Cologne: University of Cologne. Retrieved from http://kups.ub.uni-koeln.de/id/eprint/7064

Kioko, E. M., & Bollig, M. (2015). Cross-cutting ties and coexistence: Intermarriage, land rentals and changing land use patterns among Maasai and Kikuyu of Maiella and Enoosupukia, Lake Naivasha Basin, Kenya. *Rural Landscapes: Society, Environment, History, 2*(1), 1–16. https://doi.org/10.16993/rl.ad

KNBS. (1981). *Kenya population census 1979*. Nairobi: KNBS.

KNBS. (2010). *Kenya population census 2009*. Nairobi: KNBS.

Lang, B., & Sakdapolrak, P. (2014). Belonging and recognition after the post-election violence: A case study on labour migrants in Naivasha, Kenya. *Erdkunde, 68*(3), 185–196. https://doi.org/10.3112/erdkunde.2014.03.03

Lembcke, L. (2015). *Social-ecological change and migration in South-East Lake Naivasha*. Cologne: Cologne African Studies Centre.

Little, P. D. (2014). *Economic and political reform in Africa: Anthropological perspectives*. Bloomington: Indiana University Press.

LNROA. (1993). *A three phase environmental impact study of recent developments around Lake Naivasha*. Nairobi: John Goldson Associates. Retrieved from ftp://ftp.itc.nl/pub/naivasha/PolicyNGO/LNROA1993.pdf

Mavuti, K. M., & Harper, D. M. (2006). The ecological state of Lake Naivasha, Kenya, 2005: Turning 25 years research into an effective Ramsar monitoring programme. In E. Odada & D. O. Olago (Eds.), *Proceedings of the 11th World Lakes Conference* (Vol. 2, pp. 30–34). Retrieved from http://www.oceandocs.net/handle/1834/2127

Mbogo, S. (2008, May 28). Sector braves crisis to post growth. *Business Daily*, p. 7.

Meagher, K., Mann, L., & Bolt, M. (2016). Introduction: Global economic inclusion and African workers. *The Journal of Development Studies, 52*(4), 471–482. https://doi.org/10.1080/00220388.2015.1126256

Ministry of Economic Planning and Development. (1965). *Kenya population census 1962*. Nairobi: MEPD.

Moore, H. L., & Vaughan, M. (1994). *Cutting down trees: Gender, nutrition, and agricultural change in the Northern Province of Zambia, 1890–1990*. Portsmouth, NH: Heinemann.

Morgan, W. T. W. (1963). The 'White Highlands' of Kenya. *The Geographical Journal, 129*(2), 140–155.

Munene, M. (2013, February 24). Every business Nielsen touched was left in ruin. *Daily Nation*, p. 10.

Mwangi, M. (2007, August 18). Naivasha Town: Where poverty and affluence live side-by-side. *Daily Nation*, p. 26.

Mwangi, M. (2008, February 2). Post-election chaos: Violence ruins the party for Naivasha flower companies. *Daily Nation*, p. 24.

Mwangi, N. (2019). 'Good that you are one of us': Positionality and reciprocity in conducting fieldwork in Kenya's flower industry. In L. Johnstone (Ed.), *The politics of conducting research in Africa* (pp. 13–33). Cham: Springer International Publishing.

Mwathi, M., & Njuguna, M. (1996, April 7). Company sacks striking workers. *Daily Nation*, p. 4.

Mwembe, K. wa. (1979, August 19). Flower power! A fast blooming money-spinner for Kenyan economy. *Daily Nation*, p. 23.

Ngesa, M., & Mwangi, M. (2005, May 17). Scramble for land spells doom. *Daily Nation*, p. 6.

Njuguna, M. (2006, August 4). Delamare farm workers live under fear after violent raids. *Daily Nation*, p. 24.

Oberlé, P. (1990, April 18). On safari: Lake Naivasha and Hells Gate. *Daily Nation*, pp. 14–16.

Odingo, R. S. (1971). *The Kenya Highlands: Land use and agricultural development*. Nairobi: East African Publishing House.

Okanga, D. (2008, October 19). Fujo za Naivasha zilikuwa ni kulipiza kisasi mauaji [Chaos in Naivasha was a retaliation for killings]. *Taifa Leo*, p. 4.

Okeyo, V. (2013, September 16). The tragedy of the flowermen. *Daily Nation*, p. 10.

Okeyo, V. (2014, March 6). From flowers to tourism, Naivasha is a gem. *Daily Nation*, p. 14.

Ombuor, J. (1996, December 27). No longer an island. *Daily Nation*, p. 7.

Ominde, S. H. (1968). *Land and population movements in Kenya*. London: Heinemann.

Omondi, G. (2007, November 7). Burying the hatchet after a history of feuds. *Business Daily*, p. 18.

Omondi, G. (2010, February 22). State drops L. Naivasha water use control plan. *Business Daily*, p. 1.

Omosa, M., Kimani, M., & Njiru, R. (2006). The social impact of codes of practice in the cut flower industry in Kenya. Natural Resources Institute and DFID. Retrieved from http://projects.nri.org/nret/final_kenya_main_report.pdf

Opala, K. (2007, April 2). Naivasha's withering rose: Flower companies threaten to move to Ethiopia as workers and council protest. *Daily Nation*, pp. 4–5.

Police rout gun gang. (1962, February 9). *Daily Nation*, p. 1.

Police shoot suspect dead. (2005, April 3). *Daily Nation*, p. 15.

Public tasks facing private companies. (1987, June 5). *Daily Nation*, p. 6.

Redfern, P. (2006, November 30). Kenya plays down crisis in flower industry. *The East African*, p. 29.

Republic of Kenya. (1973). *The National Assembly. Official Report. Vol. XXX. Fourth session, Tuesday, 12th June, 1973 to Friday, 27th July, 1973*. Nairobi: Republic of Kenya.

Republic of Kenya. (2008). *Report of the Commission of Inquiry into post election violence*. Nairobi: Government Printer. Retrieved from http://kenyalaw.org/Downloads/Reports/Commission_of_Inquiry_into_Post_Election_Violence.pdf

Riisgaard, L., & Gibbon, P. (2014). Labour management on contemporary Kenyan cut flower farms: Foundations of an industrial-civic compromise. *Journal of Agrarian Change, 14*(2), 260–285. https://doi.org/10.1111/joac.12064

Riungu, C. (2005, August 1). Flower firms scramble for control of export market. *The East African*, p. 17.

Riungu, C. (2007, March 12). Now, world's biggest solar greenhouse opens in Naivasha. *The East African*, p. 31.

Rural road worrying traders. (1986, February 13). *Daily Nation*, p. 3.

Seal, M. (2011). *Wildflower: The extraordinary life and mysterious murder of Joan Root* (Paperback ed.). London: Orion Books Ltd.

Sorrenson, M. P. K. (1967). *Land reform in the Kikuyu country: A study in government policy*. Nairobi: Oxford University Press.

Spencer, I. (1980). Settler dominance, agricultural production and the Second World War in Kenya. *The Journal of African History, 21*(04), 497. https://doi.org/10.1017/S0021853700018715

Stoof-Leichsenring, K. R., Junginger, A., Olaka, L. A., Tiedemann, R., & Trauth, M. H. (2011). Environmental variability in Lake Naivasha, Kenya, over the last two centuries. *Journal of Paleolimnology, 45*(3), 353–367. https://doi.org/10.1007/s10933-011-9502-4

Thomson, J. (1887). *Through Masai land: A journey of exploration among the snowclad volcanic mountains and strange tribes* (New and revised ed.). London: Gilbert and Rivington.

Union appeals to govt over workers' welfare. (1998, July 11). *Daily Nation*, p. 15.

Waajiriwa watoroka mashamba ya maua [Employees escape from flower farms]. (2008, February 6). *Taifa Leo*, p. 24.

Wachira, G. (1972, April 23). Virus fear to crop. *Daily Nation*, p. 1.

Wachira, M. (2011, May 5). Success smells sweet in the land of flowers. *Daily Nation*, p. D.

Whitaker, M., & Kolavalli, S. (2006). Floriculture in Kenya. In V. Chandra (Ed.), *Technology, adaptation, and exports: How some developing countries got it right* (pp. 335–367). Washington, DC: The World Bank.

Worthington, S., & Worthington, E. B. (1933). *Inland waters of Africa*. London: Macmillan and Co.

CHAPTER 3

Coming to Naivasha: Finding a Place to Stay and a Place to Work

When I arrived, I lived with my relative.
—Flower farm worker Gabriel

The vast majority of people living in the workers' settlements and on flower farm compounds have migrated to the area, either on their own as an adult or during their childhood with their parents. Only 8.0% of the 176 respondents in the survey that I carried out named either Naivasha, one of the settlements around the lake, or one of the villages in the lake's hinterland as their place of birth.[1] Another 22.2% stated they were born nearby, in another part of the former Rift Valley Province. Most others originated from a region in the former Western and Nyanza provinces (31.8% and 25.0% respectively).[2] Bungoma, Kakamega, Kisii, and Siaya are regions that were frequently mentioned. Moreover, Table 3.1 shows that many of the migrants moved relatively recently to the place where they lived at the time of the interview.

This chapter therefore addresses questions such as: who are the labour migrants? Why do they decide to come to Naivasha, and what are their aspirations for their stay there? How do they find a roof over their heads and a job upon arrival? And what role do the farms as well as migrant workers' social networks play within these processes?

Before discussing these questions in more detail, I first introduce three female flower farm workers whose varying positions in Naivasha have

G. Kuiper, *Agro-industrial Labour in Kenya*,
https://doi.org/10.1007/978-3-030-18046-1_3

Table 3.1 Period of moving to the current place of residence ($n = 176$)

Period	*Number of respondents*	*%*
Before 1995	9	5.1
1995–1999	18	10.2
2000–2004	39	22.2
2005–2009	35	19.9
2010–2015	65	36.9
Never moved/year unknown	10	4.8

shaped my understanding of migration processes and of migrants' possibilities on the job market.

3.1 Three Workers

There are two women—Flora and Lucy—who played a crucial role during my fieldwork, who figuratively speaking helped me "arriving" in Naivasha and who inevitably also figure prominently in this book. Their life stories can function as ethnographic vignettes, as these stories reflect aspects of the life of every migrant worker living in the settlements around Lake Naivasha. At the same time, the position of these two women is not representative of the position of all migrant workers. At the end of the section, I introduce Glory, another female farm worker, whose story contrasts to that of Flora and Lucy in many ways. Moreover, my conversations with this woman—although friendly in nature and informed by curiosity from both sides—were based in an unequal and ephemeral relationship between interviewer and interviewee. This interview is representative for the way I interacted with most interlocutors, more so than the endurable and more reciprocal relationships I developed with Flora, Lucy, their families, and a few others. As I agree to Davies (2008, p. 93) assertion that ethnographers' "personal relationships with informants are a part of their data, a very fundamental basis of their analysis", I now turn to introducing these three women.

3.1.1 Flora

I was introduced to Flora already during my first short visit to Naivasha in November 2013. She was employed at Sharma Farm and I met her through the assistant I worked with at the time, a former employee of

Sharma Farm himself. We visited Flora at her rental house in Kihoto, the workers' settlement next to Naivasha Town. This was the first time I entered a house in one of the workers' settlements. I noted afterwards in my diary that the house looked much better than what I had expected beforehand, after having read the available grey literature on these settlements. To my surprise, Flora had a sofa and a television.

I started to meet Flora on a regular basis during later periods of fieldwork. She contributed to my research through our numerous conversations. Moreover, she assisted me with finding interview partners and accompanied me on a trip to Kisumu, where she introduced me to three of her former colleagues from Sharma Farm. Flora's frankness and sensitivity enabled us to develop an uncomplicated friendship, despite our different backgrounds and different positions in life. This friendship has been a tremendously important resource during my research.

Flora was born in a village in Narok County in 1987. Her father worked as a foreman on construction sites and resided in Nairobi. Her mother stayed with the children on the family plot in Narok, where she cultivated land and kept a few cows. Flora went to a primary school at a few kilometres' distance from their home, and later on moved to a secondary boarding school in Narok Town. After finishing school, she worked in the administration department of a local hospital before she decided to pursue a certificate in catering in Nairobi. Even after obtaining this certificate, she only found casual jobs, and she finally decided to move to Naivasha to try her luck there in 2006. She moved in with a friend from Narok. After three months, she found a permanent job at Sharma Farm and moved into her own rental room. She started as a general worker on the farm and after three years got promoted to quality controller. Her task was to inspect the harvested flowers and spot any deficiencies caused by, for instance, pests or careless handling of the flowers. Finally, she became a supervisor in 2014 and had 27 people working in her greenhouse. Flora told me she was glad that she only had worked as a general worker for a few years. She thought the work would make you stupid if you did it for a long period of time.

Flora explicitly identifies as a Maasai. Only when I visited her parental home in March 2015 did I learn that her father was half-Kikuyu and had grown up with his mother in a Kikuyu household in Kiambu. He had only moved to his (Maasai) father's plot in Narok County when he had inherited it upon his father's death. He had married a Maasai woman there. We went to visit them to attend a planned meeting between Flora's family and the prospective family-in-law of one of her sisters. During our visit, I noticed that another sister of Flora frequently switched from speaking Swahili to speaking Kikuyu, not Maa. She lived in Nairobi, was working in an office there, and was married to a Kikuyu man. When I visited this sister in Nairobi, I noticed that she had cut flowers in her house as a decoration, a rare sight in Kenya and a sign of her aspiration to be part of Kenya's middle class. It was interesting to see how Flora and her sister had different socioeconomic positions and related differently to their mixed ethnic background.

One reason for this might be the different ethnic backgrounds of their respective husbands. Flora met her husband James at her workplace. James is a Luo and his family originates from Kisumu County. James himself was born in Limuru, which is located between Naivasha and Nairobi, in 1978. He also grew up there. His father was working in a shoe factory and the family lived on the company compound. The family only went back to Kisumu when James was in secondary boarding school. Consequently he never lived on his family's plot. After finishing school, James became a professional football player and played for several premier league teams in Kenya and Uganda. The last team he played for was the professional soccer team of Sharma Farm in Naivasha. He played there from 2004 to 2011, when he was forced to quit because of a sustained injury. He then got a job in the packhouse there. He also continued to be involved in football, as he aspired a professional career as a football coach and trained local teams.

Although Sharma had a workers' compound, James and Flora decided not to stay there because they did not want to depend too much on the farm. Instead, they both received a housing allowance, with which they could pay the rent for a house in Kihoto, the workers' settlement next to Naivasha Town. They made use of the company buses to get to work. They lived in a relatively well-equipped, two-room brick apartment with an inside bathroom (without running water) in a compound with only four houses.

Flora and James' life in Naivasha has been far from smooth. Their daughter was born in early 2008 at the time of the post-election violence, which was a hectic and frightful time for this multi-ethnic family. They fled to Nairobi and later to Kisumu, until the calm was restored after several months. They initially returned to the rental house they had resided in but did not trust their neighbours and decided to move to another house in Kihoto. James told me that during this violent period, it helped him that many people knew him as a football coach. Being a Luo, he could otherwise have been a target early on.

A few years after the post-election violence, Flora and James got in serious financial trouble when Sharma Farm went bankrupt. They lacked a stable income and even lost their claims to service payments for retirement and the savings that they had with SACCO, the saving cooperative connected to the farm. These were substantial amounts: Flora told me she alone had already saved around 90,000 Kenyan shilling (KES) with the SACCO.[3] After losing their jobs at Sharma Farm, Flora and James eventually found other ways to make a living. The financial losses they had suffered made them decide not to apply for a flower farm job again. Their experiences with working for a flower farm contrast to the stable livelihood of Lucy.

3.1.2 Lucy

I met Lucy on my first day of observation on Karibu Farm. The production manager took me to the greenhouse where Lucy was the supervisor and told her to show me the work procedures there. Although I tried to introduce myself properly and to explain what I had come to do, Lucy did not really listen. Her remarks in the following days revealed that she simply assumed I was a Dutch intern on my way to become a flower farm manager, as there had been a few before (although previous interns had all been male). For two full working days, she showed me the work in the greenhouse in the same way as she would have done to a management intern. After those two initial days, I also spent time elsewhere on the farm. Nevertheless, every time I visited Karibu, I would pass by Lucy's greenhouse to greet her. It only dawned on her then, after I surprised her with my strange questions, that I was not about to become a manager but was a researcher. Once she realized I was interested in the social side of things, more so than in the crop, she started to suggest departments within the farm and organizations in the neighbouring settlement Kasarani that I could visit. After two months she also invited me to her home. I therefore still regularly visited her whenever I was in Kasarani, even after finishing my visits to Karibu Farm.

Lucy was born in Bungoma County in western Kenya. After having finished secondary school in 2006, she came to the settlement Kasarani, where one of her uncles was living, to look for work. She was employed by Karibu Farm in the same year. Lucy started out as a general worker in the nursery department, where new seedlings were being produced, until this department was closed down. Due to the knowledge she had gained in that specialized greenhouse, she could become a supervisor in a regular greenhouse in 2009, a position that she has held since.

I noticed that Lucy was committed to her work. She enjoyed the process of cultivating plants. She also was respected and liked by most of her colleagues. She was especially close to some of the other supervisors, probably due to their peculiar position between management and general workers. Lucy also participated in several small groups (*vyama*) of around six colleagues who would exchange goods such as sugar or oil, or small amounts of money. She was furthermore an active member of the company SACCO and was part of one of the SACCO's committees.

Lucy had met her husband George in Kasarani. George was born there. His father had been working in the irrigation department of a nearby ranch. George moved to their "home" in western Kenya with his mother and siblings in 1998 because there was no possibility at that time to go to secondary school in the vicinity of Kasarani. He came back to the settlement only a few years later, after finishing school in 2003. He started working for Karibu Farm on short contracts. After that, he found a permanent job in another nearby flower farm and eventually became a supervisor in the packhouse there.

Lucy, George, and their two young sons lived in a one-room brick apartment on a plot with around ten other rooms located in the middle of Kasarani. Just as many other people did, they had divided up their room in three parts with curtains and sheets. They owned two beds, a sofa set, and a small TV. They paid rent, including water on the plot, although they depended on a water supply by Karibu Farm and on private water vendors for accessing drinking water. Lucy and George could have moved to a flower farm compound, since George worked for a farm that provided housing. However, Lucy refused to move to a neighbourhood where everybody else would work for another farm than she did.

Lucy called me by my name but nevertheless still sometimes told her young son to say hello to "the *mzungu*". Despite her use of this othering term and her obvious pride in having a European friend, we somehow were still able to bridge some of the social and economic distance between us. Perhaps this was so because she had embraced the role of being the expert who had taught me the work. Perhaps it was also related to my status of being a student, as Lucy supposed that I was therefore not wealthy. She once asked me whether my parents had paid for my fieldwork, and was visibly relieved on behalf of my parents when I explained to her that it was paid for by the university. On one occasion, I gave her a lift to Naivasha Town when I left Kasarani on a Saturday afternoon. She wanted to go to the supermarket, a trip that she undertook at least once a month to buy staple food in bulk, which was cheaper than buying food in small quantities in Kasarani. When we arrived in Naivasha Town and I dropped her off, she took a crumpled note of 200 KES out of her handbag and gave it to me, "to buy a soda". The amount was more than what the fare for the *matatu* (public transport minibus) would have cost her. I was baffled, moved, and also amused by this gesture, as this financial reciprocity was something I—as a well-funded European student—did not expect to experience in Naivasha. I simply took the note and thanked her.

3.1.3 Glory

I am aware that my perspective on the inhabitants of the low-income settlements around Naivasha has been shaped by my relationship to Flora and Lucy, especially since there are some similarities between them. Both of these women lived in a workers' settlement, not on a farm compound. They belonged to the same generation, in fact the same as mine. Both had a husband who was also employed by a flower farm. Furthermore, both worked as a supervisor in a greenhouse, and were therefore examples of workers who had managed to move upwards, at least at some point in time. The majority of the inhabitants of the settlements never managed to get this far. I also met many of these less fortunate migrant workers but these were often one-time or two-time encounters. In what follows I introduce one of them, Glory.

Glory was a general worker on Karibu Farm. She had been born into a Kikuyu family in Ndabibi, a village in the hinterland of Lake Naivasha, in 1959. Her father had been working as a manual labourer on the ranch of a European settler and later turned to farming on his own plot of land, which her mother had been doing throughout. Glory's brothers later had inherited this plot and she herself did not own any land in Ndabibi. After she got married, she lived in several villages in the hinterland of Lake Naivasha. Her husband, with whom she had six children, was a mechanic. However, he developed eye problems and there was no money to pay for a proper operation. He could no longer work, and Glory and her family decided to move to Kasarani in 2003.

Glory entered formal employment only then and worked as a bean harvester on one of the nearby vegetable farms. In 2008, while being almost 50 years of age, she got the chance to work for Karibu Farm as a general worker in a greenhouse, which she has done since. For a long time she and her family lived in a house constructed with wattle and daub, without electricity, which until recently was common in Kasarani. However, in 2015, their landlord needed the room for himself and told them to move. Glory was not able to find another rental wattle-and-daub house, which she preferred because it was more affordable. She and her family had no choice but to move to a brick house with electricity. This was of course comfortable but they also paid a higher rent: 3300 KES per month. This was much more than the 2000 KES housing allowance that Glory received. She explained: "I did not get [an affordable house], so what should I do? Will I not just squeeze myself, even if I do not have it? Because I will not stay outside."

Glory participated in a saving group where women bought chicken (to rear) together and she was an active member of the Full Gospel Church, where she went to every afternoon after finishing work. And despite her tight budget, Glory tried to save money through participating in the SACCO of Karibu Farm. However, she had not been able yet to save enough money to purchase her own plot. When I asked Glory whether she sometimes visited her home village Ndabibi, only a few kilometres away, she replied:

> I do not even go. You know it is far, and sometimes you have this money of 300, but the fare to go and come back is 600. Now even before I arrive, I just look at that mountain, and I go back home. I stay very long [without going]. A year can pass without me going. And I like it [there]. But if I look at that mountain, I think I cannot cross it. It is far.

When I asked Glory whether she had plans to retire, as she was almost 60 years of age, she replied that she could not afford to as long as her school-going children (at the time still three of them) depended on her for food, school fees, and shelter: "you just push yourself forward." Her preference would be not to work but she simply could not afford to retire. Furthermore, she would like to buy a plot of land, wherever, but she simply did not have the money to do so. Whereas many of the inhabitants of the settlements I spoke to had a clear idea of where they wanted to go after retirement, even if they had not yet realized their plans, Glory did not put much thought into such day-dreams. She had little hope of being able to buy a plot in the future and it made little sense to make plans for such an unlikely event.

The last question I asked during the interview was where Glory would like to be buried. Most interviewees whom I asked that question replied that if possible, they would like to be buried on their own plot of land. But Glory gave me the following answer:

> My burial? Let me laugh. All these things are just funny. Because now if you don't have a plot, won't you just be buried at the cemetery? It is better you are gone and you will not wake up. It is up to those who remain behind, I will be gone. What should I do?

This final remark of Glory—"What should I do?"—summarized the interview, from which transpired the feeling of being stuck. She had no other option than to continue working for the flower farm, even though she would like to retire. She could not even afford to regularly visit her nearby village of origin. Glory's situation contrasted with the more secure position of Lucy and the aspirations for the future of Flora. This precariousness also heavily shaped my interview with Glory, in the same way as it shaped my encounters with other struggling residents. I felt presumptuous and voyeuristic when I prompted Glory to tell me her life story. I do not know whether she felt the same about my role but I could tell she felt uncomfortable herself towards the end of the interview. My questions about land ownership and family relations had confronted her with her own unfortunate position.

The contrasting positions of Flora, Lucy, and Glory indicate that not all workers achieve what they hoped for when they decided to move to Naivasha. What reasons do migrant workers have to take this step in the first place?

3.2 The Decision to Move

For the Kenyan context, especially the migration of Luo from western Kenya to cities such as Nairobi and Mombasa has been studied extensively. It has been established that many of them migrate with the intention of returning to their region of origin later in life (Oucho, 1996). The Luo consider the region Siaya to be their "homeland": "Everyday life for the Luo outside Siaya is affected by connections with and images of Siaya; everyday life inside Siaya is affected by the fact of the diaspora" (Cohen & Atieno Odhiambo, 1989, p. 4). Some of the villages and towns in Siaya (already then) were dependent on remittances. Cohen and Atieno

Odhiambo (1989) furthermore found that family networks were assisting in the process of migration and were actively maintained with that purpose. Oucho (1996, p. 56) stated: "Wherever they are, the Luo are 'men of two worlds.'"

Being part of "two worlds" is not unique for the Luo. It is common among many of the ethnic groups represented in present-day Naivasha. This specific type of "stretched-out" return migration has developed since colonial times and is rooted in longer histories of mobility in relation to land tenure relations specific to Kenya. For these "translocal" migrants, residing in Naivasha for many years does not imply permanent settlement there (McGarrigle & Ascensão, 2017). However, it is important to note that there exist additional patterns of labour migration. An example from colonial times is the squatter system, popular among the Kikuyu, who thus became used to more permanent forms of migration (Kanogo, 1987). Although migration thus is a central theme, not all migrants had the same background or the same motives in coming to Naivasha.

Migrants' move to Naivasha is regularly interpreted one-dimensionally, as simply being driven by the lack of economic options elsewhere; see, for instance, Seal (2011, p. xiv) on "impoverished migrant workers". Farm managers also stated that people come to Naivasha in search of work. They referred to the unfavourable economic situation in the most common regions of origin, where few jobs are available and land is scarce. Similarly, both a general worker and a supervisor of Karibu Farm told me literally: "We come here to work." In contrast, only 9 of the 22 respondents in the ego-centred network analysis I conducted mentioned a job search as the primary reason for migrating, as summarized in Table 3.2.[4] Others, for instance, had initially come to visit relatives and then had decided to stay in Naivasha. Notably, three respondents (all women) had sought refuge in Naivasha for either domestic or political violence. Whereas many labour migrants fled from Naivasha in early 2008, one of the respondents arrived in Naivasha in the same period, after she had been displaced from her home somewhere else in the Rift Valley Province. Another respondent came to escape a bad marriage: she did not want to depend on her parents after her divorce and decided to look for an independent life away from home. In short, some migrants had other reasons than pure economic necessity to come to Naivasha. For them, it was a place to make a new start.

The majority of the migrants arrive in Naivasha when they are young adults. These young migrants do not usually aspire to work for a horticultural farm all their lives but plan to make some quick money and to look

Table 3.2 The 22 respondents in the ego-centred network analysis and their move to Naivasha

	M/F	*Year of birth*	*County of birth*	*Occupation*	*Move*	*Reason for moving to Naivasha*	*Contact person*
1	M	1986	Meru	Flower farm	2009	Came to visit and stayed	Sibling
2	M	1980	Bungoma	Flower farm	2008	Came to visit and stayed	Friend
3	F	1978	Nakuru	Hotel	2007	Came with parents	Parents
4	M	1980	Nyamira	Security guard	2010	Job transfer	Company
5	F	1972	Laikipia	None	1995	To look for a job	Sibling
6	F	1978	Bungoma	Flower farm	2012	Fled from violence	Sibling
7	M	1984	Vihiga	Small business	2003	To look for a job	Sibling
8	F	1982	Kisii	Small business	2005	Fled from violence	Sibling
9	M	1966	Homa Bay	Flower farm	1991	To look for a job	Sibling
10	F	1967	Nakuru	Vegetable farm	2007	Fled from violence	Sibling
11	M	1988	Bungoma	Flower farm	2014	To look for a job	Relative
12	M	1973	Narok	Flower farm	2003	To look for a job	Relative
13	F	1992	Murang'a	None	2015	Came to get married	Spouse
14	F	1977	Nyandarua	Vegetable farm	2012	To look for a job	Sibling
15	M	1990	Naivasha	Casual labour	–	–	–
16	F	1983	Homa Bay	Flower farm	2004	To look for a job	Sibling
17	M	1986	Kisumu	Flower farm	2010	To look for a job	Friend
18	F	1983	Naivasha	None	–	–	–
19	F	1975	Nakuru	Teacher	1985	Came with parents	Parents
20	F	1988	Nyandarua	Flower farm	2003	Came with parents	Parents
21	F	1988	Kakamega	Flower farm	2012	Came to get married	Relative
22	F	1989	Kakamega	Small business	2012	To look for a job	Friend

for other income-generating activities afterwards, either in Naivasha or elsewhere. An important group of fresh recruits are school-leavers, who lack the funds to continue with their studies. One employee of Sharma Farm, for instance, told me he came to Naivasha when his parents could no longer pay for his school fees. He then came to work for the same farm as his brother did, for what he thought would be a period of three months. Nineteen years later he was still there.

For others, (temporary) migration simply is a part of life. It is normal for young people to spend at least several years away from "home". Many of the labour migrants in Naivasha had—like Flora's and Lucy's husbands—spent little time in the region of origin of their parents and had lived elsewhere during their childhood because their parents had also been labour migrants. In such a context, and as argued by Ross and Weisner in their study on migrants in Nairobi (1977, p. 364): "[i]dentifying precisely the migration decision or even the actual act of migration (...) is difficult."

Nevertheless, individual factors such as region of origin and age clearly influence migrant workers' aspirations and shape their decision to come to Naivasha. Gender also plays a role here. Remarkable in the case of present-day Naivasha is that labour migration is not only a valid or even expected possibility for young men but also for many young women. In colonial Kenya, the government implicitly defined migrants as "male" and settlers would only enter into agreements with male squatters. Women could only migrate to the ranches in the role of wives (Cooper, 1996, p. 266; N. Nelson, 1992, p. 120). In cases where women migrated to the city on their own, they had few opportunities to find official employment and had to resort to informal income-generating activities (Bujra, 1975). "All told, men's opportunities (access to jobs, cash crops, skills, education), mobility and productivity increased during the colonial period while those of women decreased" (N. Nelson, 1992, p. 119). Also in the period after independence, there was only a minority of elite and trading women who could afford to migrate independently of men. The majority of migrants were men, who sometimes left their wife and children behind in the village of origin to take care of the family plot. They thus also avoided the high cost of living in the urban areas. In this manner, families could depend on both the men's urban income and the women's farming activities. However, this was only possible for those who owned a plot of land. The landless—many of whom were Kikuyu—often came to the cities with their wife and children (Oucho, 1996, pp. 54–55; Ross & Weisner, 1977, pp. 371–372).

This literature thus indicates that Kenyan women in urban areas for a long time had to choose between marriage and economic independence within the insecure informal sector. But many women in agro-industrial Naivasha at the beginning of the twenty-first century do not primarily depend on a husband or on a small-scale business. They are themselves engaged in formalized wage labour. Managers of three different Naivasha flower farms mentioned 40–60% female workers on their respective farms. It was estimated by both Dolan, Opondo, and Smith (2003, p. 28) and Kazimierczuk, Kamau, Kinuthia, and Mukoko (2018, p. 34) that 60% of the workforce of the flower industry as a whole is female. The number of women employed in the industry should come as no surprise when these percentages are compared to overall employment rates in Kenya, as recorded in the most recent census of 2009. It was not uncommon at all (anymore) for women to work: 48.1% of the working population was female (KNBS, 2010). And whereas there had been a gender imbalance in Naivasha's population in 1962 (only 85 women for every 100 men), the census of 2009 showed there were just about as many women as men living in Naivasha, indicating an increase in female migration (KNBS, 2010; Ministry of Economic Planning and Development, 1965). These changing migration patterns fit into a new gendered division of labour in global industries (Mills, 2003). Few of these global industries are located on the African continent, but see, for example, Coplan (2001) and Orton, Barrientos, and McClenaghan (2001) on female wage labour in South Africa in the 1990s. Thus, female wage labour has become increasingly normal.

Although, when seen from this angle, there was not a remarkably large number of women migrating to Naivasha, NGO and media reports on the flower industry emphasized the employment of women and took it as an indication that conditions in the industry were exploitative. In such accounts, women were portrayed as extremely vulnerable (Hivos, n.d.). An article in a Kenyan newspaper stated: "the majority of poor people in Naivasha are women who have lost their husbands to HIV and Aids. (…) Being single mothers, they have little to complain about as some of them have a modest education and prefer half a loaf of bread than none at all" (M. Mwangi, 2007). Although some of the working women are indeed single mothers who came to Naivasha from pure economic necessity, there are more diverse reasons for women (just as for men) to migrate and to engage in wage labour. Moreover, as pointed out by Nici Nelson (1992), it is difficult to distinguish economic reasons from more personal reasons. Yet these reasons are partly influenced by gender. As described above, some women looked for shelter in Naivasha after they fled political or domestic violence. Others got married to someone living there and therefore relocated. The other way around, it is rare for a man to move to the place where his new wife is living. Some of the women who moved to get married simply took care of the house, another option that is not open to men. Others decided to look for a job themselves in order to have their own income. Thus, even though (labour) migration has become a valid option for both men and women, the decision to migrate is nonetheless shaped by gendered identities. At the same time, the choice of women to look for wage labour employment is not by necessity a sign of vulnerability. It can also be a positive choice. Farm worker Dennis, for instance, told me (in his wife's presence) that his wife had followed him to Naivasha and, once there, had decided to look for a job herself. As Dennis continued to pay the rent, she could retain most of her own salary, which enhanced her independence. Intrahousehold dynamics are therefore important in assessing working women's position (Friedemann-Sánchez, 2009; Mills, 2003; Wolf, 1992).

While I have discussed the diverse reasons for moving away from one's region of origin, the question remains why migrants with no skills in horticulture choose to come to Naivasha, instead of moving to Nairobi or a town in their region where they could also find a job. Again, there are diverse motivations. Flower farm supervisor Gabriel, who had started as a general worker, mentioned the relative affordable cost of living in Naivasha compared to Nakuru or Nairobi. Flora likewise told me that the rent for an apartment in Nairobi could be at least three times as high as the rent for a similar apartment in Naivasha. And a skilled migrant worker who had previously worked in Nairobi told me that he had decided to move to Naivasha because he disliked getting stuck in the traffic jam in the capital city every day.

But a result from the ego-centred network analysis (see Table 3.2) is most revealing here: regardless of the reason for moving, almost all respondents already had relatives or friends living in Naivasha before they decided to come to the area themselves. As observed by Ortiz (2002, p. 401), the mobilization of networks in order to find a job in a new place of living is a common pattern in processes of labour migration in general. This also was a strategy in the "White Highlands" in colonial times: "People moved to areas where their relations had settled and initially lived with them as they sought employment" (Kanogo, 1987, p. 30). Likewise, prospective migrants in present-day Kenya mobilize networks to find a place to stay and a place to work. They tend to migrate to places they are familiar with, due to, for instance, previous visits to family. Such moves together have resulted in a system of sustained chain migration (Oucho, 1996). I found that especially in Naivasha, where few farms provide accommodation to their workers, prospective migrants regularly mobilize their networks to find a place to stay upon arrival.

3.3 Finding a Place to Stay

Fourteen of the 22 respondents in the ego-centred network analysis had relied on a family member or friend for accommodation during an initial visit or during the first weeks or months in Naivasha. Some had initially only come for a short period of time. After bringing job applications to the farms, they had returned home to wait to be called to work. Initial short-term visiting is a common migration strategy in Kenya (Oucho, 1996, p. 80; Ross & Weisner, 1977, p. 364). Others had immediately stayed and simply continued to make use of the hospitality of family members or friends until they had found a regular job and had started to receive a salary. Those migrants who were already married or had children before coming to Naivasha often decide to bring their family over once they move to their own rental house. However, Dolan et al. (2003, p. 33) describe also more unlucky migrants who are forced to continuously stay with their relatives because they move from one casual job to another. Because of the insecurity of income, they cannot afford to look for a rental house and are not able to bring their families over.

As only a handful of the larger flower farms around the lake provide housing to the workers, the majority of the flower farm employees (and all other migrants) rely on rental housing built by local landowners. Moreover, even within the farms that provide accommodation, there are a considerable number of workers who choose to stay in a rental house in one of the settlements or in Naivasha Town. They do so for various reasons. The choice is sometimes informed by a lack of facilities on certain farm compounds. For instance, electricity was cut off on the Sharma Farm compound at the time of the farm's financial troubles. The choice to stay "outside" can also be a matter of status. Especially among the supervisors, clerks, and lower managers, it is considered more prestigious to stay in Naivasha Town. Or workers simply take the housing allowance as an opportunity to supplement their salary. One of the employees of Karibu Farm commented on the nice housing provided by a neighbouring farm, yet at the same time said he preferred to receive a housing allowance while paying a low rent for a house of poor quality in Kasarani. In this way, there was some money left every month, which he could spend otherwise. Finally, the decision not to stay in a *kambi* could be informed by an implicit wish to evade control over one's daily life and a reluctance to depend fully on the farm. Several workers told me they had decided to move out of a *kambi* because certain economic activities, such as selling vegetables in the evening hours or keeping livestock, were restricted there, or because they were not allowed to freely receive guests at their home. Similarly, respondents in a focus group discussion carried out by Gibbon and Riisgaard (2014, p. 109) stated they experienced living on a farm's compound as being "socially and economically restrictive". Furthermore, workers I spoke to in Naivasha seemed to realize that staying on a farm made them even more vulnerable if they were to lose their job. Indeed, according to the CBA, an employee should be given only a one-month notice to vacate the company house when the contract ended (AEA & KPAWU, 2011, sec. 12(c)).[5] When I told Lucy about the employees of Sharma Farm who had been summoned to leave their homes after the farm closed down, she said that this risk was one of the reasons she had refused to move to the compound of the farm where her husband George works. It would make them too dependent on that one company. However, it has to be noted that not all workers disliked living in a *kambi*. Several workers told me they preferred the security and ease of staying there, or the vicinity to one's place of work.

In any case, as most farms did not even have a *kambi*, the majority of the labour migrants ended up in a one-room apartment in one of the unplanned settlements. Construction sites were omnipresent and yet it was not easy to find a well-located and affordable rental house. When I asked how they had found their apartment, residents said they had relied on hearsay in their workplace, had asked around at construction sites, or had made use of the services of a housing agency, where they would pay a small fee.

Housing agencies have become a blooming business in Naivasha Town and at South Lake. One of the housing agents, a woman in her thirties, explained that small-scale landowners, especially those not living in Naivasha themselves, prefer an agent to handle the cumbersome business of collecting the monthly rents. The agency takes on the risk of non-payment and retains a percentage of the rents as a commission for this service. Agents struggle to acquire enough plots to manage. On the other hand, it is not difficult for them to find tenants, as there are always plenty of people looking for a place to stay. Consequently, the agencies are quite strict with late payments. The agencies have a penalty system with fines, and ultimately evict tenants who fail to pay. At the time that Flora and James did not receive their salaries from Sharma Farm, Flora said she was happy they had not rented their apartment through an agent. They would have been evicted, as they had failed to pay the rent before the fifth of the month (as was the rule) several times. Because they personally knew their landlord and had always paid on time before, they could negotiate with him and were allowed to pay later. Such an arrangement for later payment would not have been possible with an agent. Hence, the establishment of these agencies increased the insecurity of tenants.

The need to pay a monthly rent is one of the factors that made life in the workers' settlements expensive and stressful. The average reported monthly rent in the survey was 1529 KES, with a range from 400 to 4500 KES. The rent would depend on, for instance, the material of the walls (quarry stones or wattle-and-daub) and on the location and neighbourhood. Houses located far away from the Moi Lake Road would usually be more affordable because houses located close to the road are favoured. One of the employees of Karibu Farm rented a house in Tumaini, the neighbourhood in Kasarani located on the largest distance to the main road, and complained about the walking distance. It took her 25 minutes to get to work in the morning instead of the 10 minutes it would take her if she would have lived close to the road. In fact, a few months later she moved to a more expensive rental house located very close to the Moi Lake Road. In the settlement Karagita, living close to the road meant living close to the stops of the farms' staff buses. This saved the workers time and it also was deemed safer. Flower farm worker Dennis, who lived in Mirera, east of Karagita, told me he would walk the 20 minutes to the main road and back to accompany his wife whenever she was working late in the packhouse and returned at dusk or later. He considered it too dangerous for a woman to walk through Karagita on her own at night. Such considerations influence the average rents in different neighbourhoods within the settlements.

After arriving in Naivasha, the migrants do not necessarily stay in one house for the whole period of their stay: many of them continue to move within the wider Naivasha area. They could decide to move again, sometimes several times, depending on the house they stayed in (for instance, because their rent was increased, or because an opportunity arose to get a house in a better location), a change in household composition (for instance, because of getting married or getting a child), or a change in job (for instance, because of moving to a farm with a workers' compound). This mobility within Naivasha is illustrated by the survey results from Sharma Farm: 13 of the 50 respondents there mentioned they had first lived and worked elsewhere in Naivasha before moving to the farm's *kambi*.

The motivations to move within Naivasha are further illustrated by the following excerpt from an interview with flower farm supervisor Gabriel, who resided in Karagita:

> Now, like I said, when I arrived I lived with my relative. From then, when I was still doing these casual jobs, I started to cooperate with my friend whom I had met there and he was also living with a relative. So I cooperated with him, we looked for a small house. Then we stayed, we stayed, until he got another job in Nakuru. So he left, and I stayed behind. But the place where we stayed, was far from Karagita. Actually, there in the back it was cheap. So once I received a permanent job, I moved to Karagita. Ya, so from there I moved only once.
>
> *And this house, did you get it by just asking around and hearing about an opportunity, or how did you get it?*
>
> No, this house was close to where I was staying. So where I was staying, it was a mud, clay, house, and there was no electricity. Although it had a cemented floor. So there I stayed all the time until last year. But when last year arrived, and actually last year I was married, so I had to move.
>
> *Oh, you married last year?*
>
> Yeah, sure. Now next door there was a plot, it was newly built, so it was just close to where I was staying. Now when [the construction] finished, I talked to the owner and he gave me one room, I got it.

In short, networks are crucial for migrant workers when looking for a (good) place to stay in Naivasha. Which role do migrant's networks and related factors such as gender play in their access to jobs? Which opportunities does the labour market in Naivasha provide, and for whom?

3.4 Finding a Job: The Naivasha Labour Market

According to one of the labour officers of Naivasha Subcounty, the flower farms are the main employer around the lake. He mentioned vegetable farms, tourism ventures, construction companies, and a brewery in Naivasha Town as other important employers. This impression was confirmed in the survey, in which 53.4% of the respondents said they worked on a flower farm while an additional 13.6% worked on a vegetable farm. In addition, 9.8% of the non-flower farm workers had worked for a flower farm previously. Others were engaged in other wage labour such as in construction, tourism, or security, or had their own small business. Table 3.3 provides an overview of survey respondents' main occupation.

Table 3.3 Main occupation in Karagita, Kasarani, and the Sharma Farm compound ($n = 176$)

Occupation	*Number of respondents*	*%*
Flower farm	94	53.4
Vegetable farm	24	13.6
Small business	17	9.7
Other contract/permanent labour	15	8.5
Housewife	7	4.0
Casual wage labour	5	2.8
Student	3	1.7
Fishing	1	0.6
Renting out rooms	1	0.6
None	9	5.1

Compared to similar low-income migrant neighbourhoods in Nakuru, where less than half of the household heads are formally employed (Owuor, 2003), there are relatively many opportunities in formal employment in Naivasha.

Thus, many of the settlements' residents end up working for a farm, either for short periods of time or as permanent employees. In 2015, there were an estimated 35,000 employees within the approximately 55 flower farms in the wider Naivasha area (including the Kinangop towards the east).[6] Some of the farms set up other economic activities and provide additional employment opportunities in, for instance, vegetable production or in the exploitation of a lodge or restaurant at their lakeside premises. The farms furthermore provide some indirect employment opportunities. Much of the material used by Karibu Farm was imported, for instance, the polythene used for the construction of greenhouses and the scissors used for harvesting. But other tools and materials were locally produced, either within the farm (e.g. tables used for the packing of flowers) or by local companies (e.g. dust coats). Local construction companies and private masons also profit from the presence of the farms. Finally, the need to provide workers with lunch creates opportunities for local businesspeople. Employees who live in a ***kambi*** or in a settlement close to their workplace can go home during the lunch break but most employees have to get their lunch in or around the farm. Some farms have canteens, where they provide basic food against subsidized prices and, in single cases, even for free. Food is cooked in large quantities in enormous pots, and lunch is served in shifts. The cooks of Karibu Farm used 25 kilograms of rice, 45 kilograms of maize flower, 30 kilograms of beans, 20 kilograms of maize, and about 30 cabbages per day. Part of this food was acquired in a supermarket in Naivasha Town but most of it was purchased from a local businesswoman in the neighbouring settlement. Also farms that do not provide lunch create an opportunity for the "self-employed", who place makeshift food stalls outside the gate of the farm or simply come to the farm with a bag of fruits or a few bottles of tea. In this way, the flower industry creates more income-generating opportunities than only the permanent job opportunities in the greenhouses and the packhouses.

Nevertheless, the farms are by no means the only possible employer, and migrants have a range of options. Figure 3.1 depicts three important economic activities that take place in Naivasha: tourism, livestock keeping, and flower farming.[7] Table 3.4 provides an overview of the jobs in Naivasha that were listed during exercises in which I asked residents of the settlements to list job opportunities there. The table includes all types of jobs that were mentioned by at least five out of the ten participating groups.[8]

Fig. 3.1 Three economic activities taking place along the South Lake Road: tourism (minivan on the left), livestock keeping, and flower farming (gate on the right)

Table 3.4 Job opportunities mentioned by at least five of the ten groups in the listing and piling exercise

Times mentioned	*Types of job*
5	Bartender; mobile money agent; selling clothes or goods in the local market
6	Baby care; construction work; vegetable farm labourer; water vending
7	*Boda boda* driver; small-scale business; *matatu* driver or tout; shopkeeper
9	Flower farm labourer; employee in a hotel, restaurant, or *hoteli*
10	Fishing

Fig. 3.2 Business opportunities in Karagita

The presence of ten thousands of migrant wage labourers creates an abundance of opportunities for small-scale business people. The services that they provide are wide-ranging, from housing agents and mobile money agents to tailors and traders in second-hand clothes to *hoteli* (local restaurants) and cyber cafes. Figure 3.2 depicts different opportunities for business in Karagita: selling clothes in the market, a petrol station, and *boda boda* (motorcycle) drivers waiting for customers. The business opportunities were also apparent when a new farm opened up in the hinterland of the lake in 2014. During a visit to the farm shortly after it had been established, I noticed there were few people living in the immediate surroundings of the farm. When I passed the farm just one year later, I found new greenhouses and new houses for the managerial staff within the premises of the farm. Moreover, I also found a small settlement that had emerged outside the farm gate. Dozens of houses and shacks had been built there and several *hoteli* were selling tea and food. A handful of second-hand clothing hawkers had positioned themselves close to the company buses used by most of the staff to be brought home in the late afternoon. The expansion of the farm thus created opportunities for small-scale business people. Figure 3.3 illustrates the opposite situation, namely the closing down of Sharma Farm: because of a lack of customers, also surrounding *hoteli* and shops had to close. These examples show the large influence of the flower industry on the overall economy in Naivasha.

The wage labour market in Naivasha is volatile, influenced by national and global economic dynamics, and heavily dependent on the performance of single middle- and large-scale farms. For example, whenever a farm would change hands, the contracts of all employees would be terminated. Usually, some or all of them would be re-hired again by the new owner. However, the workers would lose all the privileges attached to

Fig. 3.3 Closed makeshift shops outside Sharma Farm

long-term employment, such as a higher salary (see '1,300 Flower Farm Employees', 2002). The Sharma Farm financial problems had even more impact than these "regular" takeovers that occur from time to time. In this case, eventually all employees lost their job. Whenever I walked around one of the settlements with James or Flora after production in the farm had completely come to a standstill, we would meet former colleagues of theirs who were looking for ways to make a living. One was hawking clothes, another was making fishing nets, and yet another one was working at a petrol station. Others found employment on a new middle-sized flower farm that had started up around the time they had lost their jobs. Thus, whereas some job opportunities disappear, new opportunities can arise every moment. This is not only the case for the horticultural industry. Tourism is another example of a volatile sector influenced by global dynamics. At the time I conducted my fieldwork, the number of tourists to the country had decreased tremendously after a number of terrorist attacks elsewhere in Kenya. Both the employees of large hotels and small-scale entrepreneurs who organized boat rides on the lake or who worked as drivers for tourists felt the financial consequences.

The labour market thus changes over time. Moreover, job opportunities differ around the lake. Along the tarmacked South Lake Road, relatively close to Naivasha Town and with the majority of farms and hotels settled there, there is a range of opportunities for both wage labour and business. In Kasarani, at North Lake, the inhabitants depend on a small number of middle-scale employers: a handful of flower and vegetable farms and a gated community which provides employment to security guards, masons, and housemaids. This difference in dependence on horticulture along the lake also surfaced from the survey results: 67.2% of the respondents in Kasarani said they were working for a flower or vegetable farm against 49.5% of the respondents in Karagita. In addition, as argued by Kioko (2012, p. 12), even the small-scale businesses in Kasarani have been mainly fuelled by wages earned in the aforementioned firms. Lucy, whose household in Kasarani depended on the income earned on two different flower farms, put it like this: "the flowers are carrying us."

Opportunities for work furthermore differ per person. Educational level and earlier work experience of course are relevant here but also gender influences the choice of economic activity. I found that about as many female as male survey respondents were employed by a flower farm (54.1% against 52.2%). Flower farm work thus is important for both women and men. Nevertheless, it seems that men have a more diverse range of opportunities outside the farms: 20.9% of the male respondents were engaged in either permanent or casual wage labour elsewhere, against only 5.5% of the female respondents. On the other hand, 12.8% of the women reported having no income of their own, against 3.0% of the men. These differences on the labour market are influenced by women's and men's structural positions. Whereas some women have the choice to become "housewives", it is unacceptable for men to depend financially on their wife. And as pointed out by Nici Nelson (1997) for migrants in Nairobi, women on average have lower levels of education than men, which diminishes their opportunities on the labour market.

Furthermore, gendered ideas on which occupations fit which individuals shape the opportunities for women and men further. "Let me tell you, we all do all jobs these days", was what one of the women participating in the listing and piling exercise said. Nevertheless, her group in the end selected a few gender-specific jobs anyway, as all the other participating groups did. Private baby care centres, where working parents bring their children to during the day, were said to be exclusively run by women. *Boda boda* and *matatu* drivers are usually men. The most prominent example of a gender-specific occupation is fishing. This arduous and even dangerous occupation is not necessarily liked. However, it is one of the most profitable economic activities and therefore popular. Despite the ongoing controversies on poaching, I noticed fishermen were quite visible on the lake shores. Fishery allegedly provides an income to several hundreds of men in Karagita alone ('Transport Paralysed', 2015). It thus forms an important (albeit partly illegal) economic sector—in which there is little space for women, who are only involved in the trading of fish.

Regardless of these differences, securing a stable and sufficient source of income is a challenge for almost all settlement residents. Farm managers and government officials I spoke to were under the impression that the flower industry attracts far more job seekers than it can absorb. Yet the survey did not show a remarkably high unemployment rate: only 5.1% of the respondents were unwillingly employed (see Table 3.3). However, despite the range of opportunities, few of them provide a steady and proper income. The flower industry has been scrutinized for its low wages (Anker & Anker, 2014). Temporary or casual labour in other sectors provides even less income. This scarcity of well-paid jobs forces people to settle for work with either little pay or tough labour conditions, at least until they find something better. Vegetable farms easily fill their vacancies, despite the early working hours and the low salaries. Flower farms pay more but can have other disadvantages, such as being located far away from Naivasha Town and the settlements, necessitating daily commuting by staff buses. Employees of one of the vegetable farms located far away from any settlement along the non-tarmacked part of the Moi Lake Road on the west side of the lake were even more unlucky. This farm did not have staff buses and there was no regular *matatu* along this stretch. The workers were forced to either find a ride or to walk to work, leaving the house before dawn in pitch-black darkness. These women—whom I occasionally gave a ride back home when I drove back to Naivasha Town from Kasarani in the late afternoon—would have preferred to work on a farm that provides transport, but they simply had not come across that opportunity yet.

The flower industry is also well aware that employees have few other (better) options, as indicated by an excerpt from a newspaper article: "On accusation that farms pay peanuts to employees, Ms Ngige told *Business Daily* in a past interview that the industry was a mass employer of unskilled people, explaining that '80 per cent of the people employed on flower farms are unskilled. These are people who would not secure jobs anywhere else outside the farms'" (Omondi, 2007). Flower farm managers also stated that one of the advantages of Naivasha as a production location is the availability of good and affordable labour. This abundance of labour and lack of other well-paid options have weakened the room for employees to negotiate better conditions.

To cope with the low salaries and insecure circumstances, and to reduce their dependency on the farms, some migrant workers attempt to diversify their income by performing more than one economic activity. These activities sometimes take place in Naivasha itself, for example, rearing chicken, fishing, renting out a motorcycle as a *boda boda*, or cultivating (illegally) on riparian land whenever lake levels are low.[9] The type of investment that requires the most capital is the purchase of a plot of land in one of the settlements and the construction of rental houses there. A more affordable option, which has become more popular recently, is to buy or lease a *shamba* in one of the villages in the hinterland of the lake, such as Ndabibi or Moi Ndabi, with the purpose of commercial farming (Kioko, 2016, p. 18). As pointed out by Hall, Scoones, and Tsikata (2017, p. 525), renting land allows for flexibility in income-generating activities as small-scale cultivators can thus move in and out of production according to the time and capital they have available. However, land prices and rents are also on the increase in the lake's hinterland, and most migrants can only invest in land in their home area or even elsewhere, wherever plots are more affordable.

Apart from investing in livestock or land, either in Naivasha or elsewhere, some migrant workers start a small-scale business on the side. The supervisor of the night shift in Karibu Farm's packhouse made some additional money during the day with his own maize flour mill in Kasarani. Another example is Helen, a general worker in one of Karibu Farm's greenhouses. She originated from Siaya and moved to Kasarani after a divorce, where she started a business in foodstuffs. She lost her capital when she had to bridge a period without any income after she fled during the post-election violence in 2008. She was forced to look for a farm job when she eventually returned to Naivasha. However, Helen did not leave business altogether: to make some extra money, she would go to Naivasha Town on her weekly day off to buy some vegetables with her salary. She would then sell these in Kasarani every afternoon after coming back from work, thus diversifying her income.

In sum, although the labour market in Naivasha is defined by the horticultural industry, migrant workers have more options than only farm labour. Yet few of these options secure a stable and sufficient income. And whereas some are able to diversify their income, most flower farm employees either lack the time or the capital to do so. Inhabitants of the settlements frequently used the English word "hustling" when describing their economic situation. This term refers to the perseverance and patience needed when looking for a job that enables one not only to meet one's daily needs but also to make some investments for the future. The security migrant workers have when coming to Naivasha is the presence of family members or friends, not the certainty of finding a stable job.

3.5 Finding a Job: Farm's Recruitment Processes

How can migrant workers access jobs within the horticultural sector once they have arrived in Naivasha? The most visible way of looking for employment is to simply line up at the gate of a vegetable or flower farm in the morning in the hope of finding a casual job. However, procedures for getting a more permanent job on a rose farm are more formal. Family members and friends already living in Naivasha are again crucial here: not only do they provide aspirant migrants with a space of living during their job search, but they can also inform them about job openings in their own workplace. Table 3.5 shows that survey respondents who worked for a flower farm mostly had heard about the opening for their current job through a family member or friend.[10]

Table 3.5 Ways in which respondents learned about a farm vacancy ($n = 93$)

Heard about the job opening …	*Number of respondents*	*%*
… via a family member/friend	68	73.1
… via a broker	1	1.1
… via an advertisement at the gate	13	14.0
… via an open application	11	11.8

I asked John, a former employee of Sharma Farm who had returned to his region of origin Narok, whether he already knew anyone working for the farm before applying for a job there. He answered that he indeed knew many people there. They also originated from Narok and had informed him when the position as an electrician that he later obtained was advertised. John was not an exception. Three other former employees of Sharma Farm whom I interviewed in Kisumu all had found their job at the farm through either a sibling or a brother-in-law already working there. And Sharma Farm was not the only farm where personal connections were crucial in accessing jobs. Prior contacts are important in the recruitment processes of other farms as well.

The importance of personal contacts might seem odd, considering that recruitment practices in the industry have been formalized. During the mid-2000s, the majority of the farms created official human resource (HR) departments "in response to the challenges presented by certification to and implementation of social standards" (Riisgaard & Gibbon, 2014, p. 278). This formalization contradicts trends in other global industries on the African continent, where more informal labour arrangements and recruitment through brokers are on the rise (Meagher, Mann, & Bolt, 2016).

Farm managers emphasized the formality of the recruitment procedures and stated that they provide equal chances to employment. As the production manager of a new, relatively large rose farm said about the recruitment of the many workers they needed: "they only need to be able to do the work they have to do." Through these formal processes, the farms attempt to avoid accusations of nepotism or discrimination. Conversations with both managers and workers confirmed that the procedures make it difficult to acquire a job only on the basis of a recommendation and without a formal application.[11] When I asked the HR manager of Karibu Farm about the farm's recruitment procedures, she answered decisively, leaving no doubt about the formality and transparency of its procedure. She told me they would put an advertisement at the gate, people would send an application, the HR department would make a shortlist, and the general manager would conduct the job interviews and make the final decision.[12] Although the farm does not make immediate use of recommendations by workers, this system nevertheless favours those within the networks of the employees, as it is mainly current workers who will read the advertisement at the gate and who can tell their relatives and friends to apply. Some farms do not even make a public announcement. The general manager of a farm producing seasonal flowers told me that vacancies for senior positions would be put on the internet or in a newspaper. But whenever this farm needed general workers, they would use "word of mouth" and just tell current employees to announce the job openings in the settlements where they live.

Level of education plays only a minor role in recruitment processes. I found educational levels in the settlements to be modest: 43.3% of the survey respondents had finished primary school and 44.9% had a secondary school diploma. Only 6.7% had continued their studies after finishing secondary school.[13] However, the farms do not need educated or specialized staff for the majority of the available jobs. Some flower farms recently started to require secondary education, even when recruiting general workers (Gibbon & Riisgaard, 2014, p. 106). Secondary school-leavers are considered to be more reliable and disciplined than uneducated staff. On the other hand, several managers expressed the difficulties they encounter in working with people who are "too clever" for the jobs they are doing: the managers perceived of these workers as looking for "shortcuts" instead of simply doing what they are taught, or even suspected them of trying to "trick" the management. Thus, some farms continue to only require a primary school education.

Several training institutes in Naivasha Town offer short-term courses in agriculture and even specifically in floriculture, but I did not meet any flower farm workers who had taken such a course. Most employees receive their training within the farms and therefore do not benefit from such a certificate. And even vacancies for more specialized positions are regularly filled by promoting general workers who have not followed any external training. Security guards, scouts who monitor the condition of the crop, and even supervisors are often simply trained internally. Only managers are commonly required to have a diploma of a higher education institute. Nevertheless, even these managers claimed that they had learned their work primarily "in the field" and not from books. The foreign top managers sometimes have an educational background in floriculture, but it is more important that they already gained experience in flower farming before coming to Kenya. Likewise, many Kenyan managers with a diploma or degree initially had only been able to acquire a job as a supervisor or even as a general worker, as they had not gained any work experience yet. The exception to the relative unimportance of education are specialized managerial positions in, for instance, the HR department or in irrigation, which usually require a specific diploma. Yet, overall, level of education is of minor importance when looking for a job in the horticultural industry.

Moreover, whereas managers need previous work experience to acquire a job, even this is not necessary when applying for the position of general worker. Of the 94 flower farm workers interviewed for the survey, 77.7% had no experience in the flower industry before they had started their current job.[14] Some of the migrants even arrive in Naivasha without having *any* experience in formal employment. One of the employees of Karibu Farm was 29 years old when she moved from a village close to Kisumu to Naivasha in 1997. She had only finished primary school and had not been involved in any wage labour since: "at home, there is only agriculture."[15] She nevertheless could immediately start to work for a flower farm on a temporary contract and soon after was employed permanently by another farm. She is not an exception: previous working experience on a farm or even in wage labour in general is usually not a requirement. The HR manager of Karibu Farm explained that a worker typically only needs a certificate of good conduct from the police, and for some of the heavier jobs, such as spraying pesticides, a doctor's statement that one is in good health.

As a consequence of the way in which job positions are announced, farm employees often have one or several siblings, cousins, or aunts and uncles who work for the same farm. I heard of many such cases during visits to Karibu Farm, even though this farm is strict on having a formal, open application procedure. Consequently, applicants commonly originate from the same region as those already employed. Officially, region of origin—related to the more sensitive issue of ethnicity—does not play any role in recruitment processes. Managers emphasized that everyone has an equal chance to get a job on their farm, regardless of education level, ethnic background, age, or gender. But an unintended effect of the channels through which vacant positions are announced is that the desired equality did not always materialize in practice.

Furthermore, even though explicit discrimination is not acceptable, certain naturalized preferences and discourses do play a role. As Salzinger (2003, p. 36) wrote on the role of gender in recruitment practices of global factories located in Mexico: "gender intervenes because it is the terrain upon which the question of who looks like a maquila worker, and who doesn't, is decided, thus establishing the context within which hiring takes place and production is initiated." In these Mexican factories, "femininity" provided the norm for hiring, even if also some men were employed. I argue that both gender and region of origin (if not ethnicity) likewise provide an implicit norm for hiring in the case of the Naivasha flower farms, despite official procedures that try to create equal chances. Unarticulated ideas about "who looks like a flower farm worker" (and who does not) inevitably shape the recruitment practices of the farms. In practice, the formal procedures make it difficult to openly favour a certain ethnic group over another. Nevertheless, when asked to explain imbalances in their workforce, (Kenyan) HR managers regularly referred to group attributes, suggesting that certain groups are less willing or less capable of working as agricultural wage labourers than others. A former trade union official, for instance, claimed that the Maasai are not interested in working on a flower farm, since they consider the work to be "too heavy". Contrary to this statement, I met several Maasai flower farm workers. Yet, such statements indicate the prevalence of naturalized ideas on economic activities of ethnic groups. These implicit imaginations of "the worker", in combination with the practice of advertising open positions at the gate or via current employees, have resulted in an imbalanced workforce within the flower industry in general and most poignantly within some of the individual farms. For instance, of the 50 survey respondents who resided in the Sharma Farm *kambi*, 52.0% were born in the Western Province and 34.0% in the Nyanza Province.

As outlined above, farms also tend to have an unbalanced workforce when it comes to gender, with relatively many female employees. A common perception, especially on the part of NGOs, is that the flower farms hire young women because they are easily exploitable (Hivos, n.d.). Working women in other global industries have been thought of as being in a stage between school and marriage, which justifies paying them only a "single's salary" (Kim, 1997, p. 6; Wolf, 1992, p. 117). However, the position of women is different in the horticultural industry in Naivasha. First of all, farms do not only hire young women: some female respondents in the survey had already been in their thirties when they had taken up employment on a farm. And Glory, whom I introduced above, was already 44 years old when she started to work for a farm. Moreover, like Gibbon and Riisgaard (2014, p. 118), I found that even though women are overrepresented in the worst-paying positions, women and men working in the same type of job are paid equal wages. Kazimierczuk et al. (2018, p. 35) even found that women on average earn more than men in the same position due to the system of yearly wage increments. As women have fewer job opportunities outside the flower industry, they tend to work for the same farm for long periods of time, thus benefiting from the system of yearly wage increments.

The idea of a wage-earning woman, either single or contributing to a household income, is not as alien or exceptional in present-day Kenya as in some other contexts where global industries hire women (see Ong, 1987; Wolf, 1992). Lower wages for women are therefore not justified. In other words, the vulnerability of women that NGOs have presupposed is not a given; it is context-dependent (Freeman, 2000). The reason for managers of the Naivasha flower farms to prefer employing women is not that they would be cheaper or would be less inclined to resist to bad labour conditions. More subtle, context-dependent gendered ideologies play a role. In contrast to the role of ethnicity, gender is a factor that is more openly discussed. Certain types of (physically demanding) jobs are not deemed fit for women. It is plainly unthinkable to hire a woman for spraying chemicals or for working in the night shift. This gendered division of labour, which I discuss in more detail in the following chapter, has grown into a given. It was not achieved consciously but, in the words of a manager, "developed on its own".

Thus, despite the formalization, the recruitment processes do not automatically create a balanced workforce. In fact, they have quite the opposite effect. Recruitment requires little effort from the farms. Both the initial accommodation of potential workers and the advertisement of jobs is mainly taken up by the existing workforce. The dynamic system of chain labour migration that the farms depend on is not a creation of, and was also not unique for, the flower industry. It had been shaped by changing land and labour relations since colonial times, as described in the previous chapter. Global industries in other countries sometimes had to involve the local government to access labour, especially in the initial stages (see Ong, 1987; Wolf, 1992). But when the global flower industry established itself in Naivasha, it could tap into and expand on an existing system of chain labour migration in Kenya.

3.6 Finding a Job: Migrant Workers' Preferences

From a global perspective, the Naivasha flower industry might appear to be exploiting a proletarianized workforce, as labour is abundantly available. Nevertheless, on a local level, the presence of the industry implies opportunities for individuals, as also concluded by Friedemann-Sánchez (2009, p. 4) for the case of the Colombian cut flower industry. How do migrant workers in Naivasha themselves evaluate the work in the flower farms? Do they perceive of the work as exploitation or as an opportunity? How does it compare to other possibilities on the local labour market? And do those who "look like flower farm workers" in the eyes of HR managers (Salzinger, 2003, p. 36) also imagine themselves as such?

Perceptions on the industry became especially clear through the listing and piling exercises, where one participant, for instance, asked rhetorically: "is not any job good?" The goal of most migrant workers is to make a decent living, regardless of the type of job. When I met Flora for the first time, I asked her whether she liked her work on a flower farm. She laughed and then said she liked it because it helped her to survive. For her, as for many other migrants, the flower farm work is something she would resort to when there are no other, better-paying options available. Staelens, Desiere, Louche, and D'Haese (2018) likewise concluded in their article on the Ethiopian flower industry that job satisfaction is primarily related to the question whether a job covers one's basic needs. Most general workers in Naivasha are indeed not particularly attracted to the work they do. They choose this job because of the security it provides. The listing and piling exercises in Kasarani show that flower farm work is highly appreciated there because of the likelihood of getting a permanent contract. And especially for specialized positions, the labour conditions in farms are often favourable when compared to jobs elsewhere. John, who had worked as an electrician for Sharma Farm, gave the following explanation for his decision to apply for a job there:

> It was good because with Kenya Power I only got a casual job. It was not permanent. I worked for three years with Kenya Power. I waited, and then I saw they just kept on renewing the contract. Now I got this other permanent job. I saw that it was better. I left. I looked at many things. You know there was a school there, there was a house there in Naivasha with that company. Now I saw that it was better, and I came.

Fig. 3.4 The vase-life display in Karibu Farm

The choice for flower farm work is thus often based on material considerations.

Most workers are not even aware of the ultimate goal of their labour. Farms have a display in the packhouse or the offices on which the so-called vase life of the flowers is observed (see Fig. 3.4). One or two stems of each variety would be put together in a vase every day, and these would stay on the display for 14 days. This display helps in detecting diseases and weaknesses of the crop. In addition, it is a way of making the goal of flower growing comprehensible to the workers, as general manager Jan explained to me. However, the display seemed to be unsuccessful in that: surprisingly few Karibu Farm employees were aware of the purpose of flower production. They asked me what the customers in Europe do with the millions of flowers that are being shipped there every year. Even a Kenyan production manager was surprised to hear that the flowers are really only produced for aesthetic reasons. He had imagined that perhaps part of them would be used to make perfume or soap. He simply did not see the point of putting flowers into a vase on the table. As he said, his mother would not be happy at all if he would bring her flowers. She would expect sugar or clothes instead. Thus, workers who know perfectly well how to handle a plant in order to produce "good" flowers do not know what the final purpose was of the work they were doing. And even if they do, this purpose mostly does not make sense to them. However, the workers seemed not to be bothered. Their goal was to make a living, even if they had to do that through producing something that they themselves considered to be of little or no value. This lack of affinity with the final product of their work is in itself not remarkable: most of the early social scientific writings on the topic of work discussed by Spittler (2008) linked the motivation or consent to work to workers' material needs. This link to material needs also implies that work that creates a product which is "useless" in the eyes of the workers can still be considered to be embedded in wider social relations and that employees can still feel "at home" at work (Spittler, 2009).

Moreover, I found that a few workers do specifically appreciate the product. One worker, whose job it was to tidy up the greenhouses, said that he liked his work because he liked seeing how the flowers grow. And a supervisor in the Karibu Farm packhouse told me he had shortly worked in a flower shop in his hometown and had discovered there that he liked working with flowers. Especially at the supervisory and management level, working in the flower industry could be a positive choice. One manager, upon being asked whether he liked working on a flower farm, even called it his hobby. Another manager expressed his explicit interest in the industry and said he liked the dynamics, which make the work exciting. On the other hand, the general manager of a relatively small farm told me he advised his children not to look for a career in horticulture. He found it a strenuous job, as he had to navigate between the divergent interests of the workers, the company directors, and the consumer market. Lower-ranked jobs are also considered strenuous by some. Participants in the listing and piling exercises who had opted not to work for a flower farm expressed their dislike for the labour regime and the strict work rhythm on the farms. The dependency on a good relation with the supervisors and the management and the need to comply were important reasons for these respondents to choose to be engaged in small-scale business ("self-employment").

Whether someone appreciates flower farm work and the conditions attached to it partly depends on traits such as level of education, region of origin, and gender. Some people try to "escape" from flower farm work by continuing their education. It is not uncommon to study in addition to one's job: six of the survey respondents, for instance, did so at the time we interviewed them. Other, young, workers save money to pay for further education later on. However, a higher level of education does not guarantee one a better job. General workers with a relatively high education level are sometimes frustrated about the lack of opportunities. Staelens et al.

(2018, pp. 1623–1624) likewise reported that higher-educated workers in the Ethiopian flower industry were less satisfied with their low-skilled jobs than lower-educated workers. A union representative within Karibu Farm told me: "The work here is hard. A lot of us have studied but there is just no work." Others once did have a better job but had lost it. A former quality manager of a large-scale horticultural farm had to accept a job as a general worker elsewhere after having been fired. He was very unsatisfied with his new position, which in his opinion was "a woman's job". Working as a general worker clearly was a step back, and not only the lower salary but also the loss of status and influence fell hard on him.

Gendered ideas on farm work were also expressed during the listing and piling exercises, where a few men expressed their unwillingness to accept a job as a general worker. These men thought the monotonous work of harvesting in the greenhouse and grading flowers in the packhouse (i.e. preparing the flowers for shipment) was more "fitting" for women. They stated that men only accept this work because there simply are no other options.

Even though flower farm work is not appreciated by everyone, it is generally liked better than work for vegetable farms. Work there is more demanding because of early working hours: work could start as early as 5 a.m. The vegetable farms also have poorer employment conditions than flower farms, for instance, lower payment and the prevalence of temporary, instead of permanent, contracts. These discrepancies in labour conditions are especially poignant within farms that produce both vegetables and flowers. Some migrants upon arrival in Naivasha would a first make a living with a casual or temporary job on a vegetable farm, but they would usually switch whenever an opportunity would arise within a flower farm. However, some never get that chance. I was once asked by a female resident of Kasarani to recommend her to the HR manager of Karibu Farm (which I could not do, as this farm had a strict policy on not hiring on the basis of personal recommendations). She had been working on and off for (the same) vegetable farm for many years. However, being a single mother with no other source of income, she always had difficulties making ends meet during the off-season. Her request confirmed my impression that a flower farm job is more desirable than work on a vegetable farm.

Engaging in small-scale business was preferred over both types of farm work because of the freedom and independence attached to it. Discussions during the listing exercises indicated that many farm workers aspire to quit wage labour and start their own business. At the same time, they realized that business is more insecure than wage labour: one's income depends on the income of the customers. Participants in the listing exercises explained that craftsmen in Kasarani—which is not well connected to Naivasha Town—are often out of work because there are relatively few customers around. Government interference adds to this insecurity: some types of business require a costly trading licence (Kioko, 2012, p. 47). Other possible income-generating activities (such as selling *chang'aa*) are prohibited. Hence, although doing business is generally preferred over wage labour, security of employment is an important reason to appreciate flower farm work. In the Naivasha context, this type of job often simply provides the best possibility to cover one's basic needs.

3.7 Conclusion: The Use of Networks

This chapter has shown how the flower farms have drawn on historically constituted migration patterns for the recruitment of labour. I argue that the flower farms—like other global firms—depend on inequalities and hierarchies created outside of the industry itself for the mobilization of labour. "Supply chains draw upon and vitalize class niches and investment strategies formed through the vicissitudes of gender, race, ethnicity, nationality, religion, sexuality, age, and citizenship status" (Tsing, 2009, p. 158). I have discussed how some of these factors—most explicitly gender, generation, and region of origin—have been used to "produce" a labour force for the Naivasha flower farms (Freeman, 2000; Salzinger, 2003).

Moreover, answers to the questions who the migrants are, why they decided to come to Naivasha, and how they manage to find a job and a house to stay in once there indicate that recruitment by the farms also depends on individual migrants' networks and aspirations. I argue against an overly simplistic representation of the migration process in which migrants are perceived of as individuals who are "pulled" to Naivasha exclusively because of a lack of economic options elsewhere. Ortiz (2002, p. 397) pointed out that "the search for work is not an individual pursuit but an activity structured by family dynamics and by the character of migrants' social networks". That is, the decision to move is not made individually. Furthermore, labour migrants usually find work and a place to stay by mobilizing their networks. And not only is the act of moving itself shaped by migrants' social environment, their rural-based networks also continue to support migrants while they reside in urban areas (Ross & Weisner, 1977). Migrant workers' networks thus ensure the flower industry's access to a stable and experienced workforce—a crucial factor in its success, as the following chapter will argue.

Notes

1. The standardized questionnaire for the survey contained questions about respondents' personal background, their work situation and work history, and their membership of organizations. I carried out about one third of the interviews myself while the other interviews were conducted by two assistants. Respondents were selected by randomly selecting a number of blocks or lines of houses within the settlements and the farm compound, where interviews were conducted with all adult residents who were present during one of our repeated visits and who were willing to participate. The survey outcomes were analysed with the help of SPSS (versions 22, 23, and 24).
2. The non-response to this question was 2.8%.
3. The exchange rate between the Kenyan shilling and the euro was fluctuating tremendously during my stay in Kenya. When I started my long period of fieldwork, at the beginning of October 2014, the exchange rate was €1 = 113 KES. Thus, 90,000 KES was roughly equivalent to €800.
4. The ego-centred network analysis was based on data gathered through a standardized questionnaire. I interviewed 22 residents of the settlements Karagita, Kasarani, and Kihoto. The sample included both flower farm workers and other residents, whose average age was comparable to the average age in the survey (34 years against 36 years). Also the diversity in the region of origin was representative when compared to the survey results. I asked the participants about their motivations to come to Naivasha and their networks there, and about their connections to their region of origin and to other regions in Kenya. In addition, I asked them ten hypothetical questions about their support network. For the analysis of the social network questionnaires, I made use of the programs Microsoft Excel 2013 and UCINET 6 (Borgatti, Everett, & Freeman, 2002). Table 3.2 summarizes the migration background of the respondents in the ego-centred network analysis. Table 5.4 in Chap. 5 summarizes the questions and the aggregated results on the respondents' networks.
5. In this book, I refer to the full text of the Collective Bargaining Agreement (CBA) for the years 2011–2013 (AEA & KPAWU, 2011). Anker and Anker (2014, pp. 57–58) provide an overview of benefits in a more recent CBA for the years 2013–2015, which shows slight differences, such as increases in minimum wages and allowances.
6. This estimate was based on data provided by the KFC and in interviews conducted by Andreas Gemählich and myself. We gathered figures on the number of employees for 31 of the 54 farms (including plant breeders and propagators) we knew of in 2015, which gave a total of 24,695. The three largest farms in the area—with 10,000 employees in total—were all included and the missing farms were all small- to middle-scale farms. Our estimate is

comparable to the total number of 37,000 employees mentioned by Happ (2016, pp. 163–165) in his overview of the Naivasha flower farms, which he compiled with the help of a local trade union official.

7. I have taken all pictures in this book between 2014 and 2016.
8. I conducted listing and piling exercises on the different types of jobs performed in the settlements and in the flower firms. I was interested in perceptions on work and on job opportunities, and in how these perceptions varied according to variables such as place of residence and profession. For these listing and piling exercises, I organized meetings with ten groups of 3–4 participants. The core assignment was to make a list of all the possible jobs that people do who resided in the same settlement as where the participants lived. In the case of flower farm workers, I also asked them to list all the possible positions on the farm where they were working. The participants were then asked to pile the mentioned jobs and positions according to different criteria such as level of income and availability. Five groups consisted of flower farm workers whereas the other five groups mainly consisted of people with other occupations. Sampling was done in different ways: four groups were sampled by randomly asking people on the street to participate in exchange for a cup of tea or a soda in a *hoteli*. Two other groups were selected in Karibu Farm, two were formed by asking one flower farm worker to gather a few of his or her colleagues, and two groups were sampled by gathering a few of the survey respondents. Whereas the listing revealed job and business opportunities in the settlements and in the flower firms, the comments made during the piling exercises provided insights into perceptions on the different types of work.
9. See also Kioko (2012, pp. 40–50) on income diversification in the settlement Kasarani.
10. The results in Table 3.5 can be compared to results of a survey conducted by Gibbon and Riisgaard (2014, p. 106), who used somewhat different categories and did their research across the whole of Kenya: 40% of the 99 respondents were recommended by a friend or family member, 43% applied at the gate, and 14% wrote a letter responding to an advertisement.
11. This was different in the past: several workers who had found their jobs around the year 2000 told me that they had been hired simply because someone had recommended them.
12. This procedure was an exception in the sense that it was uncommon for such a high-ranked manager to be directly involved in the recruitment process.
13. The remaining 5.7% had not finished any formal education. However, some of those who had finished only primary or secondary education had gained a certificate in, for instance, tailoring or computer studies, or a driver's licence (15.7% of the respondents).
14. These numbers are comparable to results from the survey carried out by Gibbon and Riisgaard (2014, p. 105): 76.1% of the 113 flower farm

workers they interviewed across Kenya did not have previous working experience in the flower industry.

15. At least at the time she left Kisumu, she added. Mary Achieng, long-term resident of Kasarani, interview on February 11, 2015.

References

1,300 flower farm employees sacked. (2002, August 17). *Daily Nation*, p. 3.

AEA, & KPAWU. (2011). Collective Bargaining Agreement between the Agricultural Employers' Association and the Kenya Plantation and Agricultural Workers' Union. Retrieved from http://www.agriemp.co.ke/downloads/cbas/flower-growers-cba

Anker, R., & Anker, M. (2014). *Living wage for Kenya with focus on fresh flower farm area near Lake Naivasha*. Retrieved from http://www.fairtrade.net/fileadmin/user_upload/content/2009/resources/LivingWageReport_Kenya.pdf

Borgatti, S., Everett, M., & Freeman, L. (2002). *Ucinet 6 for Windows: Software for social network analysis*. Harvard, MA: Analytic Technologies.

Bujra, J. M. (1975). Women 'entrepreneurs' of early Nairobi. *Canadian Journal of African Studies, 9*(2), 213–234.

Cohen, D. W., & Atieno Odhiambo, E. S. (1989). *Siaya: The historical anthropology of an African landscape*. London: James Currey.

Cooper, F. (1996). *Decolonization and African society: The labor question in French and British Africa*. Cambridge: Cambridge University Press.

Coplan, D. B. (2001). You have left me wandering about: Basotho women and the culture of mobility. In D. L. Hodgson & S. McCurdy (Eds.), *'Wicked' women and the reconfiguration of gender in Africa* (pp. 188–211). Portsmouth, NH: Heinemann.

Davies, C. A. (2008). *Reflexive ethnography: A guide to researching selves and others* (2nd ed.). London: Routledge.

Dolan, C. S., Opondo, M., & Smith, S. (2003). *Gender, rights and participation in the Kenya cut flower industry* (NRI Report No. 2768). Chatham, UK: NRI.

Freeman, C. (2000). *High tech and high heels in the global economy: Women, work, and pink collar identities in the Caribbean*. Durham, NC: Duke University Press.

Friedemann-Sánchez, G. (2009). *Assembling flowers and cultivating homes: Labor and gender in Colombia* (1st Paperback ed.). Lanham, MD: Lexington Books.

Gibbon, P., & Riisgaard, L. (2014). A new system of labour management in African large-scale agriculture? *Journal of Agrarian Change, 14*(1), 94–128. https://doi.org/10.1111/joac.12043

Hall, R., Scoones, I., & Tsikata, D. (2017). Plantations, outgrowers and commercial farming in Africa: Agricultural commercialisation and implications for agrarian change. *The Journal of Peasant Studies, 44*(3), 515–537. https://doi.org/10.1080/03066150.2016.1263187

Happ, J. (2016). *Auswirkungen der Fairtrade-Zertifizierung auf den afrikanischen Blumenanbau. Das Beispiel Naivasha, Kenia [Effects of Fairtrade-certification on the African flower production: The example of Naivasha, Kenya]* (Vol. 4). Norderstedt: Books on Demand.

Hivos. (n.d.). Power of the fair trade flower. Retrieved January 24, 2014, from http://www.powerofthefairtradeflower.nl/

Kanogo, T. (1987). *Squatters and the roots of Mau Mau*. London: James Currey.

Kazimierczuk, A., Kamau, P., Kinuthia, B., & Mukoko, C. (2018). *Never a rose without a prick: (Dutch) multinational companies and productive employment in the Kenyan flower sector* (ASC Working Paper No. 142). Leiden: African Studies Centre.

Kim, S. (1997). *Class struggle or family struggle? The lives of women factory workers in South Korea*. Cambridge: Cambridge University Press.

Kioko, E. M. (2012). *Poverty and livelihood strategies at Lake Naivasha, Kenya: A case study of Kasarani Village*. Cologne: Cologne African Studies Centre.

Kioko, E. M. (2016). *Turning conflict into coexistence: Cross-cutting ties and institutions in the agro-pastoral borderlands of Lake Naivasha Basin, Kenya*. Cologne: University of Cologne. Retrieved from http://kups.ub.uni-koeln.de/id/eprint/7064

KNBS. (2010). *Kenya population census 2009*. Nairobi: KNBS.

McGarrigle, J., & Ascensão, E. (2017). Emplaced mobilities: Lisbon as a translocality in the migration journeys of Punjabi Sikhs to Europe. *Journal of Ethnic and Migration Studies*, 1–20. https://doi.org/10.1080/1369183X.2017.1306436

Meagher, K., Mann, L., & Bolt, M. (2016). Introduction: Global economic inclusion and African workers. *The Journal of Development Studies, 52*(4), 471–482. https://doi.org/10.1080/00220388.2015.1126256

Mills, M. B. (2003). Gender and inequality in the global labor force. *Annual Review of Anthropology, 32*(1), 41–62. https://doi.org/10.1146/annurev.anthro.32.061002.093107

Ministry of Economic Planning and Development. (1965). *Kenya population census 1962*. Nairobi: MEPD.

Mwangi, M. (2007, August 18). Naivasha Town: Where poverty and affluence live side-by-side. *Daily Nation*, p. 26.

Nelson, N. (1992). The women who have left and those who have stayed behind: Rural-urban migration in central and western Kenya. In S. Chant (Ed.), *Gender and migration in developing countries* (pp. 109–138). London: Belhaven Press.

Nelson, N. (1997). How women and men got by and still get by (only not so well): The gender division of labour in a Nairobi shanty-town. In J. Gugler (Ed.), *Cities in the developing world: Issues, theory, and policy* (pp. 156–170). Oxford: Oxford University Press.

Omondi, G. (2007, November 7). Burying the hatchet after a history of feuds. *Business Daily*, p. 18.

Ong, A. (1987). *Spirits of resistance and capitalist discipline: Factory women in Malaysia*. Albany: State University of New York Press.

Ortiz, S. (2002). Laboring in the factories and in the fields. *Annual Review of Anthropology, 31*(1), 395–417. https://doi.org/10.1146/annurev.anthro.31.031902.161108

Orton, L., Barrientos, S., & McClenaghan, S. (2001). Paternalism and gender in South African fruit employment. *Women's Studies International Forum, 24*(3–4), 469–478. https://doi.org/10.1016/S0277-5395(01)00166-2

Oucho, J. O. (1996). *Urban migrants and rural development in Kenya*. Nairobi: Nairobi University Press.

Owuor, S. O. (2003). *Rural livelihood sources for urban households: A study of Nakuru town, Kenya* (ASC Working Paper No. 51). Leiden: African Studies Centre.

Riisgaard, L., & Gibbon, P. (2014). Labour management on contemporary Kenyan cut flower farms: Foundations of an industrial-civic compromise. *Journal of Agrarian Change, 14*(2), 260–285. https://doi.org/10.1111/joac.12064

Ross, M. H., & Weisner, T. S. (1977). The rural-urban migrant network in Kenya: Some general implications. *American Ethnologist, 4*(2), 359–375. https://doi.org/10.1525/ae.1977.4.2.02a00090

Salzinger, L. (2003). *Genders in production: Making workers in Mexico's global factories*. Berkeley: University of California Press.

Seal, M. (2011). *Wildflower: The extraordinary life and mysterious murder of Joan Root* (Paperback ed.). London: Orion Books Ltd.

Spittler, G. (2008). *Founders of the anthropology of work: German social scientists of the 19th and early 20th centuries and the first ethnographers*. Berlin: LIT.

Spittler, G. (2009). Contesting the Great Transformation: Work in comparative perspective. In C. Hann & K. Hart (Eds.), *Market and society: The Great Transformation today* (pp. 160–174). Cambridge: Cambridge University Press.

Staelens, L., Desiere, S., Louche, C., & D'Haese, M. (2018). Predicting job satisfaction and workers' intentions to leave at the bottom of the high value agricultural chain: Evidence from the Ethiopian cut flower industry. *The International Journal of Human Resource Management, 29*(9), 1609–1635. https://doi.org/10.1080/09585192.2016.1253032

Transport paralysed as locals block road. (2015, January 10). *Daily Nation*.

Tsing, A. (2009). Supply chains and the human condition. *Rethinking Marxism, 21*(2), 148–176. https://doi.org/10.1080/08935690902743088

Wolf, D. L. (1992). *Factory daughters: Gender, household dynamics and rural industrialization in Java*. Berkeley: University of California Press.

CHAPTER 4

Inside the Farms: Rhythms and Hierarchies

Working with flowers is like working with people.
—Manager of a rose farm

This comparison was made by the first flower farm manager I interviewed. He said he likes his job: not one day is the same. He explained that flowers are a natural product and therefore are affected by diseases and changing weather conditions. Furthermore, the demand for flowers also fluctuates with the time of the year and the weather conditions in Europe. I could see the challenges this volatility can cause. However, I only realized much later that the unpredictability does not just derive from the delicate crop itself or from the dynamic markets. Another insecure factor is labour. Flower growing is not only *like* working with people; it also *involves* working with people.

In this chapter, we enter the farms. Following Mintz (1985), I argue that the flower farms are "industrial" in character because of the disciplined, time-conscious, and hierarchical organization of labour. The first part of this chapter discusses these three aspects of flower production in Naivasha. It furthermore describes how the production processes are influenced by the ecological characteristics of the crop. Sarah Besky (2014) studied, what she called, the "social ecology" of tea, in her book on labour relations on tea plantations in Darjeeling, India. She described the relations between the tea bushes, the Darjeeling landscape, and the labourers.

G. Kuiper, *Agro-industrial Labour in Kenya*,
https://doi.org/10.1007/978-3-030-18046-1_4

Besky argued that the ecological characteristics of tea, such as being a crop with a long life cycle, shaped the social conditions on the plantations. I likewise explore the "social ecology" of the Naivasha rose in this chapter.

Although anthropologists have studied structural relations surrounding work, work as a situated and interactional practice has received remarkably little anthropological attention (Orr, 1996; Spittler, 2009). Not only wider societal relations but also the immediate physical context in which work is carried out shapes the execution of the work. This in its turn impacts labour relations and the motivation to work. As argued by Orr (1996, p. 155): "the examination of practice reveals a complexity that cannot be seen from a distance; this complexity constrains how the work can be done and therefore has a crucial implication for those making policy about work." This chapter therefore starts with a description of the farms' layout and of the production processes.

4.1 The Layout of the Farms

The farms are vast, expansive areas. Some employees who have to move around the farm, such as those in the irrigation department, even use bicycles or motorcycles during their workday. The main production areas are the fields with the crop, mostly inside greenhouses (see Figs. 4.1 and 4.2), and the packhouses. Other buildings include toilet blocks, changing rooms, offices, storage rooms, pump and generator houses, water tanks, often a canteen, and sometimes housing for managers and supervisors. In the few cases that living quarters for general workers are provided, these are located next to the farm itself, behind a separate gate. Several farms also have a tourist lodge or a restaurant on their premises, located at some distance from the production areas and, where possible, close to the lake. Finally, some of the farms have installed environmental constructions such as wetlands.

In what follows, I describe the layout of Karibu Farm, the farm I became most familiar with. However, all farms look alike to a high degree, except that the type of crop (either roses or seasonal flowers) determines whether the farm has greenhouses or outdoor production fields.

Karibu Farm produced only roses and had eight greenhouses at the time of my fieldwork. These greenhouses all spanned several hectares and contained from one to four varieties of roses. In addition, there was one field for outdoor rose production. The fields were divided into "bays", which were numbered. Each bay consisted of six to seven beds of plants. This division assisted in the planning and organization of the work. The greenhouses

Fig. 4.1 A field in a greenhouse with young rose bushes

Fig. 4.2 A greenhouse with older rose bushes

were spacious, light, and calm. One could see the contours of objects or people outside through the polythene, and sometimes the roof would be slightly opened and one could see a strip of sky. Nevertheless, the greenhouses were enclosed environments and gave the feeling of being cut off from the world outside. There were one or two aisles running through each greenhouse, with doors on both ends. Harvested flowers were collected on several tables on these aisles. Black nets were spanned above the tables to reduce the heat of the sun on the flowers (see Fig. 4.2). After harvesting was over, the tables would be empty and the greenhouse would become very calm. Once everyone had gone into the bays for weeding or pruning, it even appeared as if there was no one there, as the rose bushes can be as tall as the workers themselves. Despite the calmness, there would be quite some sounds in the air: the singing of birds outside, the rustling of leaves, occasional talking or singing of the workers, the muffled rumble of tractors and other vehicles outside, the dripping of feeding water, and the opening and closing sound of the valve of the feeding system. When it would be raining heavily or when there would be a lot of wind, it could be noisy inside. The air was filled with a not so unpleasant smell of wet plants, sometimes mixed with fumes of the chlorine used in the water for harvested flowers. However, most overwhelming to me were not the sounds, sights, or smells but the temperature and climate. The air was dense and humid, and I always found it exhausting to be in the greenhouse for a long time. Employees would rarely complain about the physical strain of the greenhouse work, but understanding reactions to my own wish to go outside now and then revealed that I was not the only one struggling with the heat. It also makes the greenhouse an unfit working environment for people with certain health conditions. I, for instance, witnessed a discussion between a few general workers and the HR manager on the future of a colleague who was recovering from a stroke. They concluded she could probably not return to the same job due to the strain of the heat.

The packhouse where the flowers were packed for shipment was much cooler. It consisted of a large, light hall for grading with rows of tables, one table per grader. The packhouse also had two cold stores where the flowers were kept before and after grading respectively. The temperature in the grading hall would be more or less the same as the outside temperature. In the cold stores, the temperature was kept below 7 °C or even less. The packhouse thus was a cooler and therefore more comfortable working environment than the greenhouses but it was also much more hectic. Especially in farms where workers were given individual bonuses when processing more flowers than was required, some graders would work frantically. Also in the Karibu Farm packhouse—the "house of competition", as one supervisor called it jokingly—the speed of work was high. There was a steady distribution of flowers to the packing tables and from the packing tables to the cold store. There was the constant sound of buckets being put on the ground or on a cart, accompanying the music coming from the radio that was usually turned on. Despite being relatively close to each other, workers spoke little and were absorbed in their work. The discipline was literally written on the walls of some of the grading halls. The walls of the hall of Karibu Farm contained certain prohibitions ("no eating or drinking"), while Hanna Kunas reported in her unpublished thesis that the walls of the packhouse in another Naivasha farm contained proverbs. She noted that these aphorisms ("Do not simply retire from something, have something to retire to") mostly emphasized diligence. Diligence is indeed needed in the packhouses, where work takes place at a high pace.

4.2 Daily Routines: Accountability and "Responsibilization"

Working procedures are strictly regulated in all farms, in order to avoid the flowers being affected by pests and diseases. For example, anyone entering a greenhouse in Karibu Farm first had to dip the soles of their boots into a basin with disinfectant. Hygiene is crucial because fungal and bacterial diseases and insects such as mites and caterpillars can damage or even kill the plants by sucking up the nutrients. They can also leave marks and spots on the petals, which make the cut flowers unsaleable. But despite the general need for hygiene and the instalment of strict procedures, divisions of labour and daily routines differ considerably per farm. In rose farms, workers are mostly based in the same greenhouse for a long period of time. In farms that are growing seasonal flowers, workers have to rotate fields. Figure 4.3 shows a type of seasonal flower, hypericum, which unlike roses only grows in flushes. Not the flowers but the berries are the end product. It is cultivated outdoors, with the aid of artificial light in the evenings. These production conditions also shape labour routines. For instance, daily workloads in such farms are more variable and more dependent on weather conditions than in rose-producing farms.

In addition to the differences in the type of crop and concomitant differences in work routines, managers also make different choices with regard to the division of labour. Some farms split the work into separate

Fig. 4.3 A field of hypericum

tasks and let employees execute the same, single task every day. Despite the workers handling a "natural" and not an industrial product, farms with such a division of labour resemble assembly lines that can be found around the world, in which planning of the work is completely in the hands of the management (Braverman, 1998; Parry, 2012). However, such a segmented division of labour has become quite rare within the Kenyan flower industry. Gibbon and Riisgaard (2014, p. 112) described how the introduction of large polythene greenhouses created the need for stricter spraying schedules and better time management. Managers therefore increasingly prefer a division of labour in which one employee executes all tasks in a specific part of the greenhouse or can even rotate between the greenhouse and the packhouse. Increasing quality demands from the market are another reason for the preference for a so-called all-round workforce. As Whitaker and Kolavalli (2006, p. 337) explained: "product quality—including size, color, shape, and absence of disease and visual defects—determines marketability and price." Workers who handle the delicate flowers have to safeguard this quality. Labour therefore cannot be made into an "interchangeable part" in the production process (Braverman, 1998, p. 125). In contrast to the assembly lines described by Braverman and by scholars studying female labour in global factories (Fernández-Kelly, 1983; Wright, 2006), the production of flowers requires a system in which employees can be held accountable for the flowers they produce. This need for accountability has prompted what Riisgaard and Gibbon (2014, p. 268) labelled a "responsibilization" of the work.

This responsibilization can be illustrated by describing the division of labour in Karibu Farm. Employees did not simply execute a single task. Although they usually had a fixed place of work—either in one of the greenhouses or in the packhouse—those working in the greenhouse had a number of beds assigned to them in which they executed all the crop maintenance tasks. Each greenhouse also had one or two supervisors to plan and oversee the work. Yet, supervisor Lucy emphasized, when she explained the work to me, that they trained the workers to do their job "responsibly".

The day in the greenhouse would start with harvesting flowers, a task that was not restricted to a worker's "own" bay. The harvest had a specific, sometimes rotating, division of labour: some employees would enter the fields to cut the flowers, others would "size" them (i.e. sorting the flowers according to the length of the stem), and again others would wrap the piles of sorted flowers together in large bunches of 50–80 stems and prepare them for transport to the packhouse. I noticed that it was often women who did the actual cutting of the flowers and men who organized the packing and transport to the exit doors. However, this division of labour was not fixed and seemed to be more a habit than a norm.

The harvest itself is a delicate task, which starts with the decision as to which flowers are ready for harvesting. The so-called cut stage of the flowers defines when a flower should be harvested. This cut stage is measured on a scale from one to four. It is judged on sight, and one needs experience to be able to decide which flowers to harvest. Within Karibu Farm, flowers would normally be harvested when reaching cut stage two, which means that the petals have started to open up a bit. However, the cut stage could vary per variety and per order. After deciding that a certain flower is at the right stage to be harvested, the harvester has to cut it off at one centimetre above the "eye", the joint between the shoot and the stem. Cutting it off at a higher or lower point could affect either the length of the cut stem or the strength of the next shoot, which both influences the flowers' value. After cutting them off, the worker has to carry the flowers in a particular way so as not to damage the heads of the cut flowers.

The task of sizing consists of measuring flowers against a sizing board and piling them accordingly. Sizing is a monotonous task, but it provides the opportunity to talk to other employees. In the case of Karibu Farm, sizing had previously been a task for the graders in the packhouse. However, it had been moved to the greenhouse to speed up the work of the graders (see Fig. 4.2 for the sizing area in the middle of a greenhouse). The worker who was sizing also had to check for any bad stems and take them out. This rejection of flowers was checked by the supervisor: the rejected stems were counted per greenhouse and reported to the management at the end of the day, including the reasons for rejection.

After harvesting flowers in the morning, and with some varieties after a second round of harvesting after lunch, all general workers would engage in so-called cultural activities in their own designated part of the greenhouse. This part of the work includes pruning, weeding, and taking out "blind shoots", "suckers", "bullheads", and "pelican heads", which are shoots that have not developed a bud or where the bud is deformed. These activities are meant to keep the plants healthy, to avoid wasting fertilizers on non-productive parts of the plants, and to create space for new flowering shoots. As Lucy explained to me, "you produce flowers" by removing these parts. The timing of these activities is planned by the supervisors because it influences when new flowers would be ready for harvesting.[1] Pruning looks easy and the Karibu Farm employees performed it quickly. However, when I tried it myself, I soon found it requires as much accurateness as harvesting. Plants are easily damaged. Furthermore, the pruning also requires tacit knowledge: employees have to be able to recognize the diverse types of unproductive parts, and they have to know at which point they should remove them. As Lucy expressed it, a worker has to "ask questions and talk to the plant" to determine which part to take out. Lucy's explanation illustrates Spittler's (2009) assertion that the interaction with things is the essence of work.

Other, more straightforward, "cultural activities" are sweeping, as to giving bacteria and fungus no opportunity to spread, and weeding. The cultural activities are rotational and they never end. Because the plants keep on growing, there is always work to do in the greenhouse. And in addition to attending to their own designated area, Karibu Farm workers would also execute the planned activities for that day in the bays of those workers who were absent due to their weekly day off, a leave, or illness.

Another figure in the greenhouse—apart from the general workers and the supervisor—is the scout. In order to avoid damage to flowers as much as possible, it is important to detect pests and diseases early on and to spray pesticides accordingly. Time is of the essence here, and farms employ scouts to monitor the plants. Each Karibu Farm greenhouse had its own scout, who went around the whole greenhouse over the course of two working days. He or she would check for pests and diseases as well as for weeds and for problems in the irrigation system. These scouts, who need to be knowledgeable, sometimes had a certificate from an agricultural training institute. However, others had simply been general workers who were promoted when they showed that they had gained a good understanding of the plants.

On the basis of the scouts' findings, the management and the supervisor of the pesticide sprayers would make a pesticide spraying schedule. Each greenhouse would normally be attended by sprayers every other day in the afternoon, after all regular workers had left. The job of spraying is possibly the most arduous and dangerous task within the farms, not in the least because of the weight and the oppressiveness of the heavy protective clothing, which consists of an overall, a spray suit, a mask, a face shield, gloves, and gumboots. This clothing protects the sprayers, but it also makes it impossible to communicate during the job. Furthermore, the sprayers were well aware that their work is inherently dangerous, despite this equipment, because of the toxic chemicals that they could get in touch with if an accident occurs. As one of them told me: "If you mess up, you might faint."

Thus, with the exception of this delicate pest and disease control, general workers in the Karibu Farm greenhouses all were supposed to be able to execute all tasks there. Work in the packhouse was more segmented. There were almost 90 employees working in the packhouse, under 7 supervisors, who together had to execute three main tasks. Only the most visible of these tasks—"grading"—was available to women. A grader would start by taking some flowers, examining them, and removing the bad ones. These rejected flowers, just as the ones in the greenhouse, were checked and counted by a supervisor. The grader would then continue by removing excessive foliage and by putting a fixed number of flowers of the same size and the same cut stage together into bunches. The size and composition of these bunches depended on the orders and could vary per day. Finally, the grader would cut the stems of the bunched flowers to the same length and in some cases would wrap plastic sleeves around them or would attach a sachet of flower food. Creating one bunch of flowers would take around a minute. Some farms split up the job of grading into several separate tasks, executed by several employees. A few farms even have a conveyor belt along which these tasks are executed. However, Gibbon and Riisgaard (2014, p. 114) pointed out that because such a segmented division of labour requires a good coordination, most farms prefer having one individual responsible for the whole process. Indeed, in Karibu Farm, all graded bunches would be checked by a supervisor before being transported to the cold room. Any deficient bunches, for instance, those containing a flower that showed marks of a disease, would be noted down and would have to be adjusted ("rectified") by the grader.

The second activity in the Karibu Farm packhouse was to distribute the flowers from the "receiving" cold store—where the flowers that had been harvested in the greenhouses were brought to—to the packing tables, and to bring the ready bunches to the next ("dispatching") cold store. The distribution was done by the so-called runners, who were all male. Additional tasks of the runners, which they distributed among themselves, were to sweep the floor, to collect waste, and to clean buckets.

The third activity, taking place in the dispatching cold store, was the packing of the flower bunches into large boxes and loading them onto the truck to be transported to the airport. The loading of the truck was done at night, by a special team for the night shift, again consisting of only men. The packhouse thus had a more gendered and segmented division of labour than the greenhouses.

Although the large majority of flower farm workers perform one of the jobs described above in either the greenhouse or the packhouse, there are more positions within the farms. However, the exact number and the types of positions vary greatly per farm. The six groups of flower farm workers participating in the listing exercises mentioned between 12 and 28 possible jobs within the farms they worked for. Positions mentioned by all groups were general worker in the greenhouse, grader in the packhouse, manager, security guard, and sprayer. Also frequently mentioned were packer, transporter, supervisor, driver, cook in the canteen, employee in the maintenance department, and carpenter in the workshop. Differences between the listing exercises show that the work is more segmented within some farms than others. For instance, whereas the grader in the Karibu Farm packhouse would, if applicable, also put a plastic sleeve on a bunch of flowers, employees of another farm mentioned "sleeves" as a separate job. Nevertheless, there are not many examples of a different division of labour within the production departments. The largest differences are found among office and technical staff. Whereas a small- or middle-scale farm would only employ a handful of office staff, employees of Sharma Farm listed payroll clerks, data clerks, an HR manager, other managers, the accountant, and a tea girl. This farm also used to have a special department of electricians, whereas in a smaller farm electrical jobs would be executed by the general maintenance department. Furthermore, farms with a ***kambi*** need even more "non-productive" staff. Sharma Farm in the past employed doctors and nurses for the company hospital, six nursery teachers, drivers and cooks for the managers, and "welfare managers" to maintain the order on the compound. The large flower farms thus have a more segmented labour force than the smaller farms. Nevertheless, all Naivasha flower farms primarily employ "general workers" who are hired under the same conditions. This system stands in contrast to the labour system in some other global agro-industries, in which a segmentation of the workforce is an important tool in controlling labour, for instance, by employing both temporary and permanent workers who have different interests (Bolt, 2013; Moberg, 1996; Thomas, 1985).

The flower farms make use of other tools to control labour. For instance, the security guards that each flower farm employs are there not only to protect the premises from intruders (both thieves and wild animals) but also to prevent the workers from stealing and other misconduct. Karibu Farm had 41 guards, who worked in two shifts of 12 hours. There were both male and female security guards, although only men worked on the night shift. A few of the guards would be posted at the gate during the day, where they would register everyone coming in and out and search all employees before leaving the farm (the latter task made it necessary to employ female security guards). The others would guard a particular area of the farm.

Whenever I planned to visit Karibu Farm, I had to announce my visits to one of the managers. Without their consent, the security guards would not let me pass the gate. However, apart from that condition, I got the chance to freely talk to anyone on the farm and to enter most sections, except for areas with specific safety regulations such as the chemical mixing room. This freedom I had in moving around contrasted to the restrictions on the movements of the workers.[2] They were not allowed to move outside the area they worked in and a few shared spaces, such as the canteen and the changing rooms. Thus, workers' movements within the farms are subject to tight control.

4.3 Rhythms of Labour: Yielding to the Flowers and the Markets

The timing of the work is an important aspect of flower growing and structures the tightly controlled daily routines described above. As explained by Happ (2016, p. 53), the workers are in a race with time once a flower is ready for harvesting, as it loses much of its value once it starts to wither. But there are still other factors which shape the rhythms of labour within the farms.

First of all, the crop goes through a natural growth cycle. I here describe the cycle of the most prevalent crop at the time of my fieldwork: the rose. I witnessed during a visit to Karibu Farm that the planting of new seedlings by a greenhouse team only takes a few hours of steady labour. After the planting, there is little work to do in the greenhouse for some time and in Karibu Farm most of the employees would be temporarily put to work in other parts of the farm. It takes around two months from the planting of the seedlings to the harvesting of the first flush of flowers. After several flushes, during which plants produce several flowers at a time, the growth of the plants can be balanced and stabilized. Plants can then produce steadily for a period of three to six years. Whenever old rose bushes are no longer productive or when a specific variety is not popular anymore in the market, the bushes are uprooted and replaced by seedlings of the same or a different variety. These (licenced) varieties and their seedlings are acquired from, mostly Dutch-owned, breeders and plant propagators, some of which have a local branch in Naivasha.[3]

Apart from these growing cycles over longer time spans, the workload also varies on a daily basis. Supervisors have to be flexible in the planning of the work. The hours of work differ per farm and also per department, although working hours have become more standardized since an increasing number of farms participate in the Collective Bargaining Agreement (CBA). Typically, workers in the greenhouse start work at 7 a.m. They have an (unpaid) lunch break of one or two hours. The time of finishing work differs per day. There could, for instance, be more flowers to harvest after sunny days, there could be more time needed for spraying pesticides after the outbreak of certain diseases (and so less time to do other work in the greenhouse), and a specific order could also disrupt the normal work rhythm. I once witnessed in Lucy's greenhouse that a sudden request for yellow flowers made workers harvest those flowers all day long, leaving maintenance tasks for another day. This variability demands considerable flexibility of the employees, as they have to work longer hours on certain days than on others. Moreover, in farms that adhere to the CBA, (paid) overtime is mandatory when need be (AEA & KPAWU, 2011, sec. 5(c)). Supervisors in the greenhouses of Karibu Farm nevertheless attempted to balance the work over the week in order to attain the basic 46 hours negotiated in the CBA (AEA & KPAWU, 2011, sec. 3(a)). The reason for this is that paying out overtime is expensive for the farm. However, in the packhouse it is not possible to avoid overtime. Employees typically start work there at 8 a.m., after the first flowers have been harvested. They never know beforehand at what time they will finish. The working hours depend entirely on the number of flowers produced on a certain day, and packhouse workers can leave work as late as 9 p.m.

The pressure of the flexibility demanded from the employees is alleviated through weekly days off and several types of leave. Every employee, regardless of the department he or she is working in, has a fixed day off—"a day to sleep", as one employee called it—per week.[4] Employees cannot choose this day freely as work in the greenhouses and the packhouses has to continue seven days a week, even on national and religious holidays. However, some groups of workers, such as sprayers and employees in the maintenance department, have Sunday as a fixed day off. In addition to this weekly day off, there are several types of leave. A common reason for absence is illness, but one could not simply call in sick. Sick leave in Karibu Farm was only given when employees filled out a sick sheet and went to the dispensary nearby. Other types of leave in farms adhering to the CBA are the annual leave of 24–26 days, a maternity leave of 3 months, a paternity leave of 2 weeks, and unpaid "compassionate" leave in case of, for example, bereavement (AEA & KPAWU, 2011, sec. 7–10). Most of these leaves are also prescribed by the Employment Act 2007 and its revised version of 2012. With regard to these regulations, the CBA therefore largely followed national legislation.

As sprayers have to execute their work outside of normal working hours, they have a specific rhythm of work, which also differs per farm. Karibu Farm worked with a rotational system, in which one team would do the spraying for three months, after which a second team would take over for the same period of time. The reason for rotating was that the work of spraying is heavy and hazardous. In the period that the sprayers received other tasks, they performed regular work in the greenhouse or the packhouse, in the cold stores, or in the maintenance department. In addition, even in those three months of spraying, the sprayers did regular work for three hours in the morning, would then go on a long break, and only sprayed for several hours in the late afternoon, when other employees had already left the greenhouses. Management created this schedule in order to have the sprayers work the same amount of hours as other employees. Not all farms give their sprayers double tasks to compensate for short working days, and the Karibu Farm sprayers complained about it. However, as it was up to the management to set working hours and schedules, there was little they could do.

The farms require flexibility on the part of the employees not only with regard to working hours but also with regard to the content of the work. General workers cannot choose freely in which part of the farm they want to work: "that's why they are called general workers," as one supervisor told me. They can express their preferences, and their wishes would sometimes be taken into account. One employee of Karibu Farm told me she had requested to work in the open production area: "There is wind there." Other employees had requested to work in the packhouse because of the opportunity to earn bonuses. Nevertheless, the final decision remains with management.

One's workplace is also not fixed. Workers can be deployed in another department temporarily, either for just a day when work pressure is high in a particular area or for longer time, for example, when the plants in a greenhouse are being uprooted and replaced. When I conducted interviews for a total network analysis within a greenhouse in Karibu Farm, I was confronted with the unstable composition of such working teams. I had to finalize these interviews as soon as possible: some of the team members rotated every three months between working in the greenhouse and in the pesticide spraying department, while others were at some point permanently transferred to another greenhouse or to the packhouse. Not all employees moved around like that. There were also team members who had been working in this same greenhouse for 12 years already. However, again, it was the management who made the decision where a worker would be placed and for what period of time.

In addition to requiring from workers that they are flexible with regard to working hours and place of work, the farms also require their workers to be punctual. It is a gross offence to be repeatedly late for work. The quality of cut flowers deteriorates quickly if they stay outside cold stores for too long. As there are several steps involved in the production process of the flowers, it is crucial that all workers start to work on time. Working hours are therefore monitored to the minute through "clocking in" systems.

The "clock" of Karibu Farm was a digital system based on fingerprints, which ensured that those who clocked in and out were really the workers themselves.

Also while at work, workers have to be punctual and quick, especially those working in the packhouse. Time pressure is increased by minimum production targets, which are common for graders. Employees get reprimanded if they do not reach those targets. On the other hand, some farms pay employees a bonus if they grade more than the minimum amount. The exact targets differ per farm and product. They can be set by either number of stems or bunches per minute, hour, or day (Anker & Anker, 2014; Gibbon & Riisgaard, 2014). The production target set for graders of Karibu Farm was 175 bunches per day. As one of the packhouse supervisors told me, these 175 bunches were "the company's flowers". Anything extra was "for the employee": he or she would get a bonus of a few shillings for every extra graded bunch. Employees regularly graded several dozen extra bunches per day and thus could increase their daily income considerably. In addition, there was a minimum target for the farm as a whole, which was 120,000 stems per day. A bonus of 750 KES per 10,000 extra stems was shared among all employees, except the supervisors, working in the packhouse on a particular day. These two bonuses would be calculated per day and then paid out together with the monthly salary. These bonuses could increase an employee's salary significantly, yet the individual production, and therefore the earned bonus, varied greatly.[5] These bonuses therefore motivate employees to work hard: packhouse workers within Karibu Farm talked little during the work and returned early to work from their (unpaid) lunch break.

The lack of freedom to schedule one's own work and one's working hours is an important reason for many to dislike flower farm work. The need to be constantly available makes it difficult to engage in additional income-generating activities and, especially for those working after regular school and day care hours, to take care of one's children. On the other hand, bonus systems and paid overtime make it possible to augment one's income. They also add a competitive element to the work, which, as argued by Roy (1960), in itself can be a source of motivation. The bonus system thus induces employees to work long hours.

To sum up, the timing of the work depends on different factors, such as the rhythms of the crop, the rhythms of the market, and increasingly on the hours of work as prescribed by the CBA and legislation. The combination of different cycles and rhythms has resulted in a complex production process which contains elements of both "task-oriented time" and "clock-time" (Heald, 1991; Thompson, 1967). The rhythm of labour is most of all characterized by a high level of discipline and compulsion. Although the CBA fixes working hours, the rhythm of the work is determined by the supervisors and the management. It varies by day, depending on the natural rhythms of the crop, on the demands of the market, and on regulations. Employees are expected to be flexible and to agree to work overtime when needed. They are furthermore required to be punctual and to work at high speed. The strict timing of the work and the high levels of discipline make that flower farming resembles industrial production (Mintz, 1985).

4.4 Farm Hierarchies: Discipline and Social Distance

The hierarchical, top-down organization of labour within the farms is another factor reminiscent of industrial production. Because the flowers are so delicate, it is not only important to control the crop itself but also important to control the labourers handling the plants and harvested flowers. The farms have a pyramid-like structure: each farm has only one or two top managers; a small group of middle-level managers, supervisors, and office staff in between; and a large group of general workers with varying tasks in the production process at the bottom. For example, a particularly small farm with 74 workers had two managers, a secretary, and two supervisors. All the other (partly permanent, partly temporary) employees were general workers. Larger farms than this one employ more skilled and semi-skilled staff in absolute numbers, and the division of labour among managers and supervisors varies greatly per farm. Nevertheless, the ratio in this small farm of over 90% of the workforce being "general workers" is representative for the industry as a whole.[6]

I learned about farm hierarchies through my own anomalous position as a *mzungu* researcher. I could not position myself as a fellow general worker, yet workers were also not familiar with an ethnographer's role. Workers would in the first instance associate me to management, which would create distance to some of them while others perceived of me as a potential intermediary who could connect them to management. I thus experienced the top-down hierarchy within Karibu Farm in my relations to workers there. But the hierarchies were also simply visible on the work floor. For one, despite the obligation to wear standardized personal protective equipment (PPE), dress could betray (income) differences between general workers and higher-level employees, especially among women. Female employees with a higher income would have more jewellery and a more expensive hair-do than general workers, who mostly would just cover their hair or have simple braids. Furthermore, the colour of PPE-parts such as dust coats could differ, even within a single farm. In some farms, the colour of the coat would signify the area of work (greenhouse or packhouse), while in Karibu Farm it signified the position of the employee, that is, either general worker or supervisor. These different colours enhance control over labour, as it is immediately apparent when someone enters an area where he or she is not working on a daily basis.

Next to this tight control over workers' movements, also the work itself is strictly monitored. Supervisors in Karibu Farm would make a short note on all the workers and their individual performance at the end of each working day. If workers made a mistake in their work or showed up late, they would receive a verbal warning from their supervisor. In case of persistent misbehaviour, an employee would be referred to the management to receive an official warning or offence sheet. After several verbal and written warnings from the HR office for the same, repeated mistake, the ultimate penalty could be dismissal. As stipulated in the CBA:

> (a) The first and second warnings shall be recorded in the employee's file. The third warning shall be copied to the Branch Secretary of the Union.
> (b) If an employee with three warnings in his/her file commits misconduct within 12 months from the date of the first warning, he/she shall be liable to termination of employment. (AEA & KPAWU, 2011, sec. 16)

I was present several times when a manager gave out a first or second warning. On one occasion, an employee who had wrapped the flowers in the greenhouse wrongly was called to the packhouse together with his supervisor and was shown his mistake. He was reprimanded in front of his colleagues, who were meanwhile continuing with their work. He was also reprimanded in front of me, which made me feel uncomfortable, as I became part of the reinforcement of farm hierarchies. However, it also showed how much this hierarchy is taken for granted. It apparently was not considered something which should be hidden from a researcher.

The on-farm hierarchies are embedded in inequalities that stretch beyond the workplace. There is a large social and economic gap between the different groups of employees of the farms. This gap is reflected in spatial disparities. The divide between top management and general workers is especially large. Workers would only meet the managers in the workplace. Foreign managers occasionally take on a patriarchal and demeaning approach towards the general workers. As one manager stated in Dutch press: "We need strict control here, sometimes it's like I have seven hundred children" (Gaarlandt, 2013; my translation from Dutch). In addition, there is also a large gap between Kenyan managers and foreign (Indian and European) managers. This distance is partly caused by the differences in authority and power between the managers, as foreigners usually are part of the top management of the farms. When visiting Karibu Farm, I noticed that all employees, regardless of their position, would get slightly nervous when general manager Jan was around. They tried at all costs to avoid making a bad impression on him. Apart from these power imbalances, there is also a social gap: most foreign managers (invariably male) do not regularly meet black Kenyans outside work but mingle with other Indians or with other expats in the area, the exception being a few European managers who married a Kenyan woman. Like the settlers a century before (Clayton & Savage, 1974, p. xiv), foreign managers mainly meet Kenyans in the context of work, in an uneven employer-employee relationship. Also physically, they have placed themselves outside the communities, as they reside either on their farms or in a gated community elsewhere in Naivasha or in Nairobi. The foreign managers are sometimes referred to by their names but when employees are talking amongst themselves or even when they were talking to me, the managers were often simply referred to as the "*mzungu*" or the "*mhindi*" (Indian person).

Middle-level and top management live either in special housing on the farm where they work or in Naivasha Town. If they are staying in town, they commute with their own car or a shared car instead of getting on a general staff bus. One manager said he was happy to live on the farm where he worked and not among the other employees in a settlement. He said his decisions at work influenced his relations in the community. Residing in the same settlement as the general workers would have complicated his job.

The same holds true for supervisors, but they are seldom provided with special accommodation. They regularly live among the other workers in the settlements. Their housing situation is symbolic for their ambiguous position within the farms and in the communities. Supervisors officially form part of the management and can, for example, not join the union. However, in practice, they are awkwardly positioned between management and workers. They often originally started out as a general worker themselves and do not have a higher education than the people they are overseeing. In addition, they spend their days among their team of workers without much contact with other supervisors or managers. I noticed during visits to Karibu Farm that, perhaps because of this position "in-between", supervisors would look for contact with each other. They would talk for a few minutes while meeting a supervisor of a neighbouring greenhouse outside, they would sit together during lunch break, and they would meet after work. They would then also discuss their job. Conversations Lucy had with fellow supervisors indicated that they were proud of their expertise in flower growing, felt their responsibilities, and liked sharing experiences with each other. At the same time, when comparing salaries, living circumstances, and their work histories, their position is more comparable to that of general workers than to that of the (top) management.

Next to the supervisors, middle-level managers have a strong presence on the work floor. They spend most of their time in the greenhouses instead of in the office, and they sometimes step in to correct the work of a general worker instead of leaving the correcting to the supervisor. This presence is perceived to be necessary. Kenyan managers, who invariably said they work under a lot of pressure, often complained to me about the difficulties they have with labour. The sudden outbreak of a disease or fluctuations in the market could lead to hectic situations, yet a larger part of the stress and strain of the managers' work stems from social aspects. It is hard to establish authority and to motivate people for their work.

The managers mentioned several reasons for the lack of motivation they perceived to be prevalent in the workforce. One Kenyan manager told me that he thought the problem was that people are unskilled and even illiterate, and therefore need guidance. Yet, on another occasion he told me that the problem is that many employees are "too bright" for the work they are doing: "they only work here because their time hasn't come yet." In the previous chapter, I described that for some employees, work in the flower farms is a positive choice, either because they like the work or, more common, because of the relatively good work conditions. Yet, managers I spoke to thought few people choose to work in the industry voluntarily. In their eyes, the farms are a last resort or a "hide-out" for the workers. The manager cited here thought it is therefore necessary to be tough, in order not to be "tricked" by the unwilling employees. He would, for instance, fire someone after making a mistake more than once, although he would always work within the limits of the law. This "toughness" and the consequent lack of space for open resistance or defiance is effective in establishing control over labour and in ensuring that workers work timely and without making mistakes.

Despite this tight control, there inevitably remains some room for cheating. Employees can decide to not follow the rules in an attempt to make their work easier. They, for example, size several flowers at the same time instead of measuring them one by one. This is not allowed because it could lead to inaccuracy and so-called down-sizing: putting all measured flowers in the category of the shortest one. Down-sizing costs money as the longer ones could be sold at a higher price. Yet, sizing several flowers at once saves time, and I noticed that many employees would do so whenever there was no supervision around.

Down-sizing is an example of what Parry (1999) called "shirking", not a conscious attempt to resist discipline. But cheating and avoiding control can occasionally also be an expression of workers' resistance to what they consider abuse of power by their superiors. I once heard about an unofficial "slow-go" in one part of a greenhouse. The employees involved thought that their new supervisor was too strict. They even claimed she "harassed" them. They decided not to work whenever she was not present in their part of the greenhouse. Their unannounced slowing down of the work was a silent way of protesting, and it took several days before the supervisor and managers realized why the work in that part of the greenhouse just did not seem to get done. As soon as the truth was out, the production manager talked to the employees. This talk must have been quite impressive: afterwards the employees were uncommonly quiet, and one of them was laughed at because she had almost started to cry. In any case, the intervention was effective in restoring work discipline. That day, all flowers were harvested before lunchtime.

Workers in this case resisted harsh treatment by a specific supervisor. There is less room for questioning the hierarchical labour relations in general, even though the strict discipline is vehemently resented by some employees. Furthermore, non-flower farm workers often motivated their choice of not applying for a flower farm job by referring to the strict discipline. As one of the participants in the listing exercise said: "if you speak out, you will be fired."[7] Some had worked for a farm for some time but had quit because of the lack of freedom they experienced in their job. There seemed to be a vicious circle in these cases, in which the perceived lack of motivation on the part of the workers was aggravated by its remedy of "tough" management.

The foreign owners and top management realized that the most important skills of their managers are social and not so much technical. One of them praised a Kenyan manager who was able to avoid giving the impression he favoured certain ethnic groups. Also, supervisors, who mostly have received no formal agricultural training, are provided with special training on industrial relations (Riisgaard & Gibbon, 2014, p. 268). As one of the supervisors explained to me, they were taught how to "stay with different people".

A point of contestation between the supervisory level and the top management of Karibu Farm was the amount of labour needed. Supervisors complained among each other about the relatively small number of employees for the load of work to be done. Some workers complained to me about their workload. However, Jan explained to me that they already worked with about twice as many employees per hectare as farms in the Netherlands did. He hired in accordance with a mathematical formula, based on, among others, the surface of a greenhouse and the production of a variety. He had decided to stick to the outcome of this formula, even if there were complaints. He thought the issue was not a lack of labour but a lack of efficiency and planning. This disagreement shows that different levels of management do not always share the same interests and the same approach to organizing labour.

Despite the large cultural and economic gaps between the different groups of managers, the supervisors, and the general workers, labour relations within most farms are not wholly antagonistic. The prevalent perception among workers of Karibu Farm was that all, from manager to worker, would benefit if the company as a whole functions well and produces many flowers, if only because this enhances job security. Lucy explained the rationale behind tasks such as pruning and weeding by saying that it would avoid losses (*hasara*) for the company. The fertilizer brought by the *mzungu* (meaning the general manager) should not be wasted on unproductive parts of the plant.

The need for strict labour control is thus evident, even to most of the workers. It is also seen as part of life. As observed by Kunas in her unpublished thesis, there is a general belief that one has to endure hardships and work hard if one wants to move up the social ladder. Diligence is seen as a virtue, and failure in life is often blamed on laziness. Kunas furthermore observed that children already become accustomed to this approach to life in Kenya's competitive school system. In that sense, the "responsibilization" of labour that Riisgaard and Gibbon (2014, p. 268) referred to, is something workers in Kenya are well prepared to adapt to, even if it sometimes also forms a source of discontent.

4.5 Unskilled Labour? The Need for Stability and Experience

Another indication that workers cope with the high levels of discipline and stark hierarchies is the tendency to work for the same farm for long periods of time. Managers reported low turnover rates, especially when compared to flower farms in Ethiopia. Permanent contracts have become more prevalent with the shift from the production of seasonal flowers to rose production. Both Lucy and the HR manager of Karibu Farm explained that some newly recruited workers turn out to be not fit for the job or cannot handle the discipline, and therefore do not receive a contract after the probation period is over.[8] However, new workers who perform well are provided with a permanent contract. This has become the norm industry-wide (Gibbon & Riisgaard, 2014, p. 110; Omosa, Kimani, & Njiru, 2006, p. 37). Consequently, 64.9% of the 94 flower farm workers in the survey reported having a permanent contract. There were no significant differences here between men and women. Kazimierczuk, Kamau, Kinuthia, and Mukoko (2018, p. 34) even reported that 80% of the labour force on the flower farms they surveyed (roughly one-third of all Kenyan flower farms) had a permanent contract.

Once employees have received a permanent contract, they often work for one and the same flower farm for many years, especially in case the farm provides accommodation. Three of the survey respondents, who all worked for Sharma Farm, had already started working there before the year 1995. I also met a number of employees of Karibu Farm who had worked for this farm ever since it started producing roses in 2002. Gibbon and Riisgaard (2014, p. 109) likewise observed a high level of employment stability, at least among those on a permanent contract, with a mean length of employment of 5.8 years. This contrasts to the mean length of employment of 1.5 years that Staelens, Desiere, Louche, and D'Haese (2018, p. 1620) found among Ethiopian flower farm workers.

As Naivasha workers usually gain considerable experience, the common label of "unskilled labour"—related to the low educational requirements for the position of general worker—can be questioned. Especially since the label has actual effects: negotiated wages for semi-skilled workers are slightly higher than wages for general workers (AEA & KPAWU, 2011, sec. 34). According to Gibbon and Riisgaard (2014, p. 108), the category of semi-skilled worker is hardly used by the farms. Even general workers with decades of experience are still labelled "unskilled". This label disguises that long-term employees do over time gain certain crucial skills and acquire tacit knowledge.

During my visits to Karibu Farm, I tried most of the tasks in the greenhouses once and performed some of the easier work several times. Only through participating in the work, I learned that most tasks are not as easy as they appear at first sight. "Participation necessarily involves confrontation with the researcher's incompetence in contrast to others' long-term embedded skills" (Okely, 2012, p. 77). This incompetence was the reason I shared the hesitance expressed by Pollert (1981, p. 6) to work along fully: "The women's work in the factory—while termed 'semi-skilled'—thoroughly intimidated me." Once I became aware of the great monetary value of the flowers and of the vulnerability of the plants, I refrained from working along, with the exception of a few light tasks with which the workers and supervisors trusted me and with which I trusted myself, such as sizing. As Parry stated (in Okely, 2012, p. 94): "But nobody was going to have me buggering up their machine!" My limited attempt to work along thus made clear that the work requires certain skills, despite low educational requirements.

Workers receive only limited training to acquire those skills. Karibu Farm organized an introductory training, mainly on health and safety, which would take only a few hours. After that, the new recruits would be trained "on the job" by supervisors for a couple of days. I witnessed Lucy providing such a training to two new employees: she showed them how to perform the diverse tasks one by one and then told them to do it themselves. She would give them a lot of encouragement: "Take your time. There is no hurry today," she told them, and "don't be afraid of the flowers." Lucy compared this training with teaching a small child how to write: you have to start from scratch because the recruits know nothing. Nevertheless, new employees are already expected to just work along after these few initial days. They are supposed to learn the work in practice over a period of two to three months and to have attained a moderate speed of work after that. Workers in more specialized positions, such as scouts, security guards, and sprayers, are also mostly trained on the job, albeit for a longer period of time. Thus, the official training provided by the farms is not extensive. Nevertheless, as I experienced, the work is not easy to master. I was told there are recruits who turn out to be unsuitable for the job and who do not get a contract after the probation period was over, either because they lack the discipline or motivation or simply because they cannot perform the work properly. The different tasks for general workers are not difficult to understand, but they all have to be executed with care. For example, Lucy introduced me to the procedure of "bending": for certain varieties of roses, the first shoot of a seedling has to be bent towards the ground. As Lucy explained to me, the goal of bending is to create a *mama* (mother) who can store food for the next shoots, the *toto* (children). By using metaphors and Swahili terms, she managed to make the procedure insightful to me and to the workers in her team. Yet, despite understanding the principle, I soon found out that bending was not easy: when not being careful, one can break the entire stem and damage the (expensive) seedling. Like bending, most tasks have to be done meticulously. At the same time, routine is needed to keep up the speed of production. These are skills that can only be acquired over time.

Furthermore, the knowledge needed for these jobs is rather particular and some of it can only be learned within the farm for which one works, due to differences in working procedures. An HR manager of one of the farms affirmed that farms like to keep turnover rates low. It saves them the cost of training: "we don't like sending people away anyhow. We train them so that we can get good returns." Friedemann-Sánchez (2009, p. 75) observed a similar attitude among flower farm managers in Colombia, who were also worried about losing trained labour. In contrast, in the *maquiladoras* on the Mexican-US border and along assembly lines in Malaysia, high turnover rates of 5–6% per month were common (Fernández-Kelly, 1983; Ong, 1987). Thus, the flower industry, which is working with a natural product in a market with high quality demands, differs from some other global industries because of its need for a stable and experienced workforce. A steady and also content workforce has become only more important with the development of the second global value chain, as retailers set higher and more specific demands with regard to the quality of the product and a swift delivery than buyers on the auction.[9]

Loss of skills is not the only reason that high turnover rates are perceived to be disadvantageous by management. Long-term employees are also perceived to be more loyal than casual or temporary labour. They are considered to be more motivated and they are always available. Even vegetable farms, which usually claim not to be able to provide the majority of their workers with permanent contracts because of the seasonal production, still prefer giving these workers at least temporary contracts for several months instead of hiring casual workers on a daily basis. As a manager of a vegetable farm said, people who know they will not have a job the next day are simply less reliable.

Remarkably, "unskilled" labourers tend to stay around much longer than more skilled employees, such as managers and technical staff, who habitually move to another farm every few years. Especially Kenyan managers used the expression of "moving to greener pastures" and said they would move if they could get a better-paid job in another farm. Others are simply looking for a new challenge. It is also common, as one of the middle-level managers in Karibu Farm told me, that a manager disagrees with a senior manager or with the company's directors and then decides to move. Thus, managers move around much more than general workers.

The decision to either move or keep one's job is primarily based on material considerations. One consideration is simply the security of a basic income that a permanent contract provides. Moreover, the system of remuneration in the industry is geared towards retaining labour. The large majority of the workers in any farm—whether working in the greenhouse, the packhouse, the cold stores, the canteen, or maintenance—would receive a fixed basic salary, plus possibly a bonus. But the "basic" salary for unskilled workers is not the same for everyone, due to considerable yearly increments. Whereas a general worker who started to work for a farm that participated in the CBA in the year 2014 would earn a basic monthly salary of 5401 KES, a fellow worker who had started in 1997 would earn 10,252 KES, almost twice as much (Anker & Anker, 2014, p. 40). Previous experience in another farm does not increase a worker's basic salary when he or she starts to work for a new farm (KHRC, 2012, p. 41). The system of yearly increments therefore forms an important incentive to keep one's job.

In this respect, the general workers differ from the skilled employees, whose salaries are not part of the CBA. They negotiate their salaries individually, and they can thus gain from moving to another farm. One supervisor told me she had decided to change her workplace because she could get a higher salary elsewhere. She had earned 15,000 KES per month plus 2500 KES housing allowance in the first farm. She negotiated 20,000 KES per month plus 3000 KES housing allowance in the second farm. Her salary was still much lower than the remuneration of top managers: according to a Kenyan manager of a relatively small farm, the gross salary for a general manager would range from 350,000 to 500,000 KES. The large differences in salary within the industry also are apparent from court cases in which employees dispute their dismissal. These court cases disclose the monthly salaries that are demanded to be compensated. Recent cases showed, for instance, a monthly wage of 7700 KES for a general worker who worked for a farm close to Naivasha Town, and a monthly wage of over 500,000 KES for a chief accountant in a rose propagation company (*Henry Isaiah Onjelo v Maridadi Flowers Limited*, 2015; *Patrick Chebos v Stokman Rozen Kenya Limited*, 2016). These indications of salaries show the great discrepancies between the income of general workers and of (top) managers. Nevertheless, as seen, the salaries of general workers could—although remaining low—increase tremendously over time.

Apart from the salary, also the gratuity that is paid when leaving the job depends on the number of years the employee has worked for a farm. As prescribed in the CBA: "An employee, whose services are terminated, is retired or resigns after five (5) years' continuous service with the Employer, shall be entitled to gratuity at the rate of twenty-two (22) days basic pay for each completed year of service" (AEA & KPAWU, 2011, sec. 24(a)). This gratuity system provides a form of security for the old age and for a future after flower farm work. The money can be used to start a small-scale business or to buy a plot of land. As workers only have a right to this payment after five years of service, the gratuity system induces some of them to stay on the job longer than they would have done otherwise. Jan, for instance, noted that some employees leave after exactly five years of service.

A final incentive to keep one's job is the possibility to participate in the Saving and Credit Co-operative (SACCO). Such a Saving and Credit Co-operative is a local phenomenon, incorporated by the farms. SACCOs differ from other saving and rotations schemes in their degree of institutionalization. They are registered groups, working under rules and regulations set by the national government and audited on a yearly basis by an external accountant. They form a more accessible option than other financial service providers such as banks. Kenyan legislation stipulates that SACCO members need to have a "common bond". Consequently, the cooperatives are mostly attached to a company or to a specific, unionized trade. From the mid-1960s, the Kenyan government has stimulated the formation of these cooperatives, and they have become especially important in urban areas (Alila & Obado, 1990).

Many of the flower farms operating in Naivasha also allow and encourage their employees to set up such a saving group. As other employers do, the farms facilitate SACCOs by providing them with office space and by deducting contributions and loan repayments from the salaries before paying them out. The volunteers leading these cooperatives deal with large amounts of money. For example, there were 24 active saving cooperatives related to a company in Naivasha Subcounty in the year 2001, with a total of 5000 members and a total saved capital of 227 million KES. The largest cooperative, which had given out loans for a total amount of 85 million

KES, was attached to a flower farm.[10] According to the cooperative officer of Naivasha Subcounty, there were 60 active SACCOs in Naivasha by the year 2015, of which 43 were attached to a flower farm.

About one-half of the Karibu Farm employees participated in the farm's SACCO, which is a large proportion of the workforce, considering that participation is only possible for those with a permanent contract. Participants also have to be able to contribute a minimum amount of savings every month. The Karibu Farm SACCO had a minimum contribution of 700 KES per month. Most participants saved 1000 KES per month or even more, which would amount to 10–20% of a month's wage. In addition to the savings, many members had an outstanding loan over which they made repayments, including a small interest. The maximum loan they could receive was 100,000 KES, to be repaid within three years' time. Consequently, many of these members had already 20–30% of their salaries cut as payments for the SACCO before they would receive their salary in their bank account. Yet, they were glad to have the opportunity: the SACCO enabled them to borrow money at times when they needed it the most, for example, when they had to pay the school fees for their children. It also enabled them to save some money for the future.

In sum, the several types of payments and the SACCO savings all increase with long-term employment and therefore form incentives for employees to stay on. The farms profit from this stable, reliable, and experienced (though "unskilled") workforce. These global firms, financed mostly from overseas and selling their flowers almost exclusively in Europe, depend on the quality of the local labour force in Naivasha for their profits. Managers occasionally acknowledged this dependency on their employees, for example, when they explained their decision to remain in Naivasha and not to move to Ethiopia. Although the lower wages and other incentives offered by the Ethiopian government are attractive to the firms, a manager working in Ethiopia stated that the workforce there lacks the skills and the discipline that the workforce in Naivasha has acquired over time.

4.6 Changing Labour Conditions: Standardization and Unionization

The fidelity of the workers to their flower farm jobs might come as a surprise to anyone familiar with the bad reputation of the farms with regard to labour conditions. However, without denying that labour rights violations occurred, it seems that labour conditions have improved drastically in recent years. Criticism has also waned (Kazimierczuk et al., 2018).

One of the Naivasha labour officers even called the flower farms good employers, because of the good system of industrial relations. He said: "We feel that the workers are well represented." How did this change come about? And is it the practices of the farms that have changed, or rather the perceptions on these practices?

Gibbon and Riisgaard (2014, p. 95) have argued that conditions started to change when the farms adopted an "industrial" and "civic" system of labour management. This system is based on the principles of efficiency and welfare instead of on traditions, as in a paternalistic system, or on the market. There has been a move towards "legalization" (Gibbon & Riisgaard, 2014, p. 121). Recruitment processes have been formalized, permanent contracts have become more prevalent, these contracts are put on paper instead of being an oral agreement, and more farms provide their employees with payslips (Dolan, Opondo, & Smith, 2003; KHRC, 2012). These developments contrast to trends towards casualization of labour in industries elsewhere. An example is the horticultural industry in southern Africa, where the traditional paternalistic system, based on personal relations between farm owners and permanent labourers, is slowly replaced by a more hybrid, market-oriented system, based on the employment of mostly casual labour (Addison, 2014a; Bolt, 2013; Du Toit, 1993). The Kenya flower farms could afford to move towards an industrial-civic system of labour management, including more permanent labour, due to the all-year-round rose production and a stable market. Moreover, they were prompted to do so because of increasing quality demands and—under influence of non-governmental organization (NGO) campaigns—a wish for better labour conditions from the market (Gibbon & Riisgaard, 2014; Riisgaard & Gibbon, 2014).

An example of a recent change in labour conditions is that farms are adopting increasingly strict health and safety regulations. They now usually adhere to the (already previously existing) national legislation and to guidelines of the World Health Organization. In the early days, not all farms provided PPEs, not even to the sprayers. Dolan et al. (2003, p. 46) noted an increased use of PPEs by the year 2002, yet 50 of the 100 workers they interviewed at that time still said that the provision of PPEs was not always adequate. By the time I was in Naivasha, some 12 years later, it had become unimaginable that an employer would not provide PPEs. The CBA confirmed that at least all unionized farms have to follow the regulations with regard to the provision of PPEs from the Occupational Health and Safety Act (AEA & KPAWU, 2011, sec. 20(a)). Karibu Farm employees were provided with dust coats, gumboots, and gloves. Workers in the open-air production received raincoats, and those working in the cold stores were provided with thick overalls. Farms have also become increasingly strict with not allowing entrance to recently sprayed areas. They, for instance, place signs at the greenhouse entrances displaying the date of spraying, the chemical used, and the time at which one was allowed to enter again. Finally, most farms have installed a health and safety committee, in which elected employees monitor the situation on the farm. However, as noted by Wilshaw (2013, p. 102), the effects of these measures have until now not been researched properly.[11]

Such changes in labour conditions are related to the two trends of standardization—an increased participation of farms in international certification schemes—and unionization. In 2011, 78 of the 177 large-scale flower farms in Kenya were certified under at least one of the three most common standards (Gibbon & Riisgaard, 2014, p. 104). The certifications have aided in the formalization of working procedures within the farms. Yet, it remains questionable how profound the changes are that they have brought about. Most of these schemes were developed by industry players (Dolan et al., 2003, p. 11). Moreover, except for the certificate from lobby organization Kenya Flower Council (KFC), these schemes originated from Europe (Kazimierczuk et al., 2018, p. 11). The Kenya Human Rights Commission (KHRC) (2012, p. 35) therefore concluded that the increase in certifications is not a worker-driven process but is a mere reaction to consumer demands. Moreover, there is no democratic control over the standards since the government is not involved in any way (Kuiper & Gemählich, 2017). One can therefore wonder whether the standards are the most adequate instruments for protecting workers. Nelson, Martin, and Ewert (2007, p. 65), for instance, observed that even though the codes of conduct they investigated covered some of the workers' concerns, such as medical care and permanent contracts, other concerns, such as a lack of childcare facilities and an inability to save money for the future, were not addressed. More profoundly, these authors asserted that inequalities in the value chain remained. Existing hierarchies largely persisted. "This finding raises the question of how far codes of practice can move beyond improving *practical* interests to making a difference to the *strategic* interests of all workers (including women, and especially casual and seasonal workers) or delivering anything approaching political 'empowerment'" (V. Nelson et al., 2007, p. 71). Moreover, it is usually the farms that are already complying with national legislation and have relatively good labour conditions that are adopting certifications, as they have to make relatively little additional investments (V. Nelson et al., 2007, p. 68). Finally, although there are a number of different certification schemes, their standards mostly set similar requirements. Thus, as Naivasha farm managers confirmed, once a farm has acquired one certificate, it takes little investment and little change in production processes to acquire another one. The effects of the standards on practices within the farms therefore seem to have been limited.

The most well-known certification scheme, Fairtrade, is the only scheme that originates from outside the industry. According to the production manager of Fairtrade Africa, who also explained the procedures described below, 15 Naivasha flower farms were Fairtrade-certified by 2015. This certification scheme pays significant attention to labour. However, when comparing the Fairtrade Standard for Hired Labour (Fairtrade International, 2014) to the CBA (AEA & KPAWU, 2011), it appears that most regulations are similar. Since only unionized farms can become Fairtrade-certified in the first place, the standard does not require drastic changes to existing practices within the applying farms. The single unique aspect of Fairtrade is the so-called premium: 10% of the price paid for every flower is transferred to a special premium account. Only a small percentage of all flowers produced by a Fairtrade-certified farm can be sold under the Fairtrade label, simply because the market is not substantial enough to sell more Fairtrade flowers. Nevertheless, these sales result in substantial sums of premium. During its first full year of Fairtrade certification, Karibu Farm, for instance, already received €45,000 in premium money. This money has to be used for projects assisting the employees, their families, and the communities they are living in. Each participating farm has a premium committee consisting of elected workers and management representatives, who together have to draft a plan for the spending of the premium money. Fairtrade prescribes a detailed framework for what such a plan should look like. It has to contain a budget, a description of the project and its execution, and an assessment of the risks (of non-execution) involved. The budget also needs to be approved by all employees of the farm during a general assembly. The procedures are so elaborate that some farms even employ a specific manager in charge of preparing the application for Fairtrade certification and of the implementation of its procedures after acquiring the certificate.[12]

Examples of common projects funded with the premium are assistance in the payment of school fees of employees' children and the organization of computer, driving, or tailoring courses for the employees themselves.

It is also common and even required to spend a percentage of the premium on promotional and "awareness" activities, such as Fairtrade shirts. Another requirement is that some of the funds should not be used for the benefit of the farm's employees only but should be spent on projects targeting the wider community. Several managers noted that these projects are generally unpopular among the workers, which some of them blamed on their employees' "selfishness". However, such a judgement does not acknowledge that most workers do not consider their neighbours in the Naivasha settlements their "community". They would prefer to use this money for projects at their "home", where they ultimately plan to move to. Although Section 2.1.14 of the Fairtrade standard allows for projects in migrants' home communities, it works with a rather restricted definition of a "migrant worker", excluding those who stay in their place of work for longer periods of time (Fairtrade International, 2014, p. 5). Naivasha's "translocal" migrant workers therefore are not allowed to direct premium money to their "home". Fairtrade's requirements thus limit workers' freedom to spend the premium money as they wish.

Yet, employees of Fairtrade-certified farms, who have to survive on a tight budget, generally appreciate the premium money, as it makes their lives slightly easier. The employees are furthermore made aware that Fairtrade increases the access to markets and therefore makes their jobs more secure. As the chair of the Karibu Farm Premium Committee told the employees during a general assembly: "Fairtrade is a market. It's a business." He added that everyone would profit from this business: the employer, the employees, and the community around the farm. However, in the same meeting it also dawned on the employees that by far not all the flowers they produced were sold as Fairtrade and contributed to the premium. One of the employees then asked what they could do to increase the sales. The answer was nothing. It all depended on what the customers wanted. This answer revealed that despite the attempts of Fairtrade to make their processes transparent and democratic, and despite the emphasis that the organization puts on the "empowerment" of workers, the ultimate power does not lie in Kenya but has been shifted to the customer in Europe.[13] Thus, although Fairtrade and other standards have some positive practical effects for the workers, they do not profoundly alter power relations within the industry. The biggest success of the standards has been the previously described change in perceptions on the industry's labour conditions.

The second process that has played a role in the formalization of the industry is the increasing importance of the trade union. The union Kenya

Plantation and Agricultural Workers Union (KPAWU), which is part of the overarching Central Organization of Trade Unions (COTU), aims to represent the workers in negotiations with the employers and in case of conflicts.[14] Its main achievement is the increased influence of the CBA. Unionized farms either follow a general CBA for the flower sector as a whole, negotiated every two years between the Agricultural Employers' Association (AEA) and KPAWU, or negotiate their own agreement with the union. According to an official of the KPAWU branch in Naivasha, about 40 of the 55 flower farms in the wider Naivasha area were unionized in 2015. Furthermore, 46 of the 94 survey respondents who worked for a flower farm were a member of the union.[15] In comparison, only 2 of the 24 respondents working for a vegetable farm were unionized. An important reason for this disparity is that most vegetable farm workers have no permanent contract and therefore cannot join the union.

The union is represented on the farms through an elected union committee consisting of employees of the respective farm, the shop stewards. KPAWU is further represented in Naivasha by a few union officials, who have their main office in the small settlement Kwa Muhia at South Lake and a branch office in Kasarani at North Lake. One of these KPAWU officials and one of the labour officers of Naivasha Subcounty explained what happens in case of a dispute. As a first step, the shop stewards try to come to an internal solution. If no solution can be found, the shop stewards involve the local KPAWU branch, and if that is not sufficient the national office of KPAWU in Nakuru. If the KPAWU officials on all levels fail to agree with the farm, the governmental labour office in Naivasha Town functions as a conciliator. Only in the rare cases that all these offices fail to settle a dispute, a case can ultimately be brought to court.

Despite this elaborate system for handling conflicts, 97% of the workers interviewed for KHRC (2012, p. 30) thought the union would or could not protect them in case of unfair dismissal. The union has also been criticized for the underrepresentation of women in its leadership, thus making it even harder for women to have their voices heard (Wilshaw, 2013). Riisgaard (2009, p. 333) and Kazimierczuk et al. (2018, pp. 36–37) noted that feelings of distrust are aggravated by the top-down structure of KPAWU and COTU. I would add that although the union is expected to be an organization representing the workers, it first of all works within the framework of the industrial relations system and therefore is instrumental in keeping labour relations peaceful. As explained by the KPAWU official, representatives would get trained after being elected. "Otherwise they'll do their own thing." Through these trainings, KPAWU avoids that individual representatives would, for instance, call for illegal strikes. In short, the union provides the only official forum through which workers can voice dissent, yet this forum is highly regulated and is—like the flower industry itself—characterized by stark hierarchies.

As Wilshaw (2013, p. 97) stated: "workers often regard the union representative as part of the grievance process rather than as a unifying voice for workers." Many employees join the union nonetheless. When asked why, survey respondents failed to provide an answer or replied they had done so because others did. The one feature which makes employment on a unionized farm truly desirable is the CBA, which is perceived to make a difference with regard to payment and labour conditions. Furthermore, also non-members on farms participating in the CBA have to pay a fee.[16] Financially, it therefore does not make a difference whether one has joined the union or not.

Remarkably, next to many regular workers, also a few of the shop stewards distrusted the KPAWU officers. They complained that the central office did little to assist them.[17] Managers are quite distrustful towards the union. Jan, for instance, told me that he appreciated the CBA, yet he also thought (certain) union representatives looked for conflicts instead of resolving them. Another manager stated that the union in Kenya is hard to negotiate with.[18] And one Dutch manager stated in the press that he does not cooperate with the trade union and rather follows the CBA voluntarily, as he thinks the union officials are only enriching themselves (Gaarlandt, 2013, p. 13).

The union itself has a confrontational approach towards criticism. It, for example, claims to be the only organization that had the right to represent workers in unionized farms. The first statement in the CBA's preamble is as follows: "Whereas by terms of Recognition the Association and the Union agree that the Association has recognized the Union as a properly constituted body and the sole labour organization representing the interests of the employees within the membership of AEA" (AEA & KPAWU, 2011). This claim is understandable for the purposes of signing a CBA, yet it also makes the union quite powerful and leaves little room for other ways of resolving conflicts within the farms. The union for a long time did not acknowledge the legitimacy of NGOs and of accrediting bodies of certificates in advocating the improvement of labour conditions within the farms ("Leave Workers Alone", 2004; Riisgaard, 2009). In sum, the increased unionization complicated power relations within the farms without necessarily empowering workers. However, at the least, the increased influence of the CBA stimulated the adherence to (legal) regulations and thus aided in improving labour conditions.

On the other hand, an unintended effect of the increasing adherence to the CBA and participation in certification schemes is that farms tend to do exclusively what is prescribed in these documents and nothing more. Whereas before, management could decide to spend a small part of the profit on "corporate social responsibility" projects and would, for example, pay for the construction of a classroom, farms that have become Fairtrade-certified tend to leave such projects to the Premium Committee. Also with regard to labour conditions, supervisors and managers primarily follow the rules in the CBA. Anything extra is perceived of as a favour. For instance, the CBA contains regulations on maternity leave and on limited working hours for nursing women (AEA & KPAWU, 2011, sec. 10). However, there are no regulations with regard to the workload of pregnant women. They sometimes are given "light duties" and are exempted from any work that involves bending over. But such measures are up to the discretion of the supervisors and are not always granted.

Apart from leaving such ungoverned grey zones that show workers' enduring dependency on the goodwill of their employers, the standards and the CBA also have had only limited effects on wage levels. Low salaries remain the main cause for discontent among the workers, even on unionized and certified farms. According to Naivasha's labour officer, the salaries are the main bone of contention in the biannual negotiations for the CBA. They are also an important target for those criticizing the industry. NGO-commissioned researchers concluded that the wages were insufficient for meeting the basic needs of workers and their families (Anker & Anker, 2014; Dolan et al., 2003). Riisgaard and Gibbon (2014, p. 277) noted that the standards focus on job security and welfare and not on higher monetary wages. Significantly, real wages have decreased rather than increased in recent years as compared to the early 2000s (Anker & Anker, 2014, p. 6; Riisgaard & Gibbon, 2014, p. 281). And although workers pay little or no taxes, the salaries are lowered further due to several deductions. There are national fees all workers have to pay, such as for the National Hospital Insurance Fund. There are also personal fees, such as the membership fee of the trade union and the payment of loans with the company SACCO.

On the other hand, workers receive several allowances on top of the salaries. For instance, Karibu Farm paid for the medical treatment of employees and also for the medical costs of their (nuclear) family members.[19] Secondly, those farms participating in the CBA pay a monthly housing allowance (1500–2000 KES) and a travelling allowance for the annual leave (2300 KES) (AEA & KPAWU, 2011, sec. 7(d), 12(a)). Section 31 of the Employment Act 2012 also requires employers to either provide accommodation or to pay a "sufficient sum, as rent, in addition to the wages or salary of the employee, as will enable the employee to obtain reasonable accommodation". Whereas the housing allowance paid by the farms covers the average rents in the settlements, Anker and Anker (2014, p. 18) have argued that these one-room rental houses are too small for a family and sometimes are of poor quality. What counts as "reasonable accommodation" thus remains vague. Nevertheless, allowances somewhat compensate for the low salaries. Finally, in addition to the salary and allowances, some farms provide benefits in kind, such as the provision of drinking water to take home or a chicken for Christmas. These are all "extras" left to the discretion of the farm managers. They also do not always fit to the needs of the workers: the mentioned chicken happened to be of a foreign breed, quite different from local chicken, and one of the farm workers was still amused when she recalled how she and her colleagues had struggled to prepare these chickens properly.

Flower farms defend themselves against criticism of the low salaries by pointing out that flower farm workers on average earn more than unskilled workers in most other economic sectors in Kenya. For example, vegetable farms pay much lower wages. Such differences in salaries even occur within single farms. According to the HR manager of a Naivasha farm that produced both flowers and vegetables, the employees in the vegetable department were paid less than their likewise "unskilled" colleagues working with flowers. Industry representatives furthermore defend the level of wages by stating that flower farms pay much more than the statutory agricultural minimum wage.[20] However, these minimum wages were set for labourers on small-scale farms in rural areas, who live in areas where the cost of living is much lower than in Naivasha (KHRC, 2012, p. 25). Thus, despite paying relatively high wages, also the flower farms do not pay a wage on which the workers and their families can reasonably be expected to live on. The average wages, even including the allowances, are considerably lower than a so-called living wage, which Anker and Anker (2014, p. 47) estimated to be 18,542 KES in the year 2014.

Managers claimed that their farm would no longer be economically viable if they would pay much higher wages. They stated that profit margins had dropped tremendously in recent years. One manager even called the debate about a living wage "dangerous", as it could lead to unrest among the workers.[21] Occasionally managers were blunter and claimed their workers simply did not need more money.[22] One of them—a European manager—asserted, specifically about Maasai:

> They are too proud for it and they don't need the money. Because if they have cows and goats they can survive. And that's also a thinking mistake from the UN because they say minimum wage per day should be one and a half or two dollars. (…) but some people can survive with nothing as long as they have their little huts and cows and goats. They don't need an income. I think it's the wrong way of thinking. It's the western way of working that things, but it doesn't always match. That's my opinion.[23]

As becomes clear from this quote, farm managers feel offended by criticism on the wage they pay or on other labour conditions. They point out that they prefer to provide many low-paid jobs than just a few highly paid positions. Managers rather point the finger at the Kenyan government for a lack of involvement and argue that they make the investments in schools, hospitals, and infrastructure that the government should make. However, the provision of some of these facilities is also the interest of the farms themselves. For example, it is advantageous to have a company hospital to judge sick leave applications and cases of accidents, rather than to depend on an external clinic or hospital for that. As asserted by a farm manager in an article in a Dutch magazine: "this way you can retain some control" (Gaarlandt, 2013, p. 12; my translation from Dutch). Thus, despite the recent move towards "legalization", some managers (both foreign and Kenyan) take on a paternalistic attitude towards their workers, which surfaces from their justification of wages and labour conditions on "their" farms.

Standards attempt to reconfigure power relations within the farms and to increase workers' say in farm policies by requiring farms to install various workers' committees. The committees usually have an advisory role to management with regard to a certain aspect of the work. The increase in committees has created quite some specific roles within the farms. When taking Karibu Farm as an example again, each greenhouse there had a union representative, a welfare representative, a gender representative, a health and safety representative, two first aiders, and a fire marshal. Each working team or department would elect a committee representative for the duration of several years. Sometimes the supervisor of the concerning team had to agree with the elected members and therefore effectively had a veto. For some of the committees the voting was done in an informal manner, either by simply appointing someone during a short meeting of the team or by lining up behind the candidate one wished to vote for (the so-called *mlolongo* system). For other committees, such as the Fairtrade Premium Committee, the elections were more formal. Election procedures included campaigns, an improvised voting booth, and a balloting box. After being elected, the representatives would receive a training of several days and afterwards would have a monthly meeting, in which now and then also a representative of the management would be present.

Whereas, wherever present, the union committee and the Fairtrade Premium Committee have to follow the procedures set by the respective organizations, the exact role of other committees differs per farm. For example, the welfare committee of some farms has quite limited task of supporting employees who have been bereaved or have fallen ill by collecting financial contributions among colleagues. In farms that are not unionized, the welfare committee has the much broader role of intermediary between the management and the workers. Because the position of committees differs per farm, their impact on practices and labour relations also varies. Generally, however, it is questionable whether they are successful in their goal of empowering workers. This can be illustrated by describing in more detail one peculiar committee, the "gender committee".

4.7 Gender on the Farms: Divisions of Labour, Sexual Harassment, and Gender Committees

In response to the global attention for the position of female workers, and under pressure of standards, farms have introduced "gender committees". To understand the varying role of these committees, one first needs to understand the gendered division of labour and the role of gendered discourses within the farms.

As women have fewer job opportunities outside the flower industry, they more heavily rely on these jobs than men do. Nevertheless, contrary to women employed by other global (agro-)industries (Ong, 1987; Samarasinghe, 1993), women in the flower farms in Naivasha are not only working in subordinate positions. There is, for instance, a substantial proportion of female supervisors. In a supervisors' meeting within Karibu Farm, I counted 5 female and 11 male supervisors. And about 30% of the managers of the farms surveyed by Kazimierczuk et al. (2018, p. 34) were female. Nevertheless, men and women do not always perform the same jobs. More specifically, even within the flower industry, certain jobs are not available to women. Tasks that are considered to be risky, dangerous, or physically demanding are given exclusively to men. Examples of such tasks are spraying pesticides, irrigation, working in night shifts, working in the cold store, and transporting flowers on a pushcart. One of the supervisors in the Karibu Farm packhouse told me, without me even asking, that there were just as many women as men working in the grading hall. He said: "As you can see we have gender equality here." However, when I asked him whether this meant that there were also women working in the cold room, he started to laugh: "Of course not." His amusement demonstrated that it is unimaginable to employ women in physically demanding jobs. Especially with regard to spraying, it was said that women are "too delicate" for the job.

This division of labour was never challenged by workers I spoke to, regardless of gender or position. "Even among workers, such gender segmentation was viewed as a natural outcome of social norms and biological difference" (Dolan et al., 2003, p. 40).[24] It is furthermore supported by NGO campaigns which have emphasized the vulnerability of women for chemicals and sometimes have made explicit references to their reproductive roles (Hivos, n.d.).

In addition to these heavy or dangerous jobs, participants in the listing and piling exercise also mentioned a few more technical positions, such as carpeting and welding, which were said to be given exclusively to men. As one of the participants remarked, these jobs are performed by women in the settlements, yet somehow they have remained a male domain within the farms.

Apart from these jobs that are clearly not available to women, there are yet other jobs that are perceived to be more fitting for the one sex or the other. Although for these jobs the gender segmentation is not always adhered to, certain patterns are discernible. "Women are concentrated in the segments of the production process that are most labour intensive and that also hold the most significance for the cosmetic quality of the final product. These include picking, packing, and value-added processing activities, which all require intense concentration and long periods of standing and bending" (Dolan et al., 2003, p. 28). Some (although by far not all) men thought the manual labour such as harvesting or grading was not "fit" for them. This perception of the work not being fit for men is reflected in the composition of greenhouse working teams, which usually consist of more women than men. There were, for instance, 21 female and 9 male employees in the greenhouse of Karibu Farm where I conducted a total network analysis. Observations during visits to other farms provided a similar picture.

Furthermore, as explained earlier, even within greenhouse teams, there are certain tasks that are more often performed by men than women and the other way around. Lucy explained to me why she allocated tasks such as wrapping the flowers in the greenhouse to men. She said that, because of their traditional household chores, women are used to small but many tasks, somewhat similar to harvesting or sizing, while men are used to bulk work. Thus, supervisors and managers sometimes connected the planning of the work to (their perception of) the gendered division of labour in the domestic domain. A Kenyan manager quoted by Nungari Mwangi (2019, p. 24) explained his preference for hiring women by referring to what he considers their traditional role in the household and their capability to suffer and obey. A Kenyan manager of European descent interviewed by Gemählich likewise justified the common division of labour within the industry by using cultural arguments:

> It's traditional that you will find most of the girls in the […] fields and the greenhouse maintenance, sprayers and truck drivers tend to be male. It has never changed. It's not about the job. It's about the man's work. So gender equality is a lot of crap in this job. It comes from the West. Just open your eyes and look at Africa. You can't just sweep it away. But there is no reason not to employ the women for weeding, because that has always been their job. You rarely find a man in the greenhouse doing the weeding. Sometimes you do.[25]

Another Kenyan manager (also of European descent) consistently talked about "our ladies" in the packhouse when he gave us a tour of the farm, even though there evidently were quite a number of men working there. Foreign managers expressed similar opinions. Jan thought Kenyan women are more "responsible" and therefore fit for precise jobs. Another Dutch flower farm manager even called Kenyan men "lazy". He would prefer to only hire women, were it not that the farm needs men for the more heavy and technical tasks.

Although these managers and supervisors all referred to what they perceived to be "Kenyan" culture, their portrayal of women echoes a gendered narrative that has played a role in recruitment and labour control practices in industries worldwide. "Women are considered not only to have naturally nimble fingers, but also to be naturally more docile and willing to accept tough work discipline, and naturally more suited to tedious, repetitious, monotonous work" (Elson & Pearson, 1984, p. 23). Whereas the managers in Naivasha did not portray women to be "naturally" docile, they portrayed them as "culturally" subordinated and as used to repetitive labour. They took this "culture" as a given that could not be changed. But as Salzinger (2003) argued, docile labour is not something that simply exists and that these farms have stumbled upon. It has to be produced, for example, by such references to cultural gender patterns. The explicit connection that managers make between women's and men's roles on the work floor and the (perceived) gender relations in Kenyan society makes it difficult for women (as well as for men) to question the division of labour within the farms.

Notably, these perceptions on gender roles are not necessarily disadvantageous for women. Wilshaw (2013, p. 85) reported that slightly more women than men receive a permanent contract. This is related to the types of tasks for which they are typically hired, which have to be executed quickly yet carefully. These jobs thus require more experience than the physically demanding jobs which are regularly given to men. And one manager explained in Dutch press that he only hired women for the more responsible jobs, even as supervisors and managers, because in his opinion they work harder than men. He also thought that he in this way can avoid having cases of sexual intimidation on the farm (Gaarlandt, 2013, p. 13).

Sexual harassment has been a central concern in criticism on the flower industry (Hivos, n.d.; Riungu, 2006; Wilshaw, 2013). The emphasis on this subject initially puzzled me because the issue of sexual harassment was hardly ever mentioned to me during my time in Naivasha. I admittedly also did not explicitly ask about this sensitive issue, and victims probably would find it difficult to talk about. Yet, workers spoke about harassment in general, in the sense of general abuse of power, as in the case of the "slow-go" described in Sect. 4.4. Wilshaw (2013, p. 86) also noted that workers themselves ranked sexual harassment as "the lowest of all challenges they faced". It made me wonder, is sexual harassment as prevalent, and also as much experienced as a problem, as critics of the industry believe?

Jacobs, Brahic, and Olaiya (2015) noted that sexual harassment in African firms has not been well researched and that there is a lack of official numbers on the prevalence of this issue. Their own research, executed in cooperation with local NGOs under the umbrella of the British organization Women Working Worldwide, was meant to generate knowledge on this subject. They interviewed employees of horticultural firms in four East African countries, amongst others 40 female employees of Kenyan firms. A minority of these respondents reported to have been bothered with offensive comments or with unwanted touching. Although sexual harassment thus occurred, the researchers noted that the mentioned cases of harassment not only took place in the workplace but also elsewhere (Jacobs et al., 2015, p. 8).

Sexual harassment was reported by workers of all seven farms in the sample of Dolan et al.'s (2003, p. 8) study. Harassment mostly took the form of only receiving benefits (including job security) in exchange for sexual favours. However, the authors did not provide a percentage of affected employees. And significantly, these authors added that there were also other forms of harassment within the farms, such as verbal abuse and corruption. At the time, there were no facilities or boards to which workers could bring a complaint on (sexual) harassment. In addition, at the time of their research, some farms had not yet formalized their recruitment processes. Supervisors could hire and fire temporary labour. With the creation of HR departments, workers have become less vulnerable to, for instance, random dismissal and therefore to harassment by superiors (Dolan et al., 2003).

Overall, it seems research has been too scanty to draw conclusions on the prevalence of sexual harassment on the farms. Apart from a lack of statistics, the issue is further complicated by the lack of a shared definition. When does coercion in a hierarchical wage labour environment turn into (sexual) harassment? As Kloß (2017, p. 399) argued: "sexual(ized) harassment is a means of sustaining (…) hegemony." Rather than being primarily about sexual attraction, it is about expressing and reassuring (both gender-based and role-based) power. Harassment thus can be used as a (systemic) tool in labour control (Jacobs et al., 2015, pp. 3–5). The attention to sexual harassment points at wider issues of (partly gendered) inequalities of power. Yet I noticed that these power imbalances are hardly discussed. The primary focus on sexual harassment might even have taken attention away from these underlying power imbalances.

Managers sometimes have denied that sexual harassment takes place on their farms or have denied responsibility for it (Dolan et al., 2003). The manager of a rose-breeding farm, for instance, stated in an interview with Gemählich (November 22, 2014): "We did not invent sexual harassment, it is a cultural thing." The manager of the South African farm where Addison (2014b) conducted his research likewise blamed transactional sex on "African culture". However, Naivasha flower farms cannot evade responsibility anymore since the industry has been under intense scrutiny for this issue.

When media attention for the concerns on sexual harassment threatened the reputation of farms in the export markets in Europe—an explicit strategy of the NGOs pushing for better labour conditions (Jacobs et al., 2015, p. 2)—farms started to adopt policies to address these concerns. The issue of sexual harassment is also addressed in the new labour legislation (Employment Act, 2012, sec. 6). The CBA requires participating farms to formulate policy on sexual harassment (AEA & KPAWU, 2011, sec. 31). The formation of gender committees was already a requirement in the Code of Practice of the KFC in the year 2006 (Riungu, 2006). Finally, the Fairtrade Standard for Hired Labour includes the obligation to implement a policy counteracting "unwanted conduct of a sexual nature", which has to include "awareness raising on what constitutes sexual harassment" (Fairtrade International, 2014, para. 3.1.6). The grievance procedure of the farms should include specifically appointed women or women's committees for cases of sexual harassment (Fairtrade International, 2014, para. 3.5.27). Thus, both NGOs and industry-based organizations heralded special trainings and the installation of women's or gender committees as the solution to harassment within the farms (Jacobs et al., 2015, p. 10).

Ironically, the focus on sexual harassment in criticism of the industry thus induced measures that focus on this single issue and that do not profoundly reshape power relations within the farms. Even more ironically, the increased awareness of sexual harassment does not always mean that complaints are taken seriously: employees of several farms told me that these accusations could also be false, uttered to discredit a manager. Twisting the original reason for establishing gender committees, one farm employee even told me that these committees exist to counteract false accusations, not to prevent sexual harassment itself.

The exact role of these gender committees thus remains vague. The gender committee of some farms does not even regularly meet, and its only function is to receive and handle reports on cases of sexual harassment. I was told that, on other farms, the committee deals with "women's problems on the work floor" in general. An example of such a problem would be when a pregnant employee feels that her supervisor gives her a too heavy workload. Dolan et al. (2003, p. 28) described a gender committee in a Fairtrade-certified farm that had a broad agenda, including stimulating women to take part in workers' committees, (sexual) health education, and the opening of a crèche. However, I did not encounter a committee with such a broad and empowering agenda during my own fieldwork. KHRC (2012, p. 39) also noted that the committees mostly focussed on single issues. Moreover, as also noted by Wilshaw (2013, p. 86), in most farms, only women can become gender representatives. I therefore found that the general perception among workers was that these committees only deal with issues relating to women, not with relations *between* women and men.

The farms also organize trainings on gender relations. These trainings are meant to teach small groups of employees about "gender equity". When I asked Lucy what she had been taught when she attended such a training, she said she had learned that women also have responsibilities and that they should not only stay at home in the kitchen. Just like the gender committees, these trainings exclusively target women: men cannot participate, and they apparently are not expected to make any contribution to "gender equity".

Hence, the instalment of gender committees designated certain issues as "women's issues" instead of enabling a discussion on broader relations of inequality that are integral to the organization of labour within the farms. Gender committees might have been able to counteract overt cases of sexual harassment but they did not profoundly change the disadvantaged position of female (as well as male) general workers and their dependence on their jobs and their managers. The KHRC (2012, p. 39) therefore concluded that gender committees only seem to exist because it is required by standards.

The HR manager of Karibu Farm invited me to attend a meeting of the gender committee in January 2015. Observing this meeting shed a new light on the functions of this committee. The chair opened the meeting by reflecting on the past year, stating there had not been many problems. "We are together with the superiors." After the opening, each representative was given time to report on any problems within their departments. These discussions showed me that the gender committee did not deal with general or structural discrimination of women or men. Instead, it assisted individual employees with specific problems. The gender representative had the task of talking to the supervisor in case an employee reported an issue. If that did not solve the issue, the representative should report it in a committee meeting and to the management. However, when I heard the issues discussed during the gender committee meeting, it dawned on me that perhaps these committees do not even exist exclusively to protect individual workers. They are also instrumental in keeping labour relations peaceful. Some employees had, for example, come to a gender representative to complain about a colleague who, according to them, regularly pretended she was ill so that she could go on sick leave and leave the work to her colleagues. The gender representatives themselves, all women who had worked for the farm for several years now, were furthermore aggrieved by the behaviour of some of the more recent employees. They called them the "digital ones" (i.e. the young ones), who came with their "behaviour from outside" and who did not listen. "If a girl gets reprimanded for making a mistake, she will just talk back. She doesn't watch her mouth. Those young educated girls have no manners." The HR manager urged the committee members to send those whose behaviour was "too much" to her. If they were still on an initial contract, they would not be hired permanently, and even those on a permanent contract could ultimately be fired for using "abusive language".[26] Significantly, she reminded the representatives that they, together with the shop stewards, are the "eyes of the management". I remembered at that point that even union representatives had not told me that they were representing the employees. Instead, they said their task was to make sure that there were good, peaceful relationships within the farm. They perceived of themselves as an intermediary between management and employees. Thus, these committees, which on paper are supposed to empower the workers, are instrumental in enhancing labour control.

4.8 Ethnicity on the Work Floor: Which Language to Speak?

Unlike gendered categories, ethnic categories (such as "Kikuyu" or "Luo") do not play an official or openly acknowledged role in recruitment processes, divisions of labour, and labour control. Ethnicity is deliberately kept out of the farms. An utmost priority of farm management, and also of lobby organizations such as the KFC, is to avoid the image of being "tribalist", that is, of favouring certain ethnic groups over others. Accusations of tribalism, for instance, with regard to recruitment practices, seemed ridiculous in the eyes of the foreign general managers. As Jan told me during an informal conversation: "Why would I care about tribe?" The managers are reluctant to become part of local political struggles, including ethnical enmities, and they manage remarkably well to stay out of it. For example, flower farms with workers' compounds were not immediately affected by the post-election violence in early 2008 and even became a safe haven for some people living around the farms. Jan said that he emphasized that employees are judged not on who they are but on how they perform. He hoped people would understand that decisions are based on the wish to increase production and to be able to pay employees their salaries, and not on ethnic considerations. He had experienced that it is important to employ managers who are able to avoid the impression of tribalism. This helped in keeping labour relations friendly and peaceful.

Nevertheless, ethnic markers inevitably seeped into the farms. An example is vernacular languages. Kenya has two official national languages, English and Swahili. But the vernacular languages of different ethnic groups also remain widely spoken. Abdulaziz (1982) described how in urban areas, with a large socioeconomic stratification and a mix of people from different backgrounds, it has become hard to predict which language people would speak to each other, sometimes even for themselves. The farms in Naivasha attempted to regulate the choice of language. In this context, where there is a risk of ethnic tensions that exist in wider society destabilizing labour relations on the farms, the choice which language to use on the work floor is not only a practical matter but can potentially take on political salience. Management therefore encourages the use of the politically neutral language Swahili.

Swahili had already been the working language on the Naivasha farms and ranches in colonial times. The settlers did not favour the population to become too educated and to learn English and would speak a pidginized version of Swahili with their employees (Abdulaziz, 1982, p. 4). Later on, English became the official language in primary and secondary school. As a consequence, many of the current farm workers in Naivasha are able to speak (some) English. They can therefore communicate with foreign managers. Management uses English or Swahili when communicating changes in policies, job vacancies, a monthly schedule of annual leaves, and dates of union meetings and soccer matches of the company team via notice boards. Sheets of papers with safety regulations are present in both languages in most greenhouses and packhouses. However, just as in colonial times, Swahili remains the language used on the farms on a daily basis. Work meetings are held in Swahili, unless a foreign manager is present. Out of the 94 flower farm workers in the survey, 76 said they spoke primarily Swahili in their workplace, while another 13 said that both English and Swahili are the working languages.

Abdulaziz (1982, p. 9) observed that in Kenya, speaking English is associated with a higher class and a higher level of education than speaking Swahili. I observed a similar difference in language use by different socioeconomic groups. However, it is not always easy to decide which language would fit to which situation, regardless of an individual's proficiency in both languages. At a meeting on Karibu Farm held in Swahili, one member of the audience suddenly started to speak English. He was laughed at for his lack of confidence in Swahili and the audience also seemed to find him presumptuous in switching to English.

Only four of the survey respondents said that they regularly spoke another language than Swahili or English on the work floor. Nevertheless, I frequently heard vernacular languages during my visits to Karibu Farm. Whereas work-related conversations were usually held in Swahili, more informal conversations at the lunch table or the exchange of greetings while passing by regularly took place in another language. One of the two groups from Karibu Farm that participated in the listing and piling exercise, by coincidence consisted of three Kikuyu women. Significantly, they started to discuss in Kikuyu amongst themselves, until I asked them to switch to Swahili. Hence, vernacular languages were frequently spoken within this farm.

I also asked respondents in the total network analysis which language they regularly spoke with each of their colleagues working in the same greenhouse, including their supervisor and the scout.[27] Swahili was by far the most commonly used language. Notably, English was not mentioned once, confirming my impression that this language is primarily used among and with top managers. More surprisingly, only 11 of the team of 30 workers said to speak exclusively Swahili with colleagues, despite Swahili being the official working language. All others (occasionally) spoke a vernacular language with one or more colleagues. Figure 4.4 shows which languages, apart from Swahili, were spoken in this greenhouse.[28] Ties indicate either the assertion to speak a certain language with another person oneself or being named by someone else as an interlocutor in that language (or both). The graph shows that only one person never spoke a vernacular language with colleagues in her greenhouse. She told me no one else spoke her vernacular language Nandi. The graph furthermore shows that some, who came from a mixed ethnic background, even spoke several vernacular languages at work, with different colleagues.

In line with official farm policy, both the union representative in the greenhouse and Yvonne, the supervisor, stated that it is not appropriate to speak a language that other colleagues do not understand. On the other hand, another employee took the plurality of languages as something positive: she said she taught colleagues from other ethnic backgrounds some of her vernacular, and they taught her theirs. Furthermore, Yvonne was pragmatic in her use of languages. She would speak another language with

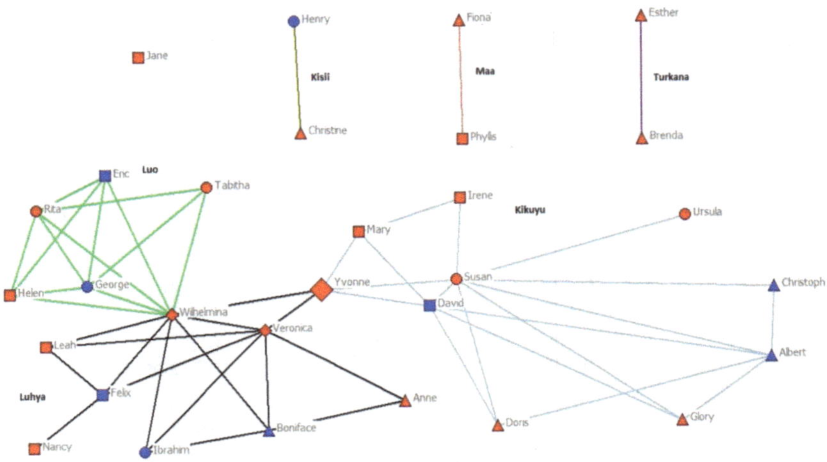

Fig. 4.4 The vernacular languages spoken by workers interviewed for the total network analysis, which they spoke in addition to the shared language Swahili. Developed using UCINET for Windows (Borgatti, Everett, & Freeman, 2002)

an employee if he or she would more readily understand her explanation in that language than in Swahili. For many employees, Swahili is their second or third language and they speak it imperfectly. One of the migrant workers, who got trained within Karibu Farm at the time of my visits, had arrived straight from a rural area close to Lake Victoria, after finishing secondary school. His supervisor had to explain the work to him in English, which he spoke well, whereas his knowledge of Swahili was limited. However, after a few months, his immediate colleagues commented that he had become a "local" (*mwenyeji*) and joked that he now was "bothering" them in Swahili all the time.

Thus, although Swahili is used as the everyday working language, the additional use of vernacular languages indicates that farms are not successful in completely eliminating ethnic markers from their farms. Farms with a workers' compound also allow employees to organize themselves along ethnic lines when it comes to non-political groups such as *vyama* and burial organizations. Moreover, I did hear occasional accusations of HR managers being ethnically biased. Nevertheless, ethnicity does not play any official role in farm policies. Ethnicized recruitment or an ethnicized division of labour is not a common strategy in labour control, unlike in some other global factories such as the factory in Malaysia described by Ong (1987, p. 158). Whereas managers use references to "Kenyan culture" to justify the gendered division of labour, they at the same time try to keep the politically more explosive category of ethnicity, with its potential for violence, out of the farms.

4.9 Conclusion: Disciplined Labour

This chapter has discussed the disciplined work processes, strict but varying rhythms of labour, and pervasive hierarchies that account for the "agro-industrial" nature of the Naivasha flower farms (Mintz, 1985). These labour conditions are partly shaped by the crop's "social ecology" (Besky, 2014). The perishability of the crop and its relative long life cycle call for a stable, experienced workforce. The fact that roses are not seasonal flowers also makes permanent employment more feasible for the farms (Gibbon & Riisgaard, 2014).

The increased provision of more permanent contracts is remarkable considering trends towards flexibilization and the casualization of labour in other global (agro-)industries, such as South African horticultural farms (Addison, 2014a; Bolt, 2013; Hall, Scoones, & Tsikata, 2017; Ortiz, 2002). The concept of "precarity" has recently been used to describe deteriorating labour conditions and increasing feelings of insecurity among employees worldwide. It draws attention to both social-economic conditions and ontological experiences. Although useful, Millar (2014) emphasized that in cities such as Rio de Janeiro, where she conducted her research, this "precarity" has for many residents always been the norm. In other words, it is not a new phenomenon. Moreover, I would argue that although they are perhaps exceptions, some workers in global industries experience more security in their jobs than previously. Hoffmann (2018) presented a case that shows a trend contradictory to increasing precarity, namely an increase in regularization and (job) security. This increased regularization only applied to some of the workers, depending on the type of job and—due to an ethnicized division of labour—the ethnicity of the worker. In the case of Naivasha, the general trend towards more permanent labour, stemming from the ecological characteristics of the crop combined with market demands for increasingly perfect flowers, has been more inclusive. Such processes challenge generalizing claims on developments in global capitalistic processes.

As the farms have an increasing interest in retaining the workers they already employed, they provide not only permanent contracts but also certain material incentives, such as considerable yearly increments when continuing to work for the same farm. The recent processes of standardization and unionization, induced by pressure from the markets, have meant a further improvement of labour conditions. Nevertheless, I have also discussed that these processes have not significantly altered the stark hierarchies within the flower industry.

The final two sections of the chapter have discussed how differences based on gender and ethnicity took on new meanings within the hierarchically organized, highly contested flower industry. For instance, culturally shaped gendered discourses have informed both the division of labour within the farms and (international) criticism of the industry. Attention to such "cultural" factors makes clear that the farms should not be analysed in isolation. The next chapter therefore shifts the attention to the workers' settlements, which are connected to the highly regulated farms but also stand in sharp contrast to them due to their seeming disorder.

Notes

1. It takes seven days after a flower or a shoot has been cut before a new shoot will come up. From that point onwards, it will take 48–60 days, depending on weather conditions and the variety, before the next flower can be harvested. This knowledge on the rhythm of the crop is important in the planning of the work. Supervisors can, for instance, plan for more red roses before Valentine's Day.
2. Rutherford (2001, p. 67) experienced the same contrast on the commercial farm in Zimbabwe where he conducted his research.
3. Whereas breeders develop new varieties, propagators produce seedlings. Some large farms breed and/or propagate themselves. Breeding and propagating requires more skill but is less labour-intensive than flower growing, and these firms employ only a small proportion of the entire Naivasha flower industry's workforce. I therefore do not discuss their production processes in detail in this book, even though they are crucial players within the cut flower value chain (Kazimierczuk et al., 2018).
4. The weekly day off was prescribed by both the Employment Act 2012 (sec. 27(2)) and the CBA (AEA & KPAWU, 2011, sec. 4).
5. There could also be minimum targets in the greenhouse. Karibu Farm had set a target of harvesting 1500 stems per day. However, this target was not coupled with a bonus system.

6. See the 94% of workers "at the base" mentioned by Friedemann-Sánchez (2009, p. 72) for the flower industry in Colombia.
7. Section 44 of the Employment Act 2012 makes it relatively easy for employers to dismiss workers, as dismissal is the ultimate form of disciplinary action. The KHRC (2012, p. 56) reported on cases in which employers had made up a reason for disciplinary action and dismissal, in order to not have to pay the workers the regular end-of-contract gratuity.
8. The CBA stipulates a regular probation period of two months (AEA & KPAWU, 2011, sec. 2). Legally, the probation period is set at a maximum of six months (Employment Act, 2012, sec. 42).
9. See Staelens et al. (2018) on similar dynamics within the Ethiopian flower industry.
10. KNA Nakuru, 15/1/Vol. 1, AR Co-operative Office, Naivasha Subdistrict, 2001.
11. Indeed, despite these improvements, I met a few former farm workers during the course of my fieldwork who had left their jobs because they felt the long-term exposure to pesticides affected their health. Interestingly, recent court cases show that a few former workers have successfully held their former employer liable for their health problems. A farm located close to Nairobi was ordered to pay damages to two former general workers in two separate cases. Their health problems were allegedly caused by exposure to chemicals and by standing in a cold environment (the packhouse) for many hours a day respectively (*Esther Wavinya Mulwa v Redland Roses Limited*, 2017; *Redlands Roses Limited v Elosy Wanja Ngai*, 2018).
12. The strict regulations did not always prevent the mismanagement or theft of premium money. A recent court case described how members of the Premium Committee of a farm in Naivasha had forged the (mandatory) signature of the general manager of the farm and had been able to steal millions of Kenyan Shillings. It took six months before the scheme was discovered (*Kenya Commercial Bank Limited v Shalimar Flowers Self Help Group*, 2018).
13. For a more elaborate discussion on the role of Fairtrade within power relations in the Kenyan flower industry, see Kuiper and Gemählich (2017).
14. A rival trade union, the Kenya Export Floriculture, Horticulture and Allied Workers Union (KEFHAU), has tried to establish itself. KPAWU disputed the registration of this new union (*David Benedict Omulama & 8 Others v Registrar of Trade Union & Another*, 2014). The large majority of the unionized flower farms were still associated with KPAWU at the time of my fieldwork.
15. Riisgaard (2009, p. 333) stated, based on interviews with a union official and two standard representatives, that only 3400 out of approximately 50,000 flower farm workers were unionized in the late 2000s. Lowthers (2018, p. 449) therefore concluded that unionization levels are extremely low in the

Naivasha flower industry. Yet, 3400 is a remarkably low number compared to my survey findings, as almost 50% of the flower farm workers indicated to be unionized. More research on levels of unionization is called for.

16. "Unionisable employees who are not members of the union shall be required to pay agency fees subject to gazettement by the Minister of Labour in accordance with Section 49 of the Labour Relations Act" (AEA & KPAWU, 2011, sec. 1). The union fee was 2% of one's gross salary for KPAWU plus 100 KES per month for COTU (KHRC, 2012, p. 30).
17. There are even occasional conflicts within the organization itself. A politically conspicuous example is the case in which the contract of a local union leader from Naivasha was terminated by the branch after he testified about the post-election violence at the International Criminal Court in The Hague (*Peter Otieno Ombude v Kenya Plantation & Agricultural Workers*, 2015).
18. Interview by Andreas Gemählich with the manager of a large rose farm, October 24, 2014.
19. Section 34 of the Employment Act 2012 stipulates that employers have to pay for medical care for their employees, insofar care is not provided for free and is not covered by any insurance scheme. However, this stipulation does not include the family members of the employees, and in that sense, farms such as Karibu Farm do more than is legally required.
20. A farm owner and the chief executive officer of the KFC in press (M. Mwangi, 2007; Riungu, 2006).
21. Interview by Andreas Gemählich with the managing director of a large rose farm, December 11, 2014.
22. Interview by Andreas Gemählich with the manager of a large rose farm, October 24, 2014.
23. Interview by Andreas Gemählich with the manager of a rose-breeding farm, November 22, 2014.
24. No one seemed to consider this naturalized division of labour to be a violation of Section 5(3)(a) of the Employment Act 2012, which explicitly banned any discrimination on the basis of sex in matters of recruitment and training.
25. Interview by Andreas Gemählich with the manager of a large rose farm, October 24, 2014.
26. Section 44 of the Employment Act 2012 confirms this statement of the HR manager.
27. I interviewed all 30 workers in one greenhouse of Karibu Farm for a total network analysis. I chose this specific greenhouse because I had spent two full days there previously for observation, and thus most respondents already knew me at the time of the interview. The interviews aimed to assess the strength and the type of connections between the workers. I analysed these interview data with the help of Microsoft Excel 2013 and UCINET 6 (Borgatti et al., 2002).

28. The red nodes represent female workers and the blue nodes male workers. The shape of the nodes indicates the area (out of three) in the greenhouse where a worker was based at the time of the interviews.

References

Abdulaziz, M. H. (1982). Patterns of language acquisition and use in Kenya: Rural-urban differences. *International Journal of the Sociology of Language, 1982*(34), 95–120. https://doi.org/10.1515/ijsl.1982.34.95

Addison, L. (2014a). Delegated despotism: Frontiers of agrarian labour on a South African border farm. *Journal of Agrarian Change, 14*(2), 286–304. https://doi.org/10.1111/joac.12062

Addison, L. (2014b). The sexual economy, gender relations and narratives of infant death on a tomato farm in Northern South Africa. *Journal of Agrarian Change, 14*(1), 74–93.

AEA, & KPAWU. (2011). Collective Bargaining Agreement between the Agricultural Employers' Association and the Kenya Plantation and Agricultural Workers' Union 2011–2013. Retrieved from http://www.agriemp.co.ke/downloads/cbas/flower-growers-cba

Alila, P. O., & Obado, P. O. (1990). *Co-operative credit: The Kenyan SACCOs in a historical and development perspective* (Working Paper No. 474). Nairobi: Institute for Development Studies.

Anker, R., & Anker, M. (2014). *Living wage for Kenya with focus on fresh flower farm area near Lake Naivasha.* Retrieved from http://www.fairtrade.net/fileadmin/user_upload/content/2009/resources/LivingWageReport_Kenya.pdf

Besky, S. (2014). *The Darjeeling distinction: Labor and justice on fair trade tea plantations in India.* Berkeley: University of California Press.

Bolt, M. (2013). Producing permanence: Employment, domesticity and the flexible future on a South African border farm. *Economy and Society, 42*(2), 197–225. https://doi.org/10.1080/03085147.2012.733606

Borgatti, S., Everett, M., & Freeman, L. (2002). *UCINET 6 for Windows: Software for social network analysis.* Harvard, MA: Analytic Technologies.

Braverman, H. (1998). *Labor and monopoly capital: The degradation of work in the twentieth century* (25th anniversary ed.). New York: Monthly Review Press.

Clayton, A., & Savage, D. C. (1974). *Government and labour in Kenya 1895–1963.* London: Frank Cass.

David Benedict Omulama & 8 Others v Registrar of Trade Union & Another (Industrial Court of Kenya) (2014). Retrieved from http://kenyalaw.org/caselaw/cases/view/94824/

Dolan, C. S., Opondo, M., & Smith, S. (2003). *Gender, rights and participation in the Kenya cut flower industry* (NRI Report No. 2768). Chatham, UK: NRI.

Du Toit, A. (1993). The micro-politics of paternalism: The discourses of management and resistance on South African fruit and wine farms. *Journal of Southern African Studies, 19*(2), 314–336.

Elson, D., & Pearson, R. (1984). The subordination of women and the internationalisation of factory production. In K. Young, C. Wolkowitz, & R. McCullagh (Eds.), *Of marriage and the market: Women's subordination internationally and its lessons* (2nd ed., pp. 18–40). London: Routledge & Kegan Paul.

Employment Act. (2012). Retrieved from http://www.kenyalaw.org/lex//actview.xql?actid=No.%2011%20of%202007

Esther Wavinya Mulwa v Redland Roses Limited (High Court of Kenya at Milimani) (2017). Retrieved from http://kenyalaw.org/caselaw/cases/view/133019/

Fairtrade International. (2014). Fairtrade Standard for Hired Labour. Version 15.01.2014_v1.0. Fairtrade International. Retrieved from https://www.fairtrade.net/fileadmin/user_upload/content/2009/standards/documents/HL_EN.pdf

Fernández-Kelly, M. (1983). *For we are sold, I and my people: Women and industry in Mexico's frontier*. Albany: State University of New York Press.

Friedemann-Sánchez, G. (2009). *Assembling flowers and cultivating homes: Labor and gender in Colombia* (1st Paperback ed.). Lanham, MD: Lexington Books.

Gaarlandt, E. (2013). Bloeiend Afrika [Blossoming Africa]. *OneWorld Dossier 6*.

Gibbon, P., & Riisgaard, L. (2014). A new system of labour management in African large-scale agriculture? *Journal of Agrarian Change, 14*(1), 94–128. https://doi.org/10.1111/joac.12043

Hall, R., Scoones, I., & Tsikata, D. (2017). Plantations, outgrowers and commercial farming in Africa: Agricultural commercialisation and implications for agrarian change. *The Journal of Peasant Studies, 44*(3), 515–537. https://doi.org/10.1080/03066150.2016.1263187

Happ, J. (2016). *Auswirkungen der Fairtrade-Zertifizierung auf den afrikanischen Blumenanbau. Das Beispiel Naivasha, Kenia [Effects of Fairtrade-certification on the African flower production: The example of Naivasha, Kenya]* (Vol. 4). Norderstedt: Books on Demand.

Heald, S. (1991). Tobacco, time and the household economy in two Kenyan societies: The Teso and the Kuria. *Comparative Studies in Society and History, 33*(1), 130–157.

Henry Isaiah Onjelo v Maridadi Flowers Limited (Employment and Labour Relations Court of Kenya at Nakuru) (2015). Retrieved from http://kenyalaw.org/caselaw/cases/view/116644

Hivos. (n.d.). Power of the fair trade flower. Retrieved January 24, 2014, from http://www.powerofthefairtradeflower.nl/

Hoffmann, M. P. (2018). From casual to permanent work: Maoist unionists and the regularization of contract labor in the industries of Western Nepal. In C. Hann & J. P. Parry (Eds.), *Industrial labor on the margins of capitalism: Precarity, class, and the neoliberal subject* (pp. 336–354). New York: Berghahn.

Jacobs, S., Brahic, B., & Olaiya, M. M. (2015). Sexual harassment in an East African agribusiness supply chain. *The Economic and Labour Relations Review, 26*(3), 393–410.

Kazimierczuk, A., Kamau, P., Kinuthia, B., & Mukoko, C. (2018). *Never a rose without a prick: (Dutch) multinational companies and productive employment in the Kenyan flower sector* (ASC Working Paper No. 142). Leiden: African Studies Centre.

Kenya Commercial Bank Limited v Shalimar Flowers Self Help Group (Court of Appeal at Nyeri) (2018). Retrieved from http://kenyalaw.org/caselaw/cases/view/163287/

KHRC. (2012). *Wilting in bloom: The irony of women labour rights in the cut-flower sector in Kenya*. Nairobi: KHRC.

Kloß, S. T. (2017). Sexual(ized) harassment and ethnographic fieldwork: A silenced aspect of social research. *Ethnography, 18*(3), 396–414. https://doi.org/10.1177/1466138116641958

Kuiper, G., & Gemählich, A. (2017). Sustainability and depoliticisation: Certifications in the cut-flower industry at Lake Naivasha, Kenya. *Africa Spectrum, 52*(3), 31–53.

Leave workers alone, Atwoli tells lobbies. (2004, August 31). *Daily Nation*, p. 17.

Lowthers, M. (2018). On institutionalized sexual economies: Employment sex, transactional sex, and sex work in Kenya's cut flower industry. *Signs: Journal of Women in Culture and Society, 43*(2), 449–472. https://doi.org/10.1086/693767

Millar, K. (2014). The precarious present: Wageless labor and disrupted life in Rio de Janeiro, Brazil. *Cultural Anthropology, 29*(1), 32–53. https://doi.org/10.14506/ca29.1.04

Mintz, S. W. (1985). *Sweetness and power: The place of sugar in modern history*. New York: Viking.

Moberg, M. (1996). Myths that divide: Immigrant labor and class segmentation in the Belizean banana industry. *American Ethnologist, 23*(2), 311–330.

Mwangi, M. (2007, August 18). Naivasha Town: Where poverty and affluence live side-by-side. *Daily Nation*, p. 26.

Mwangi, N. (2019). 'Good that you are one of us': Positionality and reciprocity in conducting fieldwork in Kenya's flower industry. In L. Johnstone (Ed.), *The politics of conducting research in Africa* (pp. 13–33). Cham: Springer International Publishing.

Nelson, V., Martin, A., & Ewert, J. (2007). The impacts of codes of practice on worker livelihoods: Empirical evidence from the South African wine and Kenyan cut flower industries. *Journal of Corporate Citizenship, 28*, 61–72.

Okely, J. (2012). *Anthropological practice: Fieldwork and the ethnographic method*. London: Berg.

Omosa, M., Kimani, M., & Njiru, R. (2006). The social impact of codes of practice in the cut flower industry in Kenya. Natural Resources Institute and DFID. Retrieved from http://projects.nri.org/nret/final_kenya_main_report.pdf

Ong, A. (1987). *Spirits of resistance and capitalist discipline: Factory women in Malaysia*. Albany: State University of New York Press.

Orr, J. E. (1996). *Talking about machines: An ethnography of a modern job*. Ithaca, NY: ILR Press.

Ortiz, S. (2002). Laboring in the factories and in the fields. *Annual Review of Anthropology, 31*(1), 395–417. https://doi.org/10.1146/annurev.anthro.31.031902.161108

Parry, J. P. (1999). Lords of labour: Working and shirking in Bhilai. *Contributions to Indian Sociology, 33*(1–2), 107–140. https://doi.org/10.1177/006996679903300107

Parry, J. P. (2012). Industrial work. In J. G. Carrier (Ed.), *A handbook of economic anthropology* (2nd ed., pp. 145–165). Cheltenham: Edward Elgar Publishing.

Patrick Chebos v Stokman Rozen Kenya Limited (Employment and Labour Relations Court of Kenya at Nairobi) (2016). Retrieved from http://kenyalaw.org/caselaw/cases/view/125507

Peter Otieno Ombude v Kenya Plantation & Agricultural Workers (Employment and Labour Relations Court at Nairobi) (2015). Retrieved from http://kenyalaw.org/caselaw/cases/view/111961

Pollert, A. (1981). *Girls, wives, factory lives*. London: The Macmillan Press Ltd.

Redlands Roses Limited v Elosy Wanja Ngai (High Court of Kenya at Nairobi) (2018). Retrieved from http://kenyalaw.org/caselaw/cases/view/152624/

Riisgaard, L. (2009). Global value chains, labor organization and private social standards: Lessons from East African cut flower industries. *World Development, 37*(2), 326–340. https://doi.org/10.1016/j.worlddev.2008.03.003

Riisgaard, L., & Gibbon, P. (2014). Labour management on contemporary Kenyan cut flower farms: Foundations of an industrial-civic compromise. *Journal of Agrarian Change, 14*(2), 260–285. https://doi.org/10.1111/joac.12064

Riungu, C. (2006, September 18). Flower farms shed bad image. *The East African*, p. VII.

Roy, D. (1960). 'Banana time': Job satisfaction and informal interaction. *Human Organization, 18*(4), 158–168.

Rutherford, B. (2001). *Working on the margins: Black workers, white farmers in postcolonial Zimbabwe*. London: Zed Books.

Salzinger, L. (2003). *Genders in production: Making workers in Mexico's global factories*. Berkeley: University of California Press.

Samarasinghe, V. (1993). Puppets on a string: Women's wage work and empowerment among female tea plantation workers of Sri Lanka. *The Journal of Developing Areas, 27*(3), 329–340.

Spittler, G. (2009). Contesting the Great Transformation: Work in comparative perspective. In C. Hann & K. Hart (Eds.), *Market and society: The Great Transformation today* (pp. 160–174). Cambridge: Cambridge University Press.

Staelens, L., Desiere, S., Louche, C., & D'Haese, M. (2018). Predicting job satisfaction and workers' intentions to leave at the bottom of the high value agricultural chain: Evidence from the Ethiopian cut flower industry. *The International*

Journal of Human Resource Management, 29(9), 1609–1635. https://doi.org/10.1080/09585192.2016.1253032

Thomas, R. J. (1985). *Citizenship, gender, and work: Social organization of industrial agriculture*. Berkeley: University of California Press.

Thompson, E. P. (1967). Time, work-discipline, and industrial capitalism. *Past & Present, 38*, 56–97.

Whitaker, M., & Kolavalli, S. (2006). Floriculture in Kenya. In V. Chandra (Ed.), *Technology, adaptation, and exports: How some developing countries got it right* (pp. 335–367). Washington, DC: The World Bank.

Wilshaw, R. (Ed.). (2013). *Exploring the links between international business and poverty reduction: Bouquets and beans from Kenya*. Oxfam. Retrieved from https://www.oxfam.org/sites/www.oxfam.org/files/rr-exploring-links-ipl-poverty-footprint-090513-en.pdf

Wright, M. W. (2006). *Disposable women and other myths of global capitalism*. New York: Routledge.

CHAPTER 5

Workers' Settlements: In Search of Order

Suddenly the world was dropped on Kasarani.
—*The first chief of Kasarani*

This chapter describes the living environment of the migrant workers in Naivasha. The tumultuous, dense, dirty settlements with a mixture of brick, wooden, and wattle-and-daub houses stand in stark contrast to the luscious green areas around tourist resorts and remaining ranches, and the highly regulated, technical, and agro-industrial environment of the flower farms. These different areas are usually only separated from each other by a single fence or by the Moi Lake Road. This vicinity makes the contrast between the farms and the settlements even more noticeable. It therefore does not come as a surprise that the informality and transiency of the settlements have played a major role in criticism of the flower industry (Anker & Anker, 2014; M. Mwangi, 2007). The question of who is responsible for the living conditions of the flower farm workers is highly contested.

Most flower farm workers are not housed by their employer, in contrast to the situation on the Naivasha ranches in colonial times and on contemporary agro-industrial enterprises elsewhere (Besky, 2014; Bolt, 2013; Kanogo, 1987). Until the 1990s, some flower farms provided accommodation in makeshift labour camps. When regulations for workers' housing became more stringent, partly due to requirements set by certification schemes such as Fairtrade, some of these *kambi* were closed. As a receiving

G. Kuiper, *Agro-industrial Labour in Kenya*,
https://doi.org/10.1007/978-3-030-18046-1_5

manager of Sharma Farm explained, maintaining and especially improving and constructing accommodation were simply too costly. Only a handful of farms continue to provide on-farm housing to general workers (assistant chief of Olkaria Sublocation, 2016; Fairtrade International, 2014; Gibbon & Riisgaard, 2014; Happ, 2016). I, therefore, do not discuss these labour compounds in detail. Instead, I focus on the settlements where the majority of the workers reside, together with those who are not employed in horticulture.

The settlements have mostly been described in generalizing terms and from the point of view of those who would like to see an "order" in these settlements. For instance, in a report in a Dutch magazine on development aid, the settlement Karagita was labelled a "slum". The author wrote that this settlement was "populated with harvesters, cutters, bundlers and packers". She thus made an explicit connection between the existence of "slums" and the flower industry (Gaarlandt, 2013, p. 10; my translation from Dutch). Local government officials are even more dismissive about these settlements and associate them with crime. This is illustrated by the following excerpt from minutes of a security meeting, where chiefs and representatives of flower farms and hotels were present: "It was also noted that criminal [*sic*] reside in those slums as houses and life is very cheap. Also it is very easy for them to intermingle with the crowd as no one is concerned with what others are doing."[1] Scientific articles have mostly simply not mentioned the settlements, or at most in general terms: "The population has increased tremendously resulting in a proliferation of unplanned settlements around the lake. These settlements are without basic amenities such as water, sanitation and waste disposal programmes" (Becht, Odada, & Higgins, 2005, p. 278). Few researchers have looked into the constitution of the perceived disorder.

This chapter investigates how and why these settlements took the shape they currently have. As argued by Appadurai (2013, p. 252), the daily order (or a lack of order) in a certain locality is not a given but is produced by social actors. In other words, daily life in the Naivasha settlements has been actively produced through imaginative actions, despite the seeming disorder of these places. The choices of residents, including the migrant workers, have influenced the settlements' configuration and the perceived disorder. This chapter therefore asks how the residents inhabit these places.

Secondly, the choices of flower farms and government officials have also shaped the settlements. As argued by Cooper (1983, p. 25), the way workers are accommodated is not a coincidence but relates to questions of labour control and to the integration of workers in a larger social order. This chapter therefore also examines how the settlements have been governed.

Finally, the development of the Naivasha settlements is also embedded in the wider context of changing land tenure relations after Kenya gained independence. The chapter starts with an introduction to this historical context before describing the development of the eight workers' settlements around Lake Naivasha in more detail.

5.1 The Establishment of Settlements in Kenya

The Kenyan state has played a central role in the redistribution of land in the former White Highlands. The government supposed that the existing large estates were more productive than smaller holdings and attempted to keep them intact. Some of the large estates were therefore sold as a whole to members of the African (political) elite. However, land was also redistributed to smallholders—both commercial farmers and subsistence farmers—through settlement schemes, such as the well-known Million Acre Scheme. Settlers for these farms were selected by state officials and were aided with loans to pay for their plot. The aim of these schemes was to enable smallholder families to be self-subsistent. In addition to the official schemes, the government stimulated the formation of private land-buying companies, which were sometimes fostered by individual politicians. Ordinary citizens could purchase shares in such a company and could thus acquire a plot together. Naivasha has largely been left out of these politically stirred redistribution efforts. There was no official settlement scheme in the vicinity of Lake Naivasha, the closest one being the scheme at the Kinangop Plateau. As described in Sect. 2.2, many of the large estates remained intact in the period after independence, even when they were taken over by new owners. Nevertheless, a few private cooperative groups acquired relatively small plots in the Naivasha area and settled there (Boone, 2012, pp. 78–82; Bradshaw, 1990; Chambers, 1969, pp. 34–39; Odingo, 1971, pp. 187–192).

There are many such privately developed settlements in Kenya, but little has been written about them. Some literature exists on "squatter settlements" worldwide (Lloyd, 1979). Squatter settlements also developed in urban areas in Kenya since the 1940s. Migrant workers in the city were expected to return to their families in the reserves. Neither employers nor the government invested sufficiently in housing for them. They ended up in settlements on squatted land, such as the current Nairobi neighbourhoods Mathare and Kibera (Obudho & Aduwo, 1989). Yet, as pointed out by Rapoport (1988), some settlements are not squatted but erected on land that is legally owned by the constructors. Also, after Kenya gained independence, the government mainly put efforts into constructing housing for middle-income groups, leaving the construction of housing of low-income groups to the private sector (Obudho & Aduwo, 1989). Consequently, settlements emerged on plots of land-buying companies and on plots of individual owners who constructed rental housing.

There is a lack of proper terminology to describe these settlements. They are not squatter settlements, as they are constructed on legally owned or accessed land. Terms such as "slums" or "informal settlements" convey the impression that the settlements are of a makeshift and temporary nature, which they are not. Moreover, as argued by Little (2014) for the term "informal sector", the use of such terms disguises linkages to "formal" economic sectors and, in the Naivasha case, to the flower farms and their workers' compounds (or the frequent absence thereof). I also did not find an appropriate Swahili term to refer to these settlements. In interviews I conducted in Naivasha and in newspaper articles, they were referred to in generic terms, such as *eneo* (area) or *mtaa* (neighbourhood or location) (see M. Mwangi, 2008). An alternative could be the term "spontaneous settlements", introduced by the architect Rapoport (1988). Yet he also points at a problem with this term: even if these areas were not planned for by the government, they are still an outcome of purposeful choices that shaped the physical environment. The difficulties in finding a proper term to describe these areas—which I for lack of a better alternative refer to as "workers' settlements"—reflect the lack of research on the topic.

The position of tenants in such settlements has received even less attention, even though their arrival overturned existing arrangements on plots owned by land-buying companies. The formal settlement schemes were intended to benefit those ethnic groups that had originally been displaced when the European settlers arrived. Anderson and Lochery (2008, p. 335) have pointed out that in practice, land was sold according to the willing-buyer-willing-seller principle. The intended ethnic homogeneous communities for these formal schemes did not come into being. This seems to have been different from the private land-buying companies. According to Odingo (1971, p. 212), these were also deliberately organized along ethnic lines, in order to create homogeneous groups in specific territories. Kanogo (1987, p. 175) asserted that these groups in practice often consisted exclusively of Kikuyu. This seems to also have been the case with at least two of the companies that settled at Lake Naivasha, Karagita (EA) Ltd. and Kihoto Farmers Company Ltd.[2] The settlements that emerged on the companies' plots thus initially were fairly homogeneous, until migrant workers started to arrive in great numbers.

5.2 The Eight Naivasha Workers' Settlements

With the arrival of migrant workers and the construction of rental housing to accommodate them, the patchworks of small private plots turned into dense residential areas. Being in the settlements is a radically different experience from being inside the farms. They form a chaotic, loud, dense, dusty, and by times smelly environment, with little vegetation. The dusty roads are scattered with potholes, and at various spots, waste water running off from plots have carved out small trenches, cutting through the roads.[3] The roads have ditches next to them filled with plastic bags and other dirt. During the day, the settlements are quiet. Whenever I went there in the morning or early afternoon, I would mainly find toddlers playing outside, small livestock dwelling on the streets, and a few men hanging around bars and *chang'aa* selling points. The tranquillity disappears in the late afternoon when farm workers return from work and children from school. The settlements then turn into bustling places. A lot of small-scale economic activity is taking place, especially along the road close to the bus drop-off points, where streams of workers are passing by on their way home.

The settlements all appear similar at first sight. The large majority of the residents are tenants of one-room apartments with shared bathrooms (World Bank, 2014). Some of these blocks of houses are makeshift, constructed with mud, wood, or iron sheets, or a combination thereof. Recently, many of these makeshift constructions have been replaced with permanent brick housing of better quality. Virtually all of the housing has roofs of corrugated iron sheets. Most of the houses also have a, sometimes dilapidated, cemented floor. Another shared characteristic is that houses in the settlements are cramped together, which increases the danger of fire and the spread of diseases such as cholera ("100 Families Homeless", 2009; Kung'u & Rogoncho, 1988; M. Mwangi, 2008). Nevertheless, I found that living conditions vary along the lake. The different settlements also have different relations to the flower industry. To show this variation, I introduce all eight settlements located close to Lake Naivasha.[4] I elaborate in most detail on Karagita and Kasarani, the two settlements where I conducted interviews for the survey and where I consequently spent most time.

5.2.1 *Karagita*

Karagita, the oldest and most infamous settlement, is situated on the south-eastern side of the lake at a ten-kilometre distance from Naivasha Town. The area around Karagita used to be called "Poverty Bay". The land had been divided into relatively small plots of 10–20 acres in the 1930s. These plots were sold to impoverished European farmers. In 1966, one of these farmers sold his plot on to Karagita (EA) Ltd., a land-buying company consisting of a group of Africans from Nairobi. The plot previously had been used for the cultivation of wheat and had only contained one permanent building, the owners' house. This house was left standing and was later turned into a community dispensary. Members of the company constructed wattle-and-daub houses and took up residence there from 1972 onwards. The European-owned farms in the plot's immediate environment mainly cultivated the fodder crop lucerne and did not provide much employment. The main economic activity for Karagita's early inhabitants was therefore informal or even illegal small businesses in *chang'aa*, fish, and firewood. The economic situation changed when the first vegetable and flower farms started up at South Lake. Although most of the members of Karagita (EA) Ltd. were not eager to work for the new farms themselves, the arrival of migrant workers opened up new business opportunities for them. The plot owners started to make some money by constructing rows of one-room shacks to rent out. The living conditions initially remained poor. Allegedly, the area became so crowded that some rooms were even rented out doubly, with a day and a night shift (assistant chief of Olkaria Sublocation, 2016; S. Higgins, 2015; P. Mburu, member of the land-buying company Karagita (EA) Ltd., interview on October 25, 2014).

Karagita already had an estimated 10,000 inhabitants by the year 1990. The landowners started to construct (brick) housing of better quality, which they could rent out for higher prices, and living conditions improved slowly. The residential area also expanded to plots north and south of the original plot, and into Mirera-Suswa cooperative farm towards the east. The original 20-acre plot was officially subdivided into 50 by 100-metre plots only in the early 1990s. These smaller plots were then sold off to both inhabitants of Karagita and outside investors (P. Mburu, 2014).[5] By 2009, Karagita, together with its neighbouring settlements—all part of Mirera Sublocation—had 39,209 inhabitants and was the largest workers' settlement in the area (KNBS, 2010).

Most of the current infrastructure in Karagita was installed only after the first migrant workers had arrived. One example is access to water. Initially, the only source of water was the lake, and the inhabitants had to pay a small amount of money to the European landowners living at the lake to pass their land to fetch water. The earliest reference to a borehole in Karagita that I could find dates back to the year 1991. Furthermore, even though other water projects have been implemented since then, accessing good, fluoride-free drinking water remains a challenge.[6] Proper sewerage and drainage also continue to be lacking. Nevertheless, other infrastructure has been in place for some time. The first primary school in Karagita area, Mirera Primary School, opened around 1980. In the year 2011, this was the primary school with the largest number of children (376) sitting for their final exams in the whole of Kenya, which illustrates how populous the area had become by then. Karagita's dispensary opened in 1991 in the former European owner's house. It was partly paid for by the government while the residents contributed through a *harambee*, a fundraising event. In recent years, also several private schools, nurseries, and clinics were established. The maintenance of roads in the settlement improved and the area became cleaner, due to a greater involvement of the local government. In the early 2000s, Mirera (including Karagita) became an official sublocation, part of the location Hell's Gate, and received its own chief and a local government office. Also, corporate actors, such as flower farms and electricity company KenGen, have initiated community projects at South Lake, including in Karagita (Kimani, 2011; Masibo, 2005; P. Mburu, 2014; "MP Thanks State", 1991).[7]

Notably, development in Karagita has been hampered by the many wrangles and disputes that have plagued the land-buying company that established the settlement. Already in 1984, there was a dispute over possible fraud with company money, and there was a conflict in 1995 about the subdivision of the first plot that the company had acquired in Naivasha. A particularly destructive case was the conflict over ownership of a neighbouring plot, which had been purchased by Karagita (EA) Ltd. later on but which was also claimed by another land-buying company. This case even led to the forced eviction of the hundreds of people staying on that plot and the demolition of housing after the court case had been concluded in favour of Karagita (EA) Ltd. in 2002. Only the mosque that had been constructed there was left standing. Even after this eviction, the case was not settled conclusively due to appeals and dragged on for many years (*Grace Wangui Mburu & another v Peter Mburu Nguri & 4 others*, 2015,

"Mystery Surrounds Fate", 1984, "Villagers Ordered", 2002).[8] The effects of this long-term insecurity over the ownership of this plot are also visible in the physical layout of the area: it contains relatively few buildings when compared to other Karagita neighbourhoods.

5.2.2 *Trading Centres DCK/Sulmac and Kongoni*

Around the same time that the first members of the land-buying company moved to Karagita, the first flower farm Dansk Chrysantemum Kulter (DCK) opened up some kilometres further along Moi South Lake Road. There have been workers' camps and some shops on and close to this farm since the early 1970s, but it took a long time before an official trading centre was established. The government started negotiations over the acquisition of a parcel of land from DCK Farm for the purpose of opening a trading centre in 1975. These negotiations continued until at least 1991. By the time I conducted fieldwork, an official trading centre—variably known as DCK and Sulmac—had been established. It consisted of a few dusty streets lined with shops, *hoteli*, and an ATM. There were only a few houses outside of farm compounds in this area. The main customers for the businesses in the trading centre were the inhabitants of the nearby Sharma Farm compound (assistant chief of Olkaria Sublocation, 2016).[9]

Also, the settlement Kongoni seems to have been waiting for the official status of trading centre for years. It had a police station since at least 1971 and thus emerged before the flower industry arrived in Naivasha. Nevertheless, it still features as only a "proposed" trading centre on a map from 1986.[10] It is located at the end of the tarmac road, a bit further from Naivasha Town then the largest flower farm, Oserian. Oserian has a workers' compound with shops and schools on-site, and like the DCK/Sulmac trading centre, Kongoni has remained small until the present day.

5.2.3 *Kihoto*

Kihoto, the populous settlement located next to Naivasha Town, has an infamous reputation comparable to that of Karagita. And just as Karagita, Kihoto also has had its share of disputes over the subdivision of the land.[11] According to Flora's husband James, Kihoto originally had been a cooperative farm, which was subdivided among the 30 Kikuyu shareholders. They all claimed a strip of land stretching towards the lake. With receding lake levels, these long strips became even longer over the years and more land was occupied, especially after the owners started to subdivide their strips of land and construct rental housing. I noticed during visits to Kihoto that the plot owners usually resided in older, sometimes wooden, more spacious houses on one side of a plot, whereas they constructed a row of brick one-room apartments and shops to rent out in another corner.

There is no commercial cultivation going on within the settlement, but the riparian land is illegally in use for small-scale farming. A flower farm was established at a strip of land immediately north of Kihoto in 1996. However, this farm had to close down in 2011 because of a land dispute. After a court order to demolish all permanent structures, the plot was ransacked by workers who had lost their jobs. Within two hours, nothing was left except for a few office buildings. The plot was left fallow and was later illegally occupied by livestock owners, who used it as a grazing area for their goats (*Geoffrey Muhoro v Lake Flowers Limited*, 2011; World Bank, 2014, p. 42). There currently are no flower farms in the direct vicinity of Kihoto, but many residents either work on a farm in the Flower Business Park close to Naivasha Town or commute to farms located at South Lake with staff buses.

5.2.4 *Kamere and Kwa Muhia*

The plot of another settlement, Kamere, located on the south-western side of the lake, was originally not owned by a land-buying company or a cooperative but by an individual. The plot of 32 acres in total was the property of a former attorney-general, Mr. Kamere, since at least 1983. In subsequent years, he subdivided and sold parts of his plot, on which a settlement developed haphazardly. The local government was not involved in this process and little infrastructure was put up in the area (Lembcke, 2015, p. 5; World Bank, 2014, p. 43).[12] When Mr. Kamere later on made a request to change the use of a neighbouring plot that also belonged to him, he was reprimanded by the town council for the way Kamere settlement had developed: "This has culminated in shanty type residential/shopping area in an otherwise high class agricultural area."[13] To make matters worse, the settlement was built on a steep hill close to the lake, and the lack of a proper sewerage or drainage system has led to problems during rainy seasons (World Bank, 2014, p. 43).[14] The settlement, with an estimated 24,000 inhabitants in the year 2015, has also been singled out as a main source of pollution of the lake (Gitonga, 2015). The settlement is nevertheless attractive to migrant workers, not only because of the presence of flower farms in its vicinity but also because it is located next to one of the few official fish landing beaches at the lake and next to a new office and staff compound of electricity company KenGen. The settlement also has a lively market along the Moi Lake Road.

As explained by Hanna Kunas in her unpublished master's thesis, the relatively small, neighbouring settlement Kwa Muhia has a similar background as Kamere. The land used to belong to a British settler, who sold it to Mr. Muhia Thuku after independence. Thuku subdivided and sold the land in parts in the early 1990s. The new owners then built rental houses on it and a small settlement came into being. The settlement is surrounded by flower farms, and the main office of Kenya Plantation and Agricultural Workers Union's (KPAWU's) Naivasha branch is located here.

5.2.5 *Kasarani*

Kasarani, which is officially called Tarabete, is located on the north-western side of Lake Naivasha, about 30 kilometres from Naivasha Town. This settlement is an exception in the sense that it was officially founded by the government in 1987. Before that, people living at North Lake mainly resided on ranches, either as employees or squatters on a European-owned ranch or, later on, as members of land-buying cooperatives which had purchased a ranch. There were originally two official trading centres in the area (Loldia and Tarabete), but both were also situated on a farm. In 1983, there were nine farms in the area with an estimated population of 3000 people. One of these farms was called Tarabete (sometimes spelled as Tarambete). This 6000-acre farm cultivated pyrethrum and held cattle and sheep. It had originally belonged to a British settler. In the 1960s, it was taken over by the Nairobi-based company Tarabete Farmers. The farm was mismanaged and understocked and was not performing well for years. In the mid-1980s, it was decided to subdivide the farm among its 182 Kikuyu members and some of these, now private, small-scale farmers continue to farm on the same plots until today. A 15-acre plot—an area of fallow land where farm residents used to go to drink *chang'aa* and play football[15]—was set aside and given to the town council to create a new trading centre in the area. The council advertised the plots in 1987. Anyone who had stayed in Naivasha for at least five years and was "financially capable" of developing a plot could be given one. The first house was built in 1988. The first inhabitants were mainly (children of) employees of the ranches in the area. It was only after a few horticultural farms were established at North Lake in the early 1990s that new migrant workers started to come to this settlement in sizable numbers. Just as plot owners in Karagita had done, those who had acquired a plot in Kasarani previously seized new economic possibilities by constructing one-room apartments to rent out ("Chotara Threatens", 1983; "Failure of Meeting", 1983; D. Gitahi, 2015; A. Sora, the first chief of Tarambete Sublocation, interview on January 22, 2015).[16]

Kasarani/Tarabete became an official sublocation (part of Malewa Location) in 1990 and has had a chief's office and an administrative police station since then (A. Sora, 2015). In addition, one of the flower farms constructed a workers' compound within the settlement (see Fig. 5.1). The houses on the compound were initially made of wood but, according

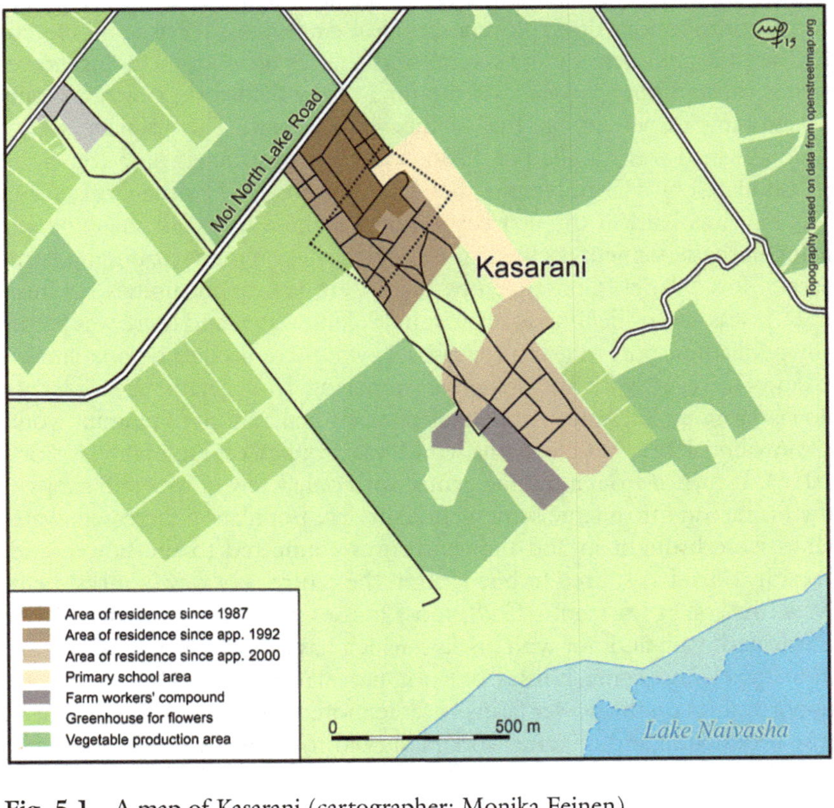

Fig. 5.1 A map of Kasarani (cartographer: Monika Feinen)

to an employee of this farm, were replaced with brick two-room apartments in order to comply with the Fairtrade standard. Overall, Tarabete Sublocation, which with regard to population primarily comprises the settlement Kasarani and the flower farm *kambi*, had 8699 inhabitants in the year 2009 (KNBS, 2010).

Kasarani developed in a more organized way than the other Naivasha settlements, most notably Karagita and Kihoto. To start with, the government intended for Kasarani to come into being and deliberately gave out plots for constructing houses. And because there had been people living on the surrounding ranches before, there were already some facilities in the area by the time a trading centre was created. This infrastructure had mainly been financed by the farms. One example is Rocco Dispensary, which started in 1976 on a plot of land donated by Rocco Farm, located at a walking distance from present-day Kasarani. It was financed by fundraising events and yearly contributions of employers and farm employees. It has continued to be the official dispensary for several of the farms around, including flower farms, throughout the years. At the time of my fieldwork, it was the only functioning dispensary in the vicinity of Kasarani. The primary school Loldia, which was founded in 1986, was also constructed on a (ten-acre) plot donated by a farm. Despite these facilities provided by the farms, life in Kasarani was hard in the first years. Initially, there were not many people living in the settlement itself and the people living on the surrounding farms earned low salaries. Consequently, there were few opportunities for business. It was also difficult to access clean drinking water, and there was hardly any public transport to go to Naivasha Town: there used to be one *matatu* a day. However, with the shift from ranching to vegetable and later on flower farming, Kasarani started to attract new generations of migrant workers. Around 1992, "suddenly the world was dropped on Kasarani" (A. Sora, 2015). It turned from a trading centre with only a few houses and shops at the main road into a large settlement. After the population increased, water tanks were brought in and the centre was connected to the power grid. Wealthy outsiders started to buy plots in the centre, as a way of investment. Nevertheless, at least until 1998, most houses were still constructed with wattle and daub and not with bricks—which has become increasingly common now—and some houses did not have latrines yet. Only when job opportunities on the flower farms became more permanent with the shift to rose production and migrant workers started to reside in the area for long periods of time did the quality of housing improve (M. Achieng, 2015; "Briefly", 1983; D. Gitahi, 2015; O. Rocco, 2015; A. Sora, 2015).[17]

Kioko (2012, p. 32) noted that, compared to the vast estates of the past and to the expansive greenhouses of the present-day flower farms, the workers' settlements are occupying little space, despite accommodating thousands of people. Figure 5.1 can illustrate this point. The map shows that Kasarani is completely hemmed in between flower and vegetable farms, the main employers. The area close to the main road was developed first and it still contains many of the original wooden and wattle-and-daub houses. The larger shops and offices—such as the local branch office of KPAWU—are also located there. The area in the middle, known as Ngurumuki, was developed more recently and primarily contains brick housing of relatively good quality. The owner of the plot in the middle has not constructed anything until now, and this plot thus awkwardly cuts the settlement into half. The area towards the south-east is officially called Tumaini but carries the nickname "Kosovo" because of the chaos and disorder there in former times, when it only had started to become an unofficial residential area. Tumaini is the least popular part of the settlement, due to the relatively large distance to the main road and the farms' entrances.

Figure 5.2 zooms in on one of the neighbourhoods in Kasarani. It shows how densely built such neighbourhoods typically are. One "arm" of the housing contains two rows of 10–14 one-room apartments. This map also shows the presence of the local government and of the flower farms. The government buildings—a brick police office and the wooden office of the chief—are centrally located, and one of the neighbouring flower farms provides drinking water at its fence bordering Kasarani.

5.2.6 KCC

KCC is the only settlement in Naivasha that is entirely located on squatted land. It has sprung up next to the former governmental milk processing plant (Kenya Co-operative Creameries), located not too far from Naivasha Town in between the Naivasha-Nakuru highway and the railway. This creamery was already established in colonial times and it had an operating milk collection depot and a packaging plant until the 1990s when the overall company collapsed (LNROA, 1993, p. 15; Odingo, 1971, p. 156). During a visit to the settlement, a former resident explained that the Naivasha plant only continued to be in use as a cooling station without any further processing, which provided few employment opportunities. The government then started to rent out the run-down brick staff housing for low rents. Furthermore, former employees also started to construct makeshift housing next to the plant on a confined plot. They informally

Fig. 5.2 Map of a Kasarani neighbourhood, demarcated in Fig. 5.1 (cartographer: Monika Feinen)

subdivided this plot among themselves. As they were only squatters on this land, they never constructed permanent housing. Initially, they used timber. As the sheds were built extremely close to each other, almost all buildings—which housed more than 3000 families—were burnt down to the ground in a large fire (Lime, 2012). Afterwards, most houses were re-built with corrugated iron sheets instead of timber. The extreme density gives the settlement a peculiar atmosphere.

Due to the settlement's squatter status, the government and surrounding employers make few investments there. The only formal infrastructure in the settlement consists of two water tanks, a public toilet block, and a nursery school. There is also a row of churches located at the entrance of the settlement, all constructed with corrugated iron sheets. Electricity is illegally diverted, as there is no official connection. After the milk processing plant had closed down, some residents started to work for the ranches and flower farms around. Some started to cultivate on another squatted plot across the Malewa River that runs north of the settlement. Others rent out sheds to migrant workers. Furthermore, the settlement is notorious for its *chang'aa* industry.

KCC forms an exception in Naivasha due to its squatter status. When comparing the living conditions in KCC to the situation in the other settlements, it is clear that its residents are in an even more precarious position.

5.3 The Economic Position of Settlements' Residents: "Hustling" and "Struggling"

Despite the varying conditions in the workers' settlements, residents are regularly glossed together as "poor" (see, for instance, M. Mwangi, 2007). Although I do not wish to deny the difficult and precarious position of many of the settlements' residents, labelling them as "poor" overlooks the means and the possibilities that they do have. It furthermore disguises internal economic differences. Neither does it do justice to residents' own conceptualizations of themselves. Residents rather perceive of themselves as "hustling" or "struggling".[18] To explore what these qualifications mean (vis-à-vis "poverty"), this section discusses the varying economic position of the settlements' residents and analyses the impact of employment by the flower industry.

Table 5.1 shows that survey respondents most commonly reported a monthly income of 5000–10,000 KES. Following the World Bank index for 2014, Kenyans with an income of less than 7708 KES are considered to be living under the poverty line (Anker & Anker, 2014, p. 44). A considerable proportion of the population of the settlements thus falls into this category. However, it is important to note those were individual incomes and not household incomes that were reported in the survey. Moreover, only the income of the main economic activity was reported. As asserted by Oucho (1996, p. 66), migrants' households in Kenya frequently do not depend solely on the wages of one household member but are also involved

Table 5.1 Monthly income of residents of Karagita, Kasarani, and Sharma Farm, correlated for gender (n = 173) (Chi-square: 11.964, p = 0.008)

Income category	*Female* (n = *108) (%)*	*Male* (n = *65) (%)*
0	13.0	6.8
Less than 5000 KES	19.4	10.1
Between 5000 and 10,000 KES	56.5	55.4
More than 10,000 KES	11.1	29.2
Total	*100.0*	*100.0*

in small-scale businesses or in farming activities in the region of origin. I likewise found that overall household incomes in Naivasha can be significantly higher in cases of two or even three income-earning adults and in cases of successful income diversification (either in Naivasha or translocally). Furthermore, there is a considerable variation with regard to the levels and the security of income and with regard to the possibilities that one has with one's income, for instance, in accessing financial institutions.

Although job opportunities differ around the lake, I did not find significant differences in reported incomes between the three places of residence included in the survey (Karagita, Kasarani, and the Sharma Farm compound). Notably, there was also no significant difference in reported income between flower farm workers and residents with other occupations. Nevertheless, farm workers have the advantage of receiving several allowances. The housing allowance, for instance, saves them the cost of paying rent. Furthermore, farm workers more often than not have permanent contracts, and therefore have a stable income. They can therefore save money with the company's Saving and Credit Co-operative (SACCO) and purchase certain luxury goods through these cooperatives. They also have better access to financial institutions, for one because most formal employers only pay out salaries on a (mobile) bank account, and not cash. This could explain why flower farm workers reported more often to own land, livestock, and other assets than settlement residents with other occupations, despite similar levels of income (see Table 5.2).

Although most of the inhabitants of the settlements are tenants there, they are not all landless. A substantial proportion of survey respondents—18.8%—reported to own a plot of land, although this plot was mostly located outside Naivasha. The same counts for (larger) livestock, for which there simply is little space in the settlements. Thus, it is

Table 5.2 Reported belongings of inhabitants of Karagita, Kasarani, and Sharma Farm, correlated for occupation ($n = 176$)

Type of possession	*Flower farm worker* (n = *94) (%)*	*Other occupation* (n = *82) (%)*
Plot of land (Chi-square: 10.513, $p = 0.010$)	27.7	8.5
Livestock (not significant)	29.8	19.5
(Mobile) bank account (Chi-square: 3.684, $p = 0.055$)	80.9	68.3
Bed in the Naivasha household (not significant)	93.6	82.9
Mobile phone (Chi-square: 2.936, $p = 0.087$)	91.5	82.9

important to note that someone who lacks access to land or other types of wealth in the settlements, and who therefore seems to be in a precarious situation, might have access to assets elsewhere.

The relatively small but influential group of local landowners who purchased their plot(s) in Naivasha between the 1960s and the 1990s have an exceptional position in the settlements. They often continue to reside in the original makeshift housing on their own plots of land, and therefore also appear "poor". In addition, they mostly have a modest economic background themselves. Nevertheless, they were suddenly in a much more secure position when land prices increased steeply and their plots became valuable. They also gained immediate wealth by the possibility to rent out shacks and houses on their plots. Despite this relative wealth, some of the landowners also engage in flower farm work. An employee of Karibu Farm even told me that one of his immediate colleagues was his landlord. There thus is no clear contrast between flower farm workers and local landowners, as these groups partly overlap.

The listing and piling exercises revealed that the settlement residents themselves make another distinction between two groups of residents. These are the wage labourers, the majority of whom are working in horticulture, and what respondents called the "self-employed", that is, those having their own small-scale business or trade. According to Kioko (2012, p. 12), who wrote about Kasarani, these two groups are dependent on each other: the workers for goods and services and the self-employed for an income. However, the distinction between these two groups is also fuzzy.

I found that many wage labourers are engaged in other income-generating activities, such as businesses or small-scale cultivation, in addition to their job. These activities take place either in the same period or at different moments in time, and either all in Naivasha or also elsewhere. An example is Lucy and her husband. They both are full-time employed by flower farms but also derive an income from their plot in western Kenya, where a relative is cultivating the land. In short, income diversification is an important strategy for economic survival in the settlements and makes it difficult to categorize distinct economic groups.

There is thus no clear correlation between level of income on the one hand and place of residence and occupation on the other. This is different for the factor gender. As indicated in Table 5.1, women in the survey sample fell more often in the lowest income categories (no income or less than 5000 KES per month) and men more often in the highest income category (over 10,000 KES per month).[19] This difference reflects the more limited job opportunities for women and the possibility for some married women to depend on their husband's income. Yet, there was generally little difference between female and male respondents with regard to the possession of assets. The only types of assets that were more often owned by men than by women were bicycles and livestock.[20] It is not common for women to ride a bicycle, and it is therefore not surprising that they did not regularly own one. With regard to livestock, Owuor (2003, p. 34) pointed out that this is often perceived to be owned by male household members, due to its cultural meanings. This observation can account for the higher percentage of male owners of livestock that I found. Perhaps surprisingly, considering that women in some communities traditionally do not inherit land, there was no significant difference between female and male respondents with regard to the access to a plot of land.[21] Perhaps some women consider their husband's or family's plots to be their own as well, yet I also met women who had been allocated a plot of family land or who had purchased a plot themselves.

The level of income and access to assets of individual migrant workers is furthermore shaped by the composition of their household. Women working in the flower industry are typically portrayed as "single mothers", who are dependent on the farms due to their responsibilities (Hivos, n.d.; M. Mwangi, 2007). The trope of the exploited "single working mother" is a recurrent theme in literature on (agro-)industry located in the Global South (Coquery-Vidrovitch, 1997, pp. 133–134; Freeman, 2000, p. 104; Ong, 1987, p. 148). However, this image is not reflected in the diverse household compositions in the Naivasha settlements. Only a minority of the households there consist of single mothers with their children.

First of all, there were not more women than men residing in the settlements. The sublocation in which Karagita is located—Mirera—had 19,554 male and 19,655 female residents in 2009. The sublocation in which Kasarani is located—Tarabete—had 4432 male and 4267 female residents (KNBS, 2010). Furthermore, as survey outcomes indicate, only a minority of the residents are single. Two-thirds of the respondents said they were married, and I found no significant difference between male and female respondents with regard to marital status.[22] Not all of the married respondents were staying with their spouse. Only 58.5% of the respondents in the survey stayed with another adult in their household in Naivasha. In a few cases, this other adult was not their spouse or partner but a relative or friend. Hence, quite a number of married couples were not residing in one house. Some of these respondents said that their spouse, typically the wife, had remained in or had returned to the region of origin, for example, because she was farming there. Lang and Sakdapolrak (2014, p. 192) found that fear of renewed ethnic violence can be another reason to not take wife and children to Naivasha. In other cases, respondents told us that their partner, typically the husband, was not residing in Naivasha and neither "at home". The husband was in those cases working elsewhere, for instance, in Nairobi. Thus, settlement residents who are married might nevertheless appear single in case they stay in Naivasha without their spouse.

The average number of children among the survey respondents who were parents was 2.7, whereas the mode was 2. Female respondents more frequently reported to have children (93.6%) than male respondents (73.1%).[23] Notably, only 57.4% of the respondents with children reported that they were staying with all of these children in their household in Naivasha at the time of the survey. Another 12.5% stayed with only one or several of their children while others stayed somewhere else. Finally, 30.1% of those respondents who had children were not staying with any of their children in Naivasha. If not staying with their parent in Naivasha, children usually stayed with their other parent, a female family member "at home", or in a boarding school.

On the other hand, some settlement residents stay with a child that is not their own, for instance, the child of a partner from a previous relationship or a child of a sibling who passed away. Some residents also accommodate adult relatives, for instance, a sibling, for a shorter or longer period of time upon their arrival in Naivasha. Kioko (2012, p. 34) furthermore found that unmarried residents sometimes share their room or apartment with a friend, a colleague, or a relative, usually of the same sex, to economize on rent. Indeed, 4.0% of the survey respondents were living together with a friend at the time of the interview.

In sum, residents' households in Naivasha do not necessarily reflect their financial responsibilities. Translocal responsibilities for children or the support they receive through a spouse who resides elsewhere are not visible when only taking their Naivasha households into account. Following Moore and Vaughan (1994, p. 225), I argue that a household should be perceived not as a coherent and stable unit but as "a nexus of overlapping interests and activities whose (sometimes very temporary) coherence is itself an achievement and not something pregiven". Decisions on labour, consumption, and residence are taken individually but also within such shifting, partly translocal households and within wider (family) networks (Friedemann-Sánchez, 2009; Ong, 1987; Wolf, 1992).

The flower farms, as the main employers in the area, impact on living arrangements. First of all, the decision to hire women has a large impact on household composition, as it makes it attractive for women to move to Naivasha, either alone or with a husband. Secondly, the increasing prevalence of permanent contracts also makes it more attractive for workers to bring their family over to Naivasha. Certain—more recent—policies of some of the farms, such as paying for the health care of dependent family members of workers, are another incentive to bring the family along. Even the absence of compounds on most farms plays a role: it gives workers more liberty in taking in relatives, which is not allowed in the *kambi*. Previously, it had not even always been allowed to bring a spouse and children along to a farm compound (Omosa, Kimani, & Njiru, 2006). Furthermore, it is possible to come to Naivasha even without finding employment on a farm.

Although there were some full-time housewives in our survey (4.0% of the respondents), the majority of the adults in the settlements, whether married or not, are involved in income-generating activities or aim to do so. Friedemann-Sánchez (2009, p. 142) concluded that the intra-household bargaining position of female flower farm workers in Colombia improved when they took up employment. The financial independence gave them the ultimate possibility to exit the household. Women in the settlements in Naivasha who earn their own income likewise have a better bargaining position than those who do not. I found in Naivasha that incomes are usually not pooled but managed individually. A flower farm owner told me that she had decided to install a cash machine on the farm premises, as she had the impression the husbands of female employees took away their money on payday. With the arrival of the cash machine, women could get the money on any day and thus were free to spend it according to their wishes. However, although there might have been cases in which a woman did not have the freedom to spend her own income, my impression of "conjugal contracts" (Li, 1998) in Naivasha is that men and women are perceived of as individuals with the rights to use their own money. There are certain expectations and patterns, such as that I heard from several couples that the men were responsible for paying the rent. When Flora and James' rent was increased with a 1000 KES per month due to renovations, Flora was not really concerned. She told me that the person who pays the rent—with whom she meant James—would figure something out. Yet, despite these expectations, women (and men) do not generally seem to lack control over their income. Nevertheless, women do not have the same level of autonomy as men, regardless of their marital status. Wilshaw (2013, p. 85) found that women on average spend a higher percentage of their income on sustaining the household than men do. Moreover, women have a double workload and are "time-poor", as they are expected to take care of the household chores in addition to their job (KHRC, 2012, p. 3; Lowthers, 2018, p. 464; Wilshaw, 2013, p. 85). This is illustrated by James' assertion that a man should not enter the kitchen, even though Flora was also employed full-time. Thus, even women who are involved in wage labour are expected to perform most of the domestic work. This is a common challenge for women working on plantations and in global firms (Freeman, 2000; Samarasinghe, 1993). The flower farms do little in the way of alleviating that gender-specific burden.

To summarize, settlement residents do not generally consider themselves to be "poor". They see possibilities for improving their situation and they are "struggling" to do so. Moreover, although gender influences individual possibilities, the trope of single women employed by exploitative farms proves to be deceptively simple. For instance, even if a woman resides alone in Naivasha, it should not be automatically concluded that she is unmarried or that she carries the responsibility for her children on her own. Migrants' household arrangements are dynamic and change over time. The households immediately observable in Naivasha should be put into wider temporal and spatial perspectives. Both internal segmentations within households and external connections to broader family networks and to employers such as the flower industry have to be taken into account when assessing the economic position of settlement residents.

5.4 The Settlements' Illicit Economies: Fish Poaching, *Chang'aa*, and Sex Work

Settlement residents' "hustle" regularly involves informal or even illegal income-generating activities. As described earlier for Karagita, residents have since the incipience of the settlements partly depended on such illicit activities for their livelihoods. They continue to do so, despite the increased employment opportunities in the area. Becht et al. (2005, p. 278) discussed the environmental consequences of activities such as cutting down trees for firewood and fish and wildlife poaching. A newspaper article described a conflict over *chang'aa* in Karagita-Mirera (M. Mwangi, 2014). And Kioko (2012, pp. 47–50) mentioned small-scale cultivation in the riparian land of Kasarani, which I also noticed taking place at Kihoto's lakeside. The cultivated land is not owned by the farmers. Moreover, cultivation (of any kind) is officially not allowed there (S. Wanjala, 2014).

Participants in the listing exercises described in Chap. 3 occasionally also mentioned illicit activities such as brewing *chang'aa*, although these were not generally recognized as "proper" job opportunities. Whenever a participant mentioned such an activity, other participants would object to calling it "work". Some of the activities were even considered an embarrassment to the settlement. The prevalence of these activities—many of which take place at night or in secrecy—is therefore hard to assess. Regardless, they contributed to the settlements' poor reputation. A government report stated: "The development of cheap informal settlements such as Karagita slums and Kihoto area have helped to fuel antisocial activities such as brewing of illicit liquor, prostitution and drug abuse."[24]

These "antisocial" activities are profitable but risky businesses. An example is fish poaching, which has been the cause of—sometimes violent—conflicts between "legal" fishermen (those with a permit) and "illegal" fishermen. These conflicts furthermore involved riparian landowners and the local government (Becht et al., 2005, p. 293; Seal, 2011). The illicit economies are also highly gendered. Whereas poaching is an exclusively male activity, typically female businesses can be just as risky. For instance, brewing *chang'aa*, mostly carried out by women, is precarious because of frequent police raids. A criminal court case involving a woman selling *chang'aa* in Karagita indicates the risks of the business. This woman was given a substantial fine of 50,000 KES or eight months of imprisonment in case she failed to pay the fine (*Mary Njeri v Republic*, 2015).

Women's participation in Naivasha's "sexual economy"—defined by Holt Norris and Worby (2012, pp. 354–355) as "mobilizing and enlisting sexual desire for economic advantage"—is even more risky. According to Lowthers (2018), who conducted research among sex workers in Naivasha, many female migrant workers supplement their—on average lower—incomes through sex work. Lowthers' research provides valuable insights into Naivasha's sexual economy, which has been heavily shaped by the attraction of—notably both male and female—migrant workers by the flower farms. The sexual economy is furthermore based on Naivasha being both a popular tourist destination and a stopover for the truck drivers who transport goods from the port in Mombasa to western Kenya and Uganda. I noticed (or suspected) the presence of sex workers during shorter research stays, when I stayed overnight in relatively cheap hotels with bars in front (some carrying suggestive names such as "Sweet Banana") and occasionally in more high-end hotels in Naivasha Town. Sex work also takes place in the settlements, as indicated by one of the groups in the listing exercises.

Lowthers (2018) asserted that some of the Naivasha sex workers are also flower farm workers, or have been so in the past. She described a (non-linear) continuum of practices, ranging from (one-time) "sex for employment" and "transactional sex relationships" (repetitive engagements with a superior to secure better working conditions and supplement income) to part-time sex work to make up for low incomes or temporary unemployment. She connects the prevalence of these practices to the conditions in the flower industry and speaks of an "institutionalized sexual economy". However, due to the nature of her research (focused on sex workers and not on flower farm workers in general, and only taking place off-farm), her understanding of labour conditions seems to be limited and heavily influenced by the stereotypes of the industry. Lowthers (2018, p. 449), for instance, states that the industry is characterized by "persistent gender discrimination", without discussing the layered and complex gender dynamics I described in Sect. 4.7. Lowthers (2018, pp. 455–456) also overestimates the percentage of women employed by the flower industry. In contrast to Lowthers' argument, I maintain that labour conditions in the industry, and recent shifts therein, *decrease* rather than increase the likelihood of sexual harassment, dependence on "employment sex", and the need to engage in sex work to supplement income earned on the flower farms.

Research on the "sexual economy" of other agro-industries on the African continent suggests that women become more dependent on sexual relations as a source of income and as a way of securing benefits when labour conditions deteriorate. Holt Norris and Worby (2012) analysed the influence of the privatization of a formerly state-owned sugar plantation on this plantation's "sexual economy". Women's increasingly insecure position after the privatization made them more likely to engage in sex against payment with men they previously would have avoided. Addison likewise (2014) interrogated how shifts in labour composition and in management practices changed the "sexual economy" of the farm in South Africa where he carried out ethnographic research. He analysed the influence of an increase in temporary labour contracts, changes in the ethnic and gender composition of the labour force (more migrant labour and more women in low-ranking positions), and the monetization of services that in the previously paternalistic system had been for free. In both the Tanzanian and the South African case, deteriorating labour conditions provided managers and supervisors with the opportunity of sexual abuse and increased women's participation in transactional sex.

In contrast to these cases, labour conditions in the Naivasha flower industry have improved in recent years, and wage levels compare favourably to other economic sectors. The increase in permanent contracts—which in contrast to Lowthers' claim (2018, p. 456) are not only awarded to men but also to women—makes women less vulnerable and enables them to refuse engagement in "employment sex" and "sex as employment". Permanent employment also enables men to bring their wives over to Naivasha, decreasing the likelihood that they engage in paid sexual relationships with other women. With regard to "sex for employment" practices, recent trends such as the increasing proportion of female supervisors and managers and the formalization of HR departments decrease the likelihood of sexual abuse on-farm.

Another major difference to the South African and Tanzanian cases is that most workers do not live on the farm. Holt Norris and Worby (2012, p. 357) argued that plantations, "in common with mines, oil rigs, and ships, are distinguished by the relative lack of distinction between the location where paid work is performed and the places where domestic and leisure activities are carried out". In contrast, the majority of the Naivasha flower farm workers live in a different space than where they work. Naivasha's sexual economy therefore does not only encompass the ordered farms but also the much less regulated settlements, where the flower farm workers reside together with non-farm workers. It furthermore encompasses other economic sectors apart from the flower industry. Notably, Lowthers (2018, p. 459) mentions that "sex for employment" is also prevalent in, for instance, the tourism sector. The exact influence of the flower industry's labour conditions on the sexual economy is therefore difficult to assess.

The flower farms actively intervene in this sexual economy. As described in the previous chapter, the farms have tried to counteract sexual harassment and "sex for employment" by installing gender committees and formalizing HR procedures. Moreover, some of the farms attempt to influence workers' reproductive behaviour by sponsoring family planning programmes offered by clinics, such as the Rocco dispensary in Kasarani (O. Rocco, 2015). Many farms also invite the Naivasha Community HIV AIDS Group (NACOHAG) and similar organizations to their farms to offer free testing to workers. In addition, NACOHAG has a clinic in Karagita that is partly sponsored by flower farms (Masibo, 2005). Representatives of NACOHAG (interview on June 25, 2015) asserted that they recently found a significantly lower proportion of workers affected than in the early 2000s, an indication of shifts in Naivasha's sexual economy.

Apart from these measurements to reduce the occurrence and the risks of sex work, along the continuum described by Lowthers (2018), among farm workers, flower farms do not intervene in the illicit income-earning activities of settlements' residents. Nevertheless, conditions on the farms—including the absence of a *kambi* in most cases—do impact (both positively and negatively) on the need for settlement residents to participate in such illicit economies.

5.5 Ethnicity in the Settlements: Mixed Marriages and Mutual Mistrust

Whereas class and gender relations within the settlements are fuzzy and dynamic, ethnic relations became more pronounced after the post-election violence in early 2008. The violence greatly disturbed the daily order in the settlements for a short period of time. What has been the role of ethnicity more recently?

According to Kioko (2016), there is a long tradition of interethnic marriages between Maasai and Kikuyu in Maiella, in the hinterland of Lake Naivasha. These connections were made possible by the mobility of these, traditionally pastoralist and trader, groups. The interethnic marriages were meant to secure influence in a community or to gain access to land. Kioko asserted that these practices have strengthened the possibility for peaceful coexistence in Maiella. Around Lake Naivasha, where many different ethnic groups are present, the situation is more complex. Whether mixed marriages have the same effect there is difficult to assess. What is clear is that interethnic marriages and being of mixed identity are not exceptional in Naivasha. Flora and James are an example of an interethnic couple. And among the respondents in the survey, 6.8% mentioned that their mother had a different ethnic background than their father. Unlike in Maiella, interethnic marriages in present-day Naivasha are usually not based on strategic considerations and are not arranged. They are closed between a man and a woman who simply have met on a flower farm or in the settlement where they rent a room. Thus, boundaries between ethnic groups are in practice not as clear-cut as the ethno-political discourse, which instigated the post-election violence, presupposes.

Interethnic couples need to find a shared language since they do not share a vernacular language. For some couples with a mixed ethnic background, such as James and Flora, Swahili and English are the only languages that both partners are able to speak. Even those who met each other in their region of origin do not always speak the same vernacular language. This was the case for flower farm worker Dennis, who met his wife during his annual leave, when she was visiting family in Dennis' region of origin. They had a different ethnic background and thus spoke Swahili to each other. Even couples who share a vernacular language, such as Kikuyu or Luhya, often (also) speak Swahili or English with each other or with their children. When asked which language or languages were spoken in the household in Naivasha, 93.2% of the survey respondents mentioned Swahili. Moreover, 64.8% of the respondents reported that Swahili was the only language spoken in his or her household. The choice of language for a specific conversation would depend on the interlocutors, the context, and even the topic. While some adults are more fluent in a vernacular language than in Swahili, their children grow up with Swahili. Despite annual visits to grandparents in the region of origin and the use of English as a primary language in school, they mostly speak Swahili with their peers and often also with their parents. As Abdulaziz (1982, p. 112) asserted for children in urban areas in Kenya: "it was becoming hard to say for certain what is [their] first language."

Kioko's study (2016) indicates that the choice for Swahili is not self-evident in a multi-ethnic environment. In Maiella, many non-Maasai land tenants learned to speak Maa, which over time replaced Swahili as the *lingua franca* there. In cosmopolitan Naivasha, none of the ethnic groups has become this hegemonic. Swahili remains the main language spoken there, both in the workplace and during leisure time.

The presence of the flower industry and its attraction of migrant workers from all over Kenya thus in some ways diffuses ethnic identities in the Naivasha settlements. Nevertheless, ethnicity has not lost all of its economic and political salience. For one, the (fuzzy) distinction between the two different economic groups identified earlier, of wage labourers on the one hand and the "self-employed" on the other, partly overlaps with ethnic affiliations. For example, a majority of the landowners in the settlements who rent out houses are Kikuyu. Furthermore, residents who belong to ethnic groups traditionally based in western parts of Kenya, such as Luo and Luhya, are fearful of investing money in starting up a business in the settlements. I met a woman, married to a flower farm worker and originating from Kakamega, who would have liked to start her own hair salon. However, she did not feel secure enough to do so in Karagita, where she resided. She explicitly referred to the (ethnicized) post-election violence of early 2008, confirming the observation of Lang and Sakdapolrak (2014, p. 192) that ethnic divisions in the settlements increased, both socially and spatially, afterwards. Migrant workers ever more perceive of Naivasha as a place of work, whereas groups who consider Naivasha to be their "home" exclude others from making such claims.

I noticed that feelings of insecurity and fear for renewed violence influenced the behaviour of migrant workers, especially when the general elections of 2017 drew closer. Some took precautions, such as moving valuable goods to the region of origin or leaving their children there instead of bringing them along to Naivasha, as also noted by Lang and Sakdapolrak (2014, p. 192) before the previous elections in 2013. And my assistant Richard—born in Naivasha in a Kikuyu family—observed an increased use of Swahili instead of vernacular languages in public areas since 2008, with the notable exception of Kikuyu. Thus, despite the increasing prevalence of permanent contracts on the flower farms, migrant workers with certain ethnic backgrounds cannot feel wholly secure in Naivasha.

On the other hand, I did not encounter "ethnic" neighbourhoods in the settlements, marked by the dominance of one ethnic group, as these are reported for other ethnically mixed towns in Kenya (Achieng', 2012).[25]

All of the housing compounds included in our survey had a multi-ethnic composition. And although migrant workers do not claim Naivasha as a home, they implicitly claim certain rights there, primarily the right to make a living. Yet, ethnic affiliations impact on the decisions residents of the settlements make, and the 2008 post-election violence seems to have exacerbated tensions between different ethnic groups in the long run.

5.6 Community Relations: Churches, "Self-help Groups", Colleagues, and Neighbours

Settlement residents attempt to live together peacefully despite this lingering mistrust and to bring some "order" to their surroundings through the participation in several types of organizations. Table 5.3 provides an overview of membership rates among survey respondents. Only a minority (15.3%), mostly those who had arrived in Naivasha recently, was not involved in any of the organizations included in the survey questionnaire.[26] Which types of organizations are important, and how do they function within the settlements and within the flower farms? And what characterizes relations between neighbours and between workmates in the settlements?

When asked about their religious affiliation, 95.5% of the respondents in the survey stated they were Christian.[27] Not all of them were church members: 55.1% of the respondents said they were an active member of a religious group. Moreover, there is not one church that could potentially unite the residents since there are many denominations. The survey respondents mentioned membership to 27 different churches. Even in the interviews with the 30 members of one working team of Karibu Farm, no less than 17 different denominations were mentioned. Some residents

Table 5.3 Membership rate of organizations, correlated for occupation ($n = 176$)

Organization	*Flower farm worker* (n = *94) (%)*	*Other occupation* (n = *82) (%)*
Religious group (not significant)	55.3	54.9
SACCO (Chi-square: 22.826, $p \leq 0.001$)	57.4	22.0
Chama/merry-go-round (not significant)	24.5	29.3
Welfare organization (Chi-square: 17.223, $p \leq 0.001$)	26.6	3.7
No membership (Chi-square: 5.166, $p = 0.023$)	9.6	22.0

Fig. 5.3 One of the many small churches in Kasarani, with a flower farm next to it

frequent international and established denominations, such as the Catholic Church, the Anglican Church, and the Pentecostal Church. Others frequent local, sometimes very small, churches, which carry imaginative names such as "Hosanna Most High Foundation", "Gethsemane Gospel", and "Repentance and Holiness". Figure 5.3 depicts a small, makeshift church building typical for such denominations.

The Catholic Church is by far the largest denomination, mentioned by 11.9% of the survey respondents as the church they frequented. This church has two parishes around Lake Naivasha and has a church building in almost every settlement. The congregations in the settlements are led by voluntary catechists. The catechist in Kasarani, for instance, earned his daily bread as a supervisor on one of the neighbouring flower farms. He explained that he did not only lead the Sunday services but also organized prayer meetings and counselling hours on weekday evenings. He thus accommodated many farm workers who did not have their day off on Sundays. The rhythm of the work within the farms thus shapes the activities of the religious groups within the settlements.

The other way around, and in contrast to the taboo on ethnicity, farms tolerate religious expressions on the work floor. Working teams start their day together with short prayers before the supervisors give instructions.

Meetings of workers' committees also start with prayers. In one farm, those working on Sundays would come 15 minutes earlier to hold a short service together. The space for religion on the work floor indicates that the farms are more than a workplace. As employees sometimes work for the same flower farm for many years or even several decades, these workplaces not only provide a steady income and some cash to invest in the future. They are also an important space within the workers' social networks, the more so since to the majority of the workers, the whole of Naivasha is a "workplace" and not a permanent home.

The incorporation of the farms within the workers' social networks is also reflected in the existence of so-called *vyama* (singular: *chama*) within the farms. These saving groups mostly take the form of so-called merry-go-rounds, in which the members rotate goods or money. *Vyama* are formed without any interference of managers or supervisors, who might not even be aware of their existence, and do not have a formal status within the farms. They are therefore more accessible than the highly institutionalized SACCOs. And whereas SACCOs are large organizations with usually at least several hundreds of participants, *vyama* are small groups of roughly 5–20 members. In one of the *vyama* of Karibu Farm employees, all the six members contributed two kilograms of sugar on a monthly basis. Each month, a different member received 12 kilograms of sugar. In another group, each member put in 500 KES every month and would get 6000 KES paid out before his or her annual leave. These groups help their members in budgeting. As Lucy explained, if she would be out of money by the end of the month, she at least still could make tea with the sugar that she received from the *chama*. Buying larger quantities at once also reduces the price of foodstuffs.

On-farm *vyama* are sometimes based in one greenhouse. Other workers prefer to form a group with colleagues from all over the farm whom they know well, rather than with their immediate colleagues. And even groups that were originally based in one greenhouse can eventually have members spread all over the farm due to the rotation of workers. Yvonne—supervisor in Karibu Farm—was even still participating in a *chama* at her former workplace, a year after she had left that farm.

In the total network analysis I carried out, I compared everyday interactions between colleagues within the greenhouse to how much they interacted with each other within the neighbouring settlement Kasarani. Levels of interaction on-farm turned out to be primarily based on the location in the greenhouse where workers were deployed. Workers mainly talked to their colleagues in the same area, especially to those harvesting in bays close to them and to those sizing the flowers. They therefore only interacted frequently with a handful of colleagues. Exceptions were those without a fixed area of work, such as the scout and the supervisor, and the female shop steward in the greenhouse, who seemed to function as a mentor for younger female colleagues. Gender thus also played a role. Men had more contact with other men, even with those who worked in a different part of the greenhouse. They would, for example, meet in the changing room.

With regard to interactions in Kasarani, the respondents mainly would meet their colleagues who also happened to be their neighbours, who participated in the same organization, or who operated a small-scale business, such as selling vegetables, in Kasarani in the evening hours. I found little overlap between these interactions in the settlement and interactions on-farm. For instance, one respondent explained that two of the other workers in the greenhouse were also her neighbours. She would sometimes ask them to lend her some money to buy food if she was penniless at the end of the month. Nevertheless, she hardly interacted with these two colleagues while at work since they were deployed in a different part of the greenhouse. Especially the position of supervisor Yvonne is remarkable: she was a central figure within the greenhouse. However, due to her habit of going to her family in Naivasha Town on her weekly day off, and perhaps also due to her senior position, she hardly had any contact with the other workers in Kasarani.

The limited relevance of these work relations for workers' networks in the settlements is related to the instability of working teams and the frequent rotating of workers. A working team based in one greenhouse initially seemed the most logical unit to be sampled as a "total network". In some ways, the working team of which I interviewed all members also seemed to be a tight-knit group. For instance, when I asked the whereabouts of a certain employee who was absent, not only the supervisor but also the general workers were able to tell me whether that person was off or on leave, and even until when in case of annual leaves. Nevertheless, I found that the process of drawing the network boundaries was not as straightforward as it had initially seemed. My approach excluded possible important connections with employees belonging to other working teams (Scott, 2013, pp. 43–44). Moreover, the instability of the team's composition caused the team to be a momentary and fluid entity, with limited relevance in labour relations and especially in relations within the neighbouring settlement.

Nevertheless, a settlement like Kasarani is completely hemmed in between farms (see Fig. 5.1). Friendships and enmities can therefore encompass both the farms and the settlement. Conflicts between neighbours potentially seep into a farm and the other way around. Management is conscious of this interconnectedness. One manager of Karibu Farm told employees during a meeting they should ask questions there and not afterwards in Kasarani. A supervisor, who had lived more anonymously in Naivasha Town before and only recently had moved to Kasarani, complained to me about the amount of gossip. One day she had eaten fish in a *hoteli* in Kasarani, and the following day a few employees, whom she had not seen at the *hoteli*, made remarks about this luxury. It thus appeared that others had been talking about her.

The relation between the settlements and the farms is less immediate at South Lake, at least for the farms without a compound, because the employees there are not all residing in the same settlement. On the other hand, a resident of Karagita who worked for a flower farm located at South Lake told me he lived in the same neighbourhood as his supervisor, and they would regularly meet outside work. He said he might even go to her house, for example, in case he wanted to ask for a day off because of an emergency. Furthermore, farms along the South Lake Road can be affected by events in the settlements, for instance, when the road is blocked by protesters ("Transport Paralysed", 2015).

All in all, work relations seem to be of limited significance in the settlements. Rather than exclusively relying on their workplace and their workmates, flower farm workers frequently participate in organizations, such as *vyama*, that are based in the settlements. Moreover, settlement-based *vyama* are relatively popular among non-flower farm workers, especially when compared to SACCOs. Table 5.3 shows that residents with other occupations participate a bit more often in *vyama* than flower farm workers. Yet, they participate less frequently in SACCOs. They often do not have the opportunity to do so, for lack of a permanent and formal employer. And whereas SACCOs have a relatively high minimum monthly contribution, due to regulations set by the government, some merry-go-rounds have very modest contributions. One survey respondent mentioned a contribution of only 20 KES per month. On the other hand, I interviewed a member of a *chama*, consisting of local businessmen and one businesswoman, which had a monthly contribution of 10,000 KES. Thus, these groups sometimes also deal with considerable amounts of money. The average monthly contribution to the SACCO among the participants in the survey was 1148 KES. The average contribution to a *chama* was slightly lower, 923 KES, yet it is still a substantial amount considering the low-income levels in the settlements. Contributions to *vyama* are often made in cash, although richer groups work with (mobile) banking accounts. In addition to rotating money or goods, some of the settlement-based *vyama* save part of the money to give out loans to their members or to invest together as a group, for instance, in a plot of land.

Membership in a *chama* is not merely a substitute for participation in a SACCO. First of all, those who cannot participate in a SACCO often also do not participate in a *chama* (40.3% of the survey respondents participated in neither), either because they do not have the financial means to do so or because they do not trust others with their savings. Furthermore, some SACCO members participate in a *chama* additionally: 8.0% of the respondents did so, presumably because a *chama* can have additional functions apart from saving money and is not tied to an employer.

More female than male survey respondents reported to participate in a *chama*, whereas on the other hand so-called welfare groups were more popular among men.[28] Like merry-go-rounds, welfare groups sometimes have a fixed monthly contribution. However, the goal and the rhythm of these organizations are different. They are meant to assist members in times of crisis, such as illness or bereavement. In some cases, the welfare committee of a farm takes on the function of such a welfare group, when the committee members collect a small contribution of all immediate colleagues of a worker who has fallen ill or has been bereaved.

The distinction between the different types of groups is not always clear-cut, and many organizations can broadly be classified as "self-help groups" that combine several functions. Such self-help groups have a long history in Naivasha and were already started in colonial times by squatters on the ranches, in order to organize schooling for their children (Kanogo, 1987, p. 74). A present-day example of a self-help group is the Lake Naivasha Disabled Environmental Group, which is based in Karagita. I interviewed two of its members, who explained that this organization was formed by a group of people with disabilities who all experienced difficulties in finding employment. The group had 17 male and 10 female members at the time of the interview. The group functioned as a merry-go-round, with a monthly contribution of 600 KES. Furthermore, they engaged in income-generating activities together. They had started out by cleaning the area around the Moi Lake Road at Karagita, for which they were paid by one of the flower farms next to the settlement. The group also started to collect garbage. In addition, the group received funding from the World Bank in 2010 to organize a meeting in Karagita on raising awareness about disabilities, and members were trained by students of Leicester University on environment-friendly activities such as recycling plastic bags and making briquettes from water hyacinth. The group has thus been quite successful in attracting sponsoring and in finding ways to collectively make some money.

Another example of a multifunctional self-help group is Huruma, a group based in Kasarani. This group had about 60 members in 2015 and functioned as a welfare group: upon bereavement or hospitalization of a member, each would contribute 200 KES (resulting in a total sum of 12,000 KES). Furthermore, each member contributed 1000 KES per month for a loan scheme and for shared savings. The group was in the process of purchasing a plot of ten acres in Moi Ndabi, an agricultural area in the hinterland of the lake, paid for with the shared savings and a loan acquired from a bank. The members planned to later subdivide this plot among themselves. Thus, this group was a *chama*, welfare group, and land-buying cooperative in one. It was organized in a formal manner. It had its own bylaws, which, for instance, made it obligatory for members to attend meetings. The pastor who had founded this group in the year 2000 had founded another multifunctional group in the year 2006, Disomne (short for "Disabled, Orphaned and Most Needy Children HIV/AIDS Group"). This group aimed to assist the guardians of around 380 orphaned or what the group leader called "needy" children. Apart from receiving monthly contributions from the guardians, this group had been successful in accessing some funds from United States Agency for International Development and from the flower farms around. It provided loans to the guardians, had purchased a *shamba* "for the children", contributed to a feeding programme in Kasarani, and paid school fees.

These two groups were led by one pastor. Two other *vyama* (merry-go-rounds with a large membership) in the same settlement were also chaired by one person, a local plot owner-cum-flower farm worker, who was in charge of collecting the money. On the other hand, only 5.1% of the survey respondents reported having a position such as chair, secretary, or committee member in an organization. This illustrates that organizations in the settlements (including churches) depend on a small number of active community leaders, despite high membership rates.

Membership to all of these organizations (unlike with SACCOs) is regularly restricted according to gender, age, or ethnic affiliation. A woman residing in Kihoto explained she participated in both a local *chama* for older women and one for younger women, as she was somewhere in between. And when I asked the farm workers interviewed for the total network analysis in which organizations based in Kasarani they participated, a number of them mentioned ethnic self-help groups, such as Mugusii Self-Help Group (with Kisii membership), LuoRet, and a newly formed Samburu group that had no name yet. Flower farms with a *kambi* also allow their employees to form *vyama* along ethnic lines. Ethnically mixed groups exist too, but these face specific challenges. The Lake Naivasha Disabled Environmental Group was, for instance, affected when some of its members left Naivasha during and after the post-election violence in 2008.

Despite such occasional drawbacks, these groups and organizations help the residents of the settlements to navigate social and economic insecurities and to reduce their dependency on the flower farms. Furthermore, they enable migrant workers to save or to make investments for the future. Nevertheless, in case of emergencies, one cannot easily borrow money from a SACCO or *chama*, due to formal and time-consuming procedures. Table 5.4 summarizes data on the support networks of the respondents in the ego-centred network analysis.[29] Only two respondents said they were able to suddenly borrow 2000 KES from their *chama*. Five had the possibility to turn to a bank because they had a regular income. Four others said they had to fall back on the services of private moneylenders in case of an emergency. The moneylenders are easily accessible in the settlements but demand high interest rates. However, quite a number of respondents also said they could borrow some money from friends or neighbours if necessary. It was remarkable that few people would turn to their family. When answering the question, many respondents expressed embarrassment in relation to borrowing money and not being self-sufficient. They would feel bad about borrowing money from someone else. One of the respondents stated she would not even lend money when she would not be able to buy vegetables. She said: "we'll just eat *ugali* [maize porridge] with salt [instead of with vegetables]."

One respondent, Lydia, who resided in Karagita, stated that she would not ask her neighbours for any kind of help, not even for borrowing a tool or kitchen utensil. She said that everyone was busy and that people "in the city" (*mjini*) do not like to depend on others. She also did not have any friends to chat with on her day off. She said she needs to wash her clothes on that day and simply wants to sleep the rest of the time. She was not alone in this isolation: a number of respondents claimed they were not talking to anyone during leisure time (see Table 5.4), which was caused by either a lack of (shared) leisure time or a lack of informal contacts. For these

Table 5.4 Aggregated answers to the questions on networks in the ego-centred network analysis ($n = 22$)

	Parent(s)	*Partner*	*Sibling(s)*	*Other relative(s)*	*Friend(s)*	*Neighbour(s)*	*Colleague(s)*	*Institutions*	*Not applicable*
1. If you need a *kitchen utensil* that you do not have yourself, whom do you go to to borrow one?	–	–	1	–	2	15	–	–	4
2. Whom do you ask for some *vegetables* if that is the only thing you are missing to cook a meal and you are out of money?	2	–	–	–	5	4	1	9	4
3. If you need *to write an official letter* and you do not know how to go about it yourself, whom do you ask for assistance?	1	2	1	3	3	3	3	1	8
4. If you suddenly need *2000 KES*, to whom or where do you go to borrow?	2	–	1	–	7	3	1	11	4
5. Whom do you most often *give money to* or send money to via mobile banking?	16	2	–	3	–	–	–	–	5

6. Who do you most often *receive money from*, in person or via mobile banking?	–	1	6	2	3	–	–	3	8
7. If you have questions about raising your children or about your relationship, whom do you go to for *advice*?	9	1	–	2	1	3	–	7	–
8. If you have *issues with a colleague* at work/ fellow business(wo) man, to whom do you go for a solution or advice?	–	–	–	–	1	–	1	19	2
9. Who do you go to if you just feel like *having a chat* in your spare time?	1	2	–	–	9	3	1	–	7
10. Is there *someone else* in your life who's important to you but who you have not mentioned yet?	–	1	–	10	1	–	–	1	9
Total	*31*	*9*	*9*	*20*	*32*	*31*	*7*	*51*	*51*

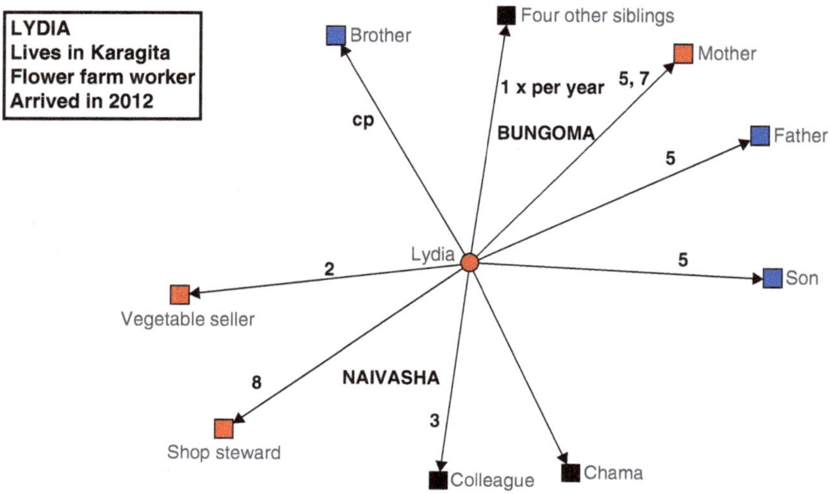

Fig. 5.4 The network of Lydia, based on her answers in the ego-centred network analysis. Developed using UCINET for Windows (Borgatti, Everett, & Freeman, 2002)

people, their network in Naivasha is primarily based in their workplace. This sole dependence on the workplace is also reflected in Fig. 5.4,[30] depicting the ego-centred network I drew based on my interview with Lydia. Even the sugar-rotating *chama* in which she participated was based in the flower farm where she worked. Lydia had originally come to Naivasha after getting divorced in Bungoma, her region of origin. She did not want to depend on her parents and followed her brother, who was working on a vegetable farm, to Naivasha. She came together with her son. However, her brother had moved back to Bungoma by the time of the interview. She had no other family in Naivasha and had made no friends. For her, "town" was a place where people have to fend for themselves. The consequence of this lack of a support network was that she, as a single mother, did not manage to pay for the education and upkeep of her teenage son in Naivasha. He had moved back to stay with his grandparents in Bungoma, where life is much cheaper.

Hence, for some migrant workers, such as Lydia, life in the Naivasha settlements (in "the city") stands in stark contrast to life in the region of origin, at "home". They have few social contacts in Naivasha. For them,

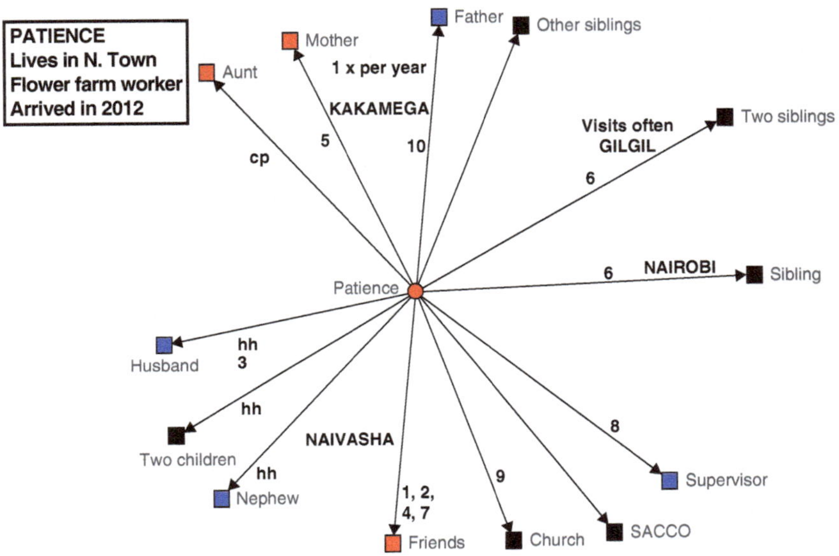

Fig. 5.5 The network of Patience, based on her answers in the ego-centred network analysis. Developed using UCINET for Windows (Borgatti et al., 2002)

the whole of Naivasha is a "workplace". They do not expect any "social order" there outside work. Nevertheless, other migrant workers establish a support network that encompasses not only their region of origin but also the settlements in Naivasha and even other places in Kenya. The network of Patience (see Fig. 5.5), who had arrived in Naivasha in the same year as Lydia, provides a good example here. Patience had originally come to Naivasha to visit her aunt. She then met her later husband and decided to stay. Although Patience retained connections with her family in Kakamega, her region of origin, and went to visit there during her annual leave, she also was closely connected to some of her colleagues and neighbours in Naivasha, whom she considered to be friends. A major difference between Patience and Lydia was that Patience was married and had a husband to fall back on. Furthermore, she was not the only one in her family who had left "home". Although her aunt had retired by the time of the interview in 2015 and had moved back to Kakamega, Patience had several siblings who were also migrant workers. In fact, she received financial support from her siblings who were living and working in Gilgil and Nairobi from time to time. Thus, her elaborate support network comprised her region of origin, other places in Kenya, and both her place of work (a flower farm) and the neighbourhood she lived in in Naivasha.

5.7 Governing the Settlements: Creating Order and Allowing for Disorder

Farm managers and government officials regularly assume that all migrant workers are like Lydia and consider Naivasha to be solely a place of work. They lament the lack of investments by settlement residents in their living environment. Karibu Farm's general manager Jan, for example, thought that Kasarani's residents could and should put more effort in making it a "proper village". Yet, in contrast to the disorder and dirtiness of the streets in the settlements, the plots themselves—especially those with brick housing and an iron gate—are usually neat and clean. The narrow central alleys of the compounds are used for doing the laundry and they are always full of clothes hung out to dry (see Fig. 5.6). Inside, the houses are also tidy, although usually stuffed with furniture and other goods. Rooms are sometimes divided into several compartments (for instance, into a sleeping and a sitting area) by curtains or bed sheets hanging down from the ceiling. Tables and sofas—when present—are adorned with embroidered cloths and pillows, and walls (including the "walls" made of curtains) are decorated with family pictures, calendars of political parties, and posters of European soccer teams. In short, residents make an effort to make their houses homely, despite the perception among farm managers and government officials that residents do not care about their living circumstances. Where does this disparity stem from? And which infrastructure is present in the settlements, and who has provided it?

As development took place haphazardly, the settlements for a long time lacked facilities such as electricity and water. More recently, infrastructure has improved (World Bank, 2014). At the time of fieldwork, all settlements—with the exception of the squatter settlement KCC—had a connection to the grid. Most plot owners had also paid for their individual plots to be connected, although sometimes tenants were disconnected again after failing to pay their own bill. Furthermore, most households still lacked access to running water on their plot. Nevertheless, whereas residents of settlements such as Karagita and Kasarani previously had depended

Fig. 5.6 Typical row of brick rental housing in Karagita

on water from the lake, there were now a number of ways to access water in the settlements, even if not on one's own plot. A non-governmental organization (NGO) called Water and Sanitation for the Urban Poor (WSUP) constructed water kiosks, selling both fluoride-free drinking water and non-treated water for lower prices. A more expensive option than getting water from a kiosk was to buy water from donkey-cart drivers who bring the water to one's doorstep. Apart from this limited access to electricity and water, other types of infrastructure, such as sewerage and drainage for waste water, were still lacking (Happ, 2016, pp. 128–141; World Bank, 2014, pp. 45–47).

A lack of management of solid waste poses a further problem in the settlements (World Bank, 2014). Due to an increase in population and an increase in wealth, the amount of garbage also increases continuously. When not removed, the waste furthermore affects the wider environment, since much of it eventually runs off into the lake. Students from the University of Bonn researched this specific issue during a field excursion

(Dittmann et al., 2016). They reported that the responsible local government department lacks the equipment and staff to put a proper waste management system in place. As with other departments, the resources for waste management did not grow (sufficiently) with the increase in population. Just as with the lack of housing, which provided an income opportunity to local landowners, private parties have taken advantage here. Several self-help groups and private companies collect garbage on a weekly basis against the payment of a fee. In Karagita, the fee per plot was 250 KES per month, boiling down to a monthly contribution of about 25 KES per household. Registered self-help groups—such as the Lake Naivasha Disabled Environmental Group introduced earlier—could sometimes keep costs low by making use of a truck of the Naivasha municipal council for the garbage collection. This truck had been purchased by the municipal council of Naivasha in 2010—with funding of the Lake Naivasha Growers' Group (LNGG), the local lobby organization of the flower farms ("Town Buys", 2010). However, by 2015, it seemed this truck was rented out to commercial companies instead of being lent out to self-help groups, as the members of the Disabled Environmental Group complained that they were not able to use it anymore. Furthermore, much of the garbage was not collected because not all tenants or landlords paid the fees (Dittmann et al., 2016, p. 28).

Solid waste management is a typical example of a type of infrastructure for which no one takes responsibility. The farms consider it to be a task of the government, the local government expects the farms to contribute because they have caused the population increase in the first place, and the residents themselves simply do not know what to do with their trash. And although the residents are the ones who have to cope with a dirty and unhealthy living environment, they are ironically enough also the ones blamed for this situation. They are perceived to lack interest in the settlements due to the common wish to ultimately move away again. However, when 24 inhabitants of Kihoto were explicitly asked about their opinion on the waste situation in Kihoto, 22 indicated that it was problematic (Dittmann et al., 2016, p. 18). And when I asked Gabriel, a resident of Karagita, about the differences in environment between Naivasha and his village of origin in western Kenya, he immediately mentioned the dirt: "OK, here in town I can say, with the high population, you find sometimes this garbage, that people carelessly throw away dirt. So you find that it is polluted almost everywhere." In other words, some of the residents consider the dirty environment to be problematic. And as a report commissioned by the World Bank (2014, p. 36) indicates, some residents are aware that the piling up of waste, the lack of (affordable) clean drinking water, and the lack of drainage pose risks to their health. However, the residents do not have the resources and the institutions to solve this, in essence logistical, issue themselves.

As the example of solid waste management illustrates, the main bone of contention between the flower farms and the local government in Naivasha is the question of who is responsible for a proper development of the settlements where the migrant workers have come to live. A planning officer of Naivasha Municipality whom I interviewed did not see the provision of affordable and good-quality rental housing for low-income workers as a priority for his office. He asserted that people who are attracted by the flower industry "fit in automatically" because they just move in with their relatives. He acknowledged that there was a problem of overpopulation in these settlements and he mentioned the example of Kamere with 40,000 inhabitants. At the same time, he blamed "urban decay" in the settlements on the attitude of the people living there. According to him, they would not want their living environment and the housing to be upgraded because that would imply higher rents, which they would not be able to afford.

The municipality thus pays little attention to the settlements. The local government is primarily present there through the lowest office in the Kenyan administrative structure, the chiefs and assistant chiefs, who are each in charge of one location or sublocation respectively. The chiefs have the duty to maintain order and can issue certain orders, for instance, in order to prohibit the damaging of public roads (Chiefs' Act, 2012, sec. 6, 10, 11). However, they are not responsible for the *creation* of such order. They are also not (financially) able to develop infrastructure in the settlements. The chief of Mirera Location even told me that his office was not constructed with government funding but was paid for by surrounding flower farms. Funding for infrastructure in the settlements thus mainly originated outside the country.

An example of such an internationally funded programme is the Kenya Informal Settlements Improvement Project (KISIP). KISIP aimed to improve settlement infrastructure in Kihoto, Kamere, Karagita, and Kasarani. The project was funded by the World Bank, the French and Swedish development agencies, and the Kenyan government. It planned to tarmac main roads within the settlements, to improve the drinking water supply, to put (better) drainage and sewerage in place, and to erect security lighting (World Bank, 2014). However, during my last visit to Naivasha in

June 2016, only the security lights were in place. There were a number of tall, extremely bright security lights in each settlement, which lit the whole settlement at night and were even visible from the other side of the lake. Notably, Lowthers (2018, p. 450), who conducted research in Naivasha a few years previous to the instalment of these lights, symbolically contrasted the "blacked-out" settlements at night to the illuminated greenhouses. This contrast had now fully disappeared, and the settlements had become much easier to surveil. Nevertheless, there were hiccups in the other construction works, which were not finished or had not even started yet.

Next to the World Bank and the previously mentioned WSUP project providing water kiosks, there are many other international NGOs operating in Naivasha. For instance, an American missionary set up a mentoring programme in the secondary school in Kasarani, and there is a feeding programme for destitute children in the same settlement, mainly financed by American donors. However, a component of the World Bank project KISIP illustrates the overlap and lack of coordination between organizations providing projects in the settlements. Part of the infrastructure that is meant to be put in place by KISIP is so-called community cookers, running on solid waste. These are meant to handle waste collected in the settlement and to provide an alternative source of fuel, more environmentally friendly than charcoal or firewood (World Bank, 2014, pp. 53–57). Although this plan sounds good on paper, the report does not mention that there is already a community cooker in Karagita, which was put in place some years ago by the Fairtrade Committee of one of the flower farms (Davis, 2011). This cooker was hardly in use in 2015. It is therefore questionable whether the community cookers by KISIP, once installed, will be of any advantage to the inhabitants of the settlements or to the local environment.

Other international NGOs active in Naivasha do not work within the settlements or with the general public but focus on environmental issues, such as water management. For instance, Imarisha, a government-funded programme, was founded in 2011 to synthesize the work of NGOs, researchers, private businesses (such as European retail chains buying flowers), and local and national government institutions with regard to the sustainable use of resources. It also involved around 50 local self-help groups with an environmental component, such as the Lake Naivasha Disabled Environmental Group and several groups of tour guides. Nevertheless, although such high-profile projects generate international funding, little of this funding is spent within the settlements due to the emphasis on conservation and protection of the environment.

Flower farms have a more visible presence within the workers' settlements than the government or NGOs do, if only by determining the rhythm of everyday life. The streets would suddenly become lively after the farms' regular working hours were over. Another example of the farms' presence is that I noticed one day that Kasarani had been infested by swarms of whiteflies, after one of the surrounding farms had sprayed pesticides to remove the flies from their crop. Farms furthermore have a presence in the settlements through the infrastructure that they sponsor there. This infrastructure is either paid from the profits of the farm or, in the case of certified farms, paid through the Fairtrade Premium. Examples are tree-planting projects, the sponsoring of clinics, and the maintenance of the Moi Lake Road. Due to the dependency on sponsoring, most facilities in the settlements—including classrooms of school, public toilets, and boreholes—have signs showing which company, NGO, or government body financed them. Lembcke (2015, p. 9) noted that, unintentionally, these signboards bear testimony to the transiency of the flower industry. Some depict names of farms that had been taken over by a new owner and had changed names a long time ago. Yet, collective memory is short. Inhabitants of the settlement named after the first flower farm, DCK, were often oblivious about the source of this name and especially of the meaning of the abbreviation.

One type of infrastructure that farms particularly like to invest in is schools for the workers' children. There had initially been few schools in the area, but new ones opened up with the increase in population. The heads of the secondary schools in Karagita and Kasarani told me these had been started in 1997 and 2009 respectively. In both cases, the start of the school had been initiated by parents of children who had finished primary school and had no possibilities nearby for further schooling. However, there are also some schools in the area that were founded (but not fully funded) by a flower farm, such as Maua ("Flowers") Primary School at South Lake. According to Happ (2016, p. 80), there were 66 public primary schools and 26 public secondary schools in Naivasha District by 2011. Furthermore, there are a number of private schools and there are possibilities for tertiary training in Naivasha Town.

Although primary education in public schools Kenya is free, parents have to provide for the obligatory uniform and in some cases pay for food provided at the schools. There is a fee for secondary education. Quite a number of farms, especially certified ones, have programmes with bursaries for the children of their employees, which cover part of the school fees.

Farms also contribute financially or materially to the schools themselves, as these receive only limited funds from the government. The workshop of Karibu Farm, for instance, fabricated benches for a nearby primary school.

Karibu Farm is also one of the many sponsors of St. Andrews, the secondary school located on a hillside at a distance of several kilometres from Kasarani. The head of school explained that it was located this far away from the settlement as it had been built on a plot that was donated through a flower farm. Its classrooms were constructed in phases with the assistance of (connections of) farms around and donations via residents of the neighbouring gated community Greenpark, a voluntary teacher from the Netherlands had collected money to buy a water tank, and the parents of the pupils had collected money to build a kitchen, a toilet block, and teachers' housing. It seemed that the head of school was almost busier with fundraising than with teaching. He even visited Germany in 2016 to thank students of a partnering school for their donations and to raise more funding. These international flows of money that are funnelled into the schools in Naivasha do not reach the region of origin of migrant workers. Hence, the presence of good schools in Naivasha is an important attraction and it is a reason to bring one's family along, especially since Kenyan parents attach great value to a good education for their children (and have done so for a long time; see Ross & Weisner, 1977, p. 363).

It is remarkable that despite the investments in the education for older children, proper day care facilities for babies and toddlers are lacking. Even though the provision of day care is an obligation under international treaties signed by Kenya and is included in the Fairtrade standard, only a few farms provide day care or pay out an allowance for that (Fairtrade International, 2014, para. 2.2.9; Happ, 2016, pp. 101–103; KHRC, 2012, p. 51). As many of the employees have migrated to Naivasha on their own, they usually do not have someone in their network there with whom they can leave their child when they are at work. Some therefore choose to leave their babies and toddlers home alone or under the supervision of neighbours, as reported by Wilshaw (2013, p. 92), or decide to leave farm labour all together and to engage in sex work, which is more flexible with regard to time (Lowthers, 2018, p. 465).

If workers can afford, they bring their small children to a private facility in their neighbourhood. About 18.2% of the survey respondents had one or more of their small children going to such a day care centre at the time of the survey. Conditions are generally poor. Children are taken care of in unhygienic private homes and are only provided with food (sometimes heated, sometimes cold) if their parents bring it with them. Parents in the survey reported an average monthly contribution of 710 KES. Conditions vary greatly, as I observed in two different private day care facilities. One was run by a woman in her own clean rental apartment in Kamere, where she took care of eight babies and toddlers. The other was a private plot of a family in Karagita, where literally dozens of children were looked after by two women in a makeshift, two-room house. Children there took their afternoon nap on cartons spread out on the floor.

This lack of proper care for the smallest children is an important point of critique on the flower industry. The presence or lack of day care is also an important consideration for the workers themselves in their employment decisions, especially for female workers. It is furthermore an important reason to let children live with relatives "at home" rather than in Naivasha (Dolan, Opondo, & Smith, 2003, p. 51; KHRC, 2012, p. 50; Wilshaw, 2013, p. 85). Yet farm managers do not acknowledge responsibility for this issue, which they consider to be private. One of the Dutch farm managers stated he admired the female employees for deciding to raise their children on their own and explained they organize themselves in groups of around eight women to provide day care. He did not mention the poor and unhygienic circumstances in many of these private day care centres and did not acknowledge that women had to bring their children there because of their work in his farm in the first place. In short, despite the emphasis on equal gender relations within the farms, the care for the small children of their employees is not something farms take responsibility for. This instance shows once more that migrant workers do desire a certain "order" in the settlements, namely proper day care for their children, but that they simply are not able to organize that in a more orderly manner. And as in the case of garbage collection, neither the flower farms nor the local government is willing or able to pay for it.

5.8 Conclusion: "Spontaneous" Settlements?

This chapter has described the physical appearance and social structure of the workers' settlements in Naivasha. The housing and infrastructure in the settlements developed haphazardly and in an uncoordinated manner. Nevertheless, I argue that they are not the outcome of chance. Rapoport (1988, p. 55) analysed what he called "spontaneous settlements" as the result of "vernacular design". Appadurai (2013, p. 252) likewise called attention to how the daily order in a specific location is produced by social actors. This chapter has discussed how settlement residents have influenced the shape these settlements took, for instance, through their income-generating activities (such as constructing rental housing) and through their participation in organizations such as churches and self-help groups.

Moreover, the chapter has drawn attention to the influence that the government, NGOs, and flower farms have on the shape of the settlements. As Cooper (1983, p. 30) noted, these settlements "are rarely as anarchic as the terms used to describe them suggest—'irregular', 'spontaneous', 'illegal'—but their social order is not the social order of state hegemony". Nor do these settlements—with their partly illicit economy—reflect the social order associated with "modern" capitalist agro-industry. Nevertheless, the government and the flower farms have shaped the physical environment of these areas, if only because they mostly do not provide housing or day care facilities. They thus do not take responsibility for the reproduction of the workforce. Stoler (1985, p. 6) has pointed out that plantations around the world "have reproduced the conditions for their existence, rarely by transforming a particular population into a full-fledged proletariat but more commonly by allowing—and more to the point frequently by *enforcing*—some degree of self-sufficiency on the part of the laboring poor" (emphasis in original). Likewise, despite flower farm managers' and government officials' disapproval of the transiency and the apparent disorder of the settlements, including their illicit economies, they have had their part in the development of these places.

This argument can be illustrated by drawing a comparison between the Naivasha flower farms and horticultural farms in Southern Africa which traditionally had a paternalistic system. Du Toit (1993, p. 315) asserted about the latter: "Farms are not factories in the field. (…) Obligations between worker and farmer extend far beyond the labour-wage nexus." More recently, the paternalistic system is slowly replaced by more impersonal, market-oriented labour regimes, which creates contestations over the extent of mutual obligations (Addison, 2014). The Naivasha flower farms have always been more industrial in nature than these farms in Southern Africa, both with regard to the organization of the work and the labour conditions. Nevertheless, the settlements depend heavily on the farms, for instance, for the creation of direct and indirect employment opportunities and for the provision of infrastructure. The extent of mutual obligations is therefore as contested in Naivasha as in the horticultural industries in Southern Africa, and this chapter has highlighted some of these points of contestation.

Notes

1. KNA Nakuru, GU/10/5/201, "Security Meeting".
2. As James told me about Kihoto. A list of Karagita plot owners in the year 1995 only contains Kikuyu names (KNA Nakuru, GU/3/36/174, "List of Plot Owners Karagita per June 24, 1995").
3. When I last visited Naivasha in June 2016, construction works to tarmac the main roads in Karagita, within the framework of the World Bank program KISIP introduced below, had started. However, construction had come to a standstill for an undetermined period of time. Moreover, there were no plans to tarmac the many smaller roads and paths within the settlements.
4. Figure 2.2 shows the location of these eight settlements. A comparison to Fig. 2.1 illustrates the rapid expansion of these settlements over the past two to three decades.
5. KNA Nakuru, GU/1/8/10, the Divisional Water Officer Naivasha, to the District Water Engineer Nakuru, "Survey of New Water Project: Karagita, Munyu and Kinamba", April 3, 1991; KNA Nakuru, GU/3/36/127, J.M. Nzukuh to the Secretary Central Authority, Nairobi, "The Land Planning Act (Cap. 303)", November 12, 1993; KNA Nakuru, GU/3/36/174, "List of Plot Owners".
6. High levels of fluoride, naturally occurring in Naivasha's groundwater, are a major health issue. It first of all makes visible who has stayed in the area for many years, as longitudinal consumption causes the teeth to turn brown. A more hazardous effect is the weakening of bones. Nic Pacini, an environmental scientist from the University of Calabria, stated at a stakeholders' meeting in Naivasha on November 26, 2014, that it is safer to drink purified lake water than water from the boreholes in the settlements because of the high levels of fluoride. His statement is significant considering the concerns among the general public (both in Kenya as in consumer markets in Europe) about the effects of pesticide use on the lake water.
7. KNA Nakuru, GU/1/8/10, "New Water Project"; KNA Nakuru, GU/1/9/44, Minutes of the Naivasha Subdivision Development Committee, January 3, 1997; KNA Nakuru, GU/9/1/202, the DO I of Naivasha Subdistrict to the DC Nakuru, "Merging of Administration Boundaries", August 10, 2004.
8. KNA Nakuru, GU/3/36/174, Chief of Hell's Gate Location to Sonrahi Surveys, Naivasha, "Sub-division of LR no. 396/31", April 22, 1995.
9. KNA Nakuru, GU/3/33/18, "DCK Trading Centre"; KNA Nakuru, GU/1/8/26, Minutes of the Naivasha Divisional Development Committee, July 26, 1991.
10. KNA Nakuru, GU/9/1/83, the DO Naivasha to the DC Nakuru, "Planning Development Data", February 23, 1971; KNA Nakuru, GU/9/1/188, "Local Authority".

11. KNA Nakuru, EA/2/19/204, E.M.O. Opar, for the Permanent Secretary of the Ministry of Lands and Settlements, to the DC, Nakuru District, "LR No. 12079 Kihoto Farmers Company Ltd", June 18, 2003.
12. KNA Nakuru, ANN/1/3/13, Agenda for the Naivasha Division Land Control Board meeting of January 26, 1983.
13. KNA Nakuru, EA/2/18/114, The Town Clerk of Naivasha to Mr. J.K. Kamere, "Change of User L.R. 9005/5 South Lake", September 18, 2000.
14. KNA Nakuru, GU/6/3/69, Minutes of Naivasha Subdistrict Development Committee, August 24, 2004.
15. This former use of the plot is why a manager of one of the surrounding farms coined the village "Kasarani". Kasarani is the name of a football stadium in Nairobi. Over the years, this nickname has become the unofficial name for the settlement (D. Gitahi, 2015).
16. *Kenya Gazette*, Notice No. 121, January 10, 1967; KNA Nakuru, ANN/1/1/63, Divisional Agricultural Office, "Minutes of Naivasha ASC meeting", October 5, 1980: 2; KNA Nakuru, ANN/1/3/23, Minutes of the Naivasha Land Control Board, July 10, 1984; KNA Nakuru, GU/3/30, The Naivasha Town Clerk, "Advertisement of Plots Tarabete Centre—Naivasha Town", August 26, 1987.
17. KNA Nakuru, GU/1/5/21, Minutes of the North Lake Harambee Dispensary Committee, March 23, 1978.
18. Hanna Kunas made the same argument and noticed the use of the same terminology in her unpublished thesis.
19. This table shows the correlation between gender and level of income. As the survey was exploratory, I chose a relatively high *p*-value and consider values under 0.1 to indicate a significant association. Keeping the limitations of such a survey in mind, I interpret the resulting numbers not as "facts" but as indications that have to be triangulated with data gathered through other methods.
20. About 15.6% of the female respondents possessed a bicycle, against 35.8% of the male respondents (Chi-square: 9.498, $p = 0.002$). Furthermore, 16.5% of the female respondents had livestock, against 38.8% of the male respondents (Chi-square: 10.997, $p = 0.001$).
21. About 17.4% of the female respondents and 20.9% of the male respondents said they owned a plot.
22. However, as explained by Oucho (1996, p. 71), finding out about marital status through a questionnaire is not as uncomplicated as it might seem. What counts as a marriage is a matter of interpretation.
23. These numbers are only indications, as some respondents might have children without acknowledging them, which is of course easier for men than for women. However, another reason for this discrepancy could be that

men on average were older when they had their first child. Female survey respondents were on average 20.8 years old when they had their first child; male respondents 24.5 years old.

24. KNA Nakuru, 15/1/Vol. 1, AR of the Probation Office, Naivasha Division, 1999.
25. The original plot that was bought by the Karagita land-buying company forms an exception here. Even though there are tenants with diverse ethnic backgrounds residing in this neighbourhood as well, the area is economically and socially dominated by the original Kikuyu landowners, many of whom continue to reside there. When we conducted the survey, my assistants and I were also confronted with much more suspicion here than in other neighbourhoods.
26. Whereas 21.5% of the 65 respondents who had arrived between 2010 and 2014 did not participate in any organization in Naivasha, this was the case for only 5.7% of the 35 respondents who had arrived between 2005 and 2009 (Chi-square: 10.250, $p = 0.068$). The questionnaire asked about membership of the trade union, religious groups, political parties, saving groups, welfare organizations, environmental organizations, and peace committees, and included the option to specify any other type of organization in which a respondent participated. Only the organizations that were mentioned most frequently are included in Table 5.3.
27. The remaining 4.5% was either Muslim or did not identify with any religion. Although there are few Muslims living in Naivasha, they have been able to construct several mosques in the area, often on a central location. For instance, the mosque in Kasarani (see Fig. 5.1 for its location) was already built in 1993, only a few years after the settlement had been founded, with the help of a donor from Kuwait (A. Sora, 2015).
28. About 33.0% of the female survey respondents were involved in a *chama* against only 16.4% of the male survey respondents (Chi-Square: 5.849, $p = 0.016$). Furthermore, 23.9% of the men were involved in a welfare organization against only 11.0% of the women (Chi-Square: 5.139, $p = 0.023$).
29. With "institution" in Table 5.4, I mean any type of formal business, organization, or government office. It can be anything from vegetable sellers (question 2) and cyber cafés (question 3) to a bank (question 4), an employer, or the chief (question 8).
30. The letters "cp" stand for contact person, that is, the person who connected Lydia to Naivasha. The numbers represent the questions in the network analysis (see Table 5.4). Red nodes stand for female *alteri*, blue nodes for male *alteri*, and black nodes for *alteri* where the gender is unknown or not applicable.

References

100 families homeless after fire guts houses. (2009, March 16). *Daily Nation*, p. 9.

Abdulaziz, M. H. (1982). Patterns of language acquisition and use in Kenya: Rural-urban differences. *International Journal of the Sociology of Language, 1982*(34). https://doi.org/10.1515/ijsl.1982.34.95

Achieng', R. (2012). *Kenya reconstructing? Building bridges of peace: Post-conflict transformation processes as human security mechanisms.* Zürich: LIT.

Addison, L. (2014). The sexual economy, gender relations and narratives of infant death on a tomato farm in Northern South Africa. *Journal of Agrarian Change, 14*(1), 74–93. https://doi.org/10.1111/joac.12008

Anderson, D., & Lochery, E. (2008). Violence and exodus in Kenya's Rift Valley, 2008: Predictable and preventable? *Journal of Eastern African Studies, 2*(2), 328–343. https://doi.org/10.1080/17531050802095536

Anker, R., & Anker, M. (2014). *Living wage for Kenya with focus on fresh flower farm area near Lake Naivasha.* Retrieved from http://www.fairtrade.net/fileadmin/user_upload/content/2009/resources/LivingWageReport_Kenya.pdf

Appadurai, A. (2013). *The future as cultural fact: Essays on the global condition.* London: Verso.

Becht, R., Odada, E. O., & Higgins, S. (2005). *Lake Naivasha. Experience and lessons learned brief.* Kosatsu: International Lake Environment Committee Foundation. Retrieved from https://worldlakes.org/uploads/17_Lake_Naivasha_27February2006.pdf

Besky, S. (2014). *The Darjeeling distinction: Labor and justice on fair trade tea plantations in India.* Berkeley: University of California Press.

Bolt, M. (2013). Producing permanence: Employment, domesticity and the flexible future on a South African border farm. *Economy and Society, 42*(2), 197–225. https://doi.org/10.1080/03085147.2012.733606

Boone, C. (2012). Land conflict and distributive politics in Kenya. *African Studies Review, 55*(1), 75–103. https://doi.org/10.1353/arw.2012.0010

Borgatti, S., Everett, M., & Freeman, L. (2002). *UCINET 6 for Windows: Software for social network analysis.* Harvard, MA: Analytic Technologies.

Bradshaw, Y. W. (1990). Perpetuating underdevelopment in Kenya: The link between agriculture, class, and state. *African Studies Review, 33*(1), 1–28.

Briefly. (1983, January 12). *Daily Nation*, p. 4.

Chambers, R. (1969). *Settlement schemes in tropical Africa.* London: Routledge & Kegan Paul.

Chiefs' Act. (2012). Retrieved from http://www.kenyalaw.org/lex//actview.xql?actid=CAP.%20128

Chotara threatens to close trading centre. (1983, May 9). *Daily Nation*, p. 3.

Cooper, F. (1983). Introduction: Urban space, industrial time, and wage labor in Africa. In *Struggle for the city: Migrant labor, capital, and the state in urban Africa* (pp. 7–50). London: SAGE.

Coquery-Vidrovitch, C. (1997). *Women in Africa: A modern history.* Westview Press.

Davis, J. (2011, March 1). Smart is when you convert. *Daily Nation*, p. 2.
Dittmann, J., Bauriedel, T., Baumeister, J., Gomm, L., Götz, J., Kempf, S., … Weiß, S. (2016). *Naivasha as a development hub: What are relevant problems related to ongoing developments in Naivasha?* (Occasional Papers of the Section for Development Geography No. 6). Bonn: University of Bonn. Retrieved from https://www.geographie.uni-bonn.de/forschung/ags/ag-geographische-entwicklungsforschung/paper-series/2occasional-paper-6-dittmann-et-al..pdf
Dolan, C. S., Opondo, M., & Smith, S. (2003). *Gender, rights and participation in the Kenya cut flower industry* (NRI Report No. 2768). NRI: Chatham, UK.
Du Toit, A. (1993). The micro-politics of paternalism: The discourses of management and resistance on South African fruit and wine farms. *Journal of Southern African Studies, 19*(2), 314–336.
Failure of meeting explained. (1983, September 17). *Daily Nation*.
Fairtrade International. (2014). Fairtrade Standard for Hired Labour. Version 15.01.2014_v1.0. Fairtrade International. Retrieved from https://www.fairtrade.net/fileadmin/user_upload/content/2009/standards/documents/HL_EN.pdf
Freeman, C. (2000). *High tech and high heels in the global economy: Women, work, and pink collar identities in the Caribbean*. Durham, NC: Duke University Press.
Friedemann-Sánchez, G. (2009). *Assembling flowers and cultivating homes: Labor and gender in Colombia* (1st Paperback ed.). Lanham, MD: Lexington Books.
Gaarlandt, E. (2013). Bloeiend Afrika [Blossoming Africa]. *OneWorld Dossier 6*.
Geoffrey Muhoro v Lake Flowers Limited (High Court of Kenya at Nakuru) (2011). Retrieved from http://kenyalaw.org/caselaw/cases/view/75475
Gibbon, P., & Riisgaard, L. (2014). A new system of labour management in African large-scale agriculture? *Journal of Agrarian Change, 14*(1), 94–128. https://doi.org/10.1111/joac.12043
Gitonga, A. (2015, May 12). Locals initiate move to clean L. Naivasha. *The Standard*.
Grace Wangui Mburu & Another v Peter Mburu Nguri & 4 Others (Court of Appeal at Nairobi) (2015). Retrieved from http://kenyalaw.org/caselaw/cases/view/108384
Happ, J. (2016). *Auswirkungen der Fairtrade-Zertifizierung auf den afrikanischen Blumenanbau. Das Beispiel Naivasha, Kenia [Effects of Fairtrade-certification on the African flower production: The example of Naivasha, Kenya]* (Vol. 4). Norderstedt: Books on Demand.
Hivos. (n.d.). Power of the fair trade flower. Retrieved January 24, 2014, from http://www.powerofthefairtradeflower.nl/
Holt Norris, A., & Worby, E. (2012). The sexual economy of a sugar plantation: Privatization and social welfare in northern Tanzania. *American Ethnologist, 39*(2), 354–370. https://doi.org/10.1111/j.1548-1425.2012.01369.x
Kanogo, T. (1987). *Squatters and the roots of Mau Mau*. London: James Currey.
KHRC. (2012). *Wilting in bloom: The irony of women labour rights in the cut-flower sector in Kenya*. Nairobi: KHRC.

Kimani, J. (2011, November 8). Wanafunzi 376 kufanya KCPE katika shule moja [376 students take KCPE in one school]. *Taifa Leo*, p. 5.
Kioko, E. M. (2012). *Poverty and livelihood strategies at Lake Naivasha, Kenya: A case study of Kasarani Village*. Cologne: Cologne African Studies Centre.
Kioko, E. M. (2016). *Turning conflict into coexistence: Cross-cutting ties and institutions in the agro-pastoral borderlands of Lake Naivasha basin, Kenya*. University of Cologne, Cologne. Retrieved from http://kups.ub.uni-koeln.de/id/eprint/7064
KNBS. (2010). *Kenya population census 2009*. Nairobi: KNBS.
Kung'u, M., & Rogoncho, D. (1988, July 27). Family of six wiped out in fire tragedy. *Daily Nation*, p. 32.
Lang, B., & Sakdapolrak, P. (2014). Belonging and recognition after the post-election violence: A case study on labour migrants in Naivasha, Kenya. *Erdkunde, 68*(3), 185–196. https://doi.org/10.3112/erdkunde.2014.03.03
Lembcke, L. (2015). *Social-ecological change and migration in South-East Lake Naivasha*. Cologne: Cologne African Studies Centre.
Li, T. M. (1998). Working separately but eating together: Personhood, property, and power in conjugal relations. *American Ethnologist, 25*(4), 675–694.
Lime, A. (2012, January 24). Squatters ordered out of rail land. *Daily Nation*. Retrieved from https://www.nation.co.ke/news/Squatters-ordered-out-of-rail-land-/1056-1313508-jrp3tc/index.html
Little, P. D. (2014). *Economic and political reform in Africa: Anthropological perspectives*. Bloomington: Indiana University Press.
Lloyd, P. (1979). *Slums of hope? Shanty towns of the third world*. Harmondsworth: Penguin Books.
LNROA. (1993). *A three phase environmental impact study of recent developments around Lake Naivasha*. Nairobi: John Goldson Associates. Retrieved from ftp://ftp.itc.nl/pub/naivasha/PolicyNGO/LNROA1993.pdf
Lowthers, M. (2018). On institutionalized sexual economies: Employment sex, transactional sex, and sex work in Kenya's cut flower industry. *Signs: Journal of Women in Culture and Society, 43*(2), 449–472. https://doi.org/10.1086/693767
Mary Njeri v Republic (High Court of Kenya at Naivasha) (2015). Retrieved from http://kenyalaw.org/caselaw/cases/view/115260
Masibo, K. (2005, March 31). Group saving lives of workers. *Daily Nation*, p. 19.
Moore, H. L., & Vaughan, M. (1994). *Cutting down trees: Gender, nutrition, and agricultural change in the Northern Province of Zambia, 1890–1990*. Portsmouth, NH: Heinemann.
MP thanks state for donation. (1991, April 8). *Daily Nation*, p. 3.
Mwangi, M. (2007, August 18). Naivasha Town: Where poverty and affluence live side-by-side. *Daily Nation*, p. 26.
Mwangi, M. (2008, April 8). Kipindupindu chawaua watu 3 katika Kasarani, Naivasha [Cholera kills three people in Kasarani, Naivasha]. *Taifa Leo*, p. 4.
Mwangi, M. (2014, October 14). Women storm den to flush out drunk husbands. *Daily Nation*.

Mystery surrounds fate of farm company's cash. (1984, July 2). *Daily Nation*, p. 4.
Obudho, R. A., & Aduwo, G. O. (1989). Slum and squatter settlements in urban centres of Kenya: Towards a planning strategy. *The Netherlands Journal of Housing and Environmental Research, 4*(1), 17–30.
Odingo, R. S. (1971). *The Kenya Highlands: Land use and agricultural development*. Nairobi: East African Publishing House.
Omosa, M., Kimani, M., & Njiru, R. (2006). *The social impact of codes of practice in the cut flower industry in Kenya*. Natural Resources Institute and DFID. Retrieved from http://projects.nri.org/nret/final_kenya_main_report.pdf
Ong, A. (1987). *Spirits of resistance and capitalist discipline: Factory women in Malaysia*. Albany: State University of New York Press.
Oucho, J. O. (1996). *Urban migrants and rural development in Kenya*. Nairobi: Nairobi University Press.
Owuor, S. O. (2003). *Rural livelihood sources for urban households: A study of Nakuru town, Kenya* (ASC Working Paper No. 51). Leiden: African Studies Centre.
Rapoport, A. (1988). Spontaneous settlements as vernacular design. In C. V. Patton (Ed.), *Spontaneous shelter: International perspectives and prospects* (pp. 51–77). Philadelphia, PA: Temple University Press.
Ross, M. H., & Weisner, T. S. (1977). The rural-urban migrant network in Kenya: Some general implications. *American Ethnologist, 4*(2), 359–375. https://doi.org/10.1525/ae.1977.4.2.02a00090
Samarasinghe, V. (1993). Puppets on a string: Women's wage work and empowerment among female tea plantation workers of Sri Lanka. *The Journal of Developing Areas, 27*(3), 329–340.
Scott, J. (2013). *Social network analysis* (3rd ed.). London: SAGE.
Seal, M. (2011). *Wildflower: The extraordinary life and mysterious murder of Joan Root* (Paperback ed.). London: Orion Books Ltd.
Stoler, A. (1985). *Capitalism and confrontation in Sumatra's plantation belt, 1870–1979*. New Haven, CT: Yale University Press.
Town buys Sh6m garbage collection vehicle. (2010, January 22). *Daily Nation*, p. 34.
Transport paralysed as locals block road. (2015, January 10). *Daily Nation*, n.p.
Villagers ordered to leave disputed plot. (2002, January 28). *Daily Nation*, n.p.
Wilshaw, R. (Ed.). (2013). *Exploring the links between international business and poverty reduction: Bouquets and beans from Kenya*. Oxfam. Retrieved from https://www.oxfam.org/sites/www.oxfam.org/files/rr-exploring-links-ipl-poverty-footprint-090513-en.pdf
Wolf, D. L. (1992). *Factory daughters: Gender, household dynamics and rural industrialization in Java*. Berkeley: University of California Press.
World Bank. (2014). *Environmental and social impact assessment for Naivasha* (Kenya—Informal Settlements Improvement Program Project: Environmental Assessment No. 11). Retrieved from http://documents.worldbank.org/curated/en/592331468050686738/Environmental-and-social-impact-assessment-for-Naivasha

CHAPTER 6

Building a Future: Preparing to Go "Home"

Let me go home to rest.
—Flower farm worker Lawrence

Workers' experiences of wage labour and of everyday life in the Naivasha settlements are heavily shaped by their migratory background and their plans for the future. Hanna Kunas reported in her unpublished thesis that almost all migrant workers she interviewed in the settlement Kwa Muhia perceived of their stay in Naivasha as temporary. Wage labour in Naivasha was for them only a means to attain other goals, such as improving material living conditions, paying for children's education, or being able to take up family responsibilities. Migrants usually planned to move back home again once these goals were reached. These findings of Kunas were confirmed during my fieldwork. Most of the migrants residing in the settlements do not perceive of Naivasha as an end station. The migrants lead "translocal" lives. They are temporarily situated in Naivasha, yet they have not settled there permanently and are ultimately "on the move". They therefore also maintain and even establish connections elsewhere (Brickell & Datta, 2011). Migration is in this context not only a strategy for survival in the present but also a way to prepare for the future (Oucho, 1996, p. 54). These imagined futures shape migrant workers' everyday life as tenants in Naivasha. As Warouw (2007, p. 118) asserted for female factory workers in Indonesia: "a worker's industrial body, her physical presence in

G. Kuiper, *Agro-industrial Labour in Kenya*,
https://doi.org/10.1007/978-3-030-18046-1_6

the factory, is constantly overshadowed by her past values and expectations of a post-factory existence."

However, post-wage labour futures can take much longer to materialize than expected beforehand. As Warouw (2007) noted, even when wage employment is regarded as a transitional stage, it can become rather constant. Ferguson (1999, pp. 123–128) elaborated on the complexities of leaving wage employment. He pointed out that colonial governments that "pushed" migrants back to the rural areas did not take into account that certain social and economic factors might make a return difficult or even impossible. Return migration has been perceived of as something to fall back on when failing to earn a wage. Ferguson argued that in the case of miners in Zambia, it was the other way around. Due to high costs of living in town, almost all retired miners left the urban areas. However, only those who had been successful in wage labour and in preparing for their retirement could make a success out of their return to their regions of origin. As Ferguson (1999, p. 165) stated: "it was not so much as a remembered past that rural life was influencing urban conduct but as an anticipated future."

Appadurai (2013, pp. 179–195) has called on anthropologists to pay more attention to the future and to future-making. He maintains that aspirations for the future are shaped by relational, permeable, and possibly contradictory norms. "Aspirations are never simply individual (as the language of wants and choices inclines us to think). They are always formed in interaction and in the thick of social life" (Appadurai, 2013, p. 187). Moreover, not everyone is equally able (or enabled) to plan the future. Appadurai thus considers aspirations to be cultural capacities. When including such capacities in our analysis, "we are surely in a better position to understand how people actually navigate their social space" (Appadurai, 2013, p. 195).

In short, the position of the migrant workers while residing in Naivasha cannot be fully understood without taking into account their plans for the future and also their varying ability to make such plans. This chapter therefore explores how various settlement residents imagined their futures and which strategies they employed to realize their plans. Before that, I address the question of what "going home"—a seemingly straightforward move—actually means in this context.

6.1 The Meaning(s) of Home

What plans do settlement residents have for the future? The usual answer I would receive when asking a resident this question was that he or she was planning to move home.[1] However, this answer proved to be deceptively simple, because what does "home" mean in this context? I found during my time in Naivasha that the meaning of the word *nyumbani* ("home") is highly ambiguous. For instance, when I asked a supervisor of Karibu Farm where his home was, he made a distinction between *kwetu* ("our place", meaning the village where he was born) and *kwangu* ("my place", meaning the town where he had bought a plot of land and built a house).

Kunas found that "home" for migrant workers in Naivasha is broadly connected to three characteristics: region of origin, where family and in-laws live, and where someone owns land. I found that these characteristics might all come together in one place, yet more often than not, they do not. Moore and Vaughan (1994, pp. 172–173) and Ferguson (1999, p. 131) pointed out for the Zambian context that the rural areas where the migrant mineworkers originated from were characterized by high levels of mobility within the region. The mineworkers therefore usually did not have one specific "home village". This is also regularly the case in the Kenyan context, where rural-rural migration is likewise common (Cohen & Atieno Odhiambo, 1989).

Interpretations of "home" are also influenced by gendered ideas. Like Glory, the flower farm worker introduced in Sect. 3.1.3, Kenyan women regularly lack access to land in their region of origin (Coquery-Vidrovitch, 1997). They therefore tend to migrate permanently, as they have no plot of land to return to, unless they purchase one themselves. Women also tend to participate in urban-based organizations, such as churches, rather than in groups organized along ethnic lines with an orientation towards maintaining rural ties (Coquery-Vidrovitch, 1997; Wurster & Ludwar-Ene, 1994). Moreover, Wurster and Ludwar-Ene (1994, p. 156) pointed out that for women, the definition of "home" can vary according to life cycle stage, while this definition is much more stable for men, at least for those men who have access to land in their region of origin. I likewise found in Naivasha that whereas a married woman can consider her husband's village of origin as her future home, a man would not commonly consider his wife's village of origin as home.

Apart from gender, ethnic identities also shape where one feels or is considered to be at home. The region that following the cultural-political discourse of ethnically defined geographical areas in Kenya is associated to someone's ethnic group is regularly deemed to be one's "home", even when one was not born there and perhaps has never lived there. Definitions of "home" can thus be influenced by a looming threat of ethnic violence in places where someone is considered (by others) to be a stranger.

In addition, vernacular languages and cultural ideas on what constitutes a community also play a role in the definition of "home", and therefore complicate the matter, as these languages and ideas are not shared among all labour migrants in Naivasha. Oucho (1996, p. 67), for instance, explained that it is of the utmost importance for Luo men to have a *dala*, which is a specific Luo concept of home. There are local political reasons for that, but also the simple need of having a place to be buried makes having a "home" important. A *dala* is established through a ritual and cannot be established in an urban area. In other words, the definition of home is not an individual venture. Cohen and Atieno Odhiambo (1989, p. 5) stated there were "pressures placed on Luo men to maintain good homes (*dala*) in the Siaya countryside, as places to be at home and to be buried, and as concrete acknowledgements of links to the past". Ritual constructions of home, such as the burying of the placenta at the parents' homestead after birth, put pressure on migrants to stay connected.

Apart from social and cultural considerations, economic factors and the presence or absence of infrastructure also influence definitions of "home". Among the Luo, constructing a *dala* in Siaya became increasingly important in the 1950s and 1960s, probably because of increased affluence and higher levels of mobility (Cohen & Atieno Odhiambo, 1989, p. 57). Likewise, and seemingly paradoxically, flower farm workers might actually have been enabled to perceive ever more of their stay in Naivasha as only temporary due to the increasing prevalence of permanent contracts. The stable income provided by the flower farms enables some workers to construct a "home" outside Naivasha.

Land prices are also crucial here. Whereas some of the migrant workers have been able to purchase a plot in the same area where their family hailed from, many others could not do so, due to land pressure in these areas. In those cases, migrants have purchased a plot elsewhere and thus established a second "home", as the previously mentioned supervisor had done. In sum, the definition of one's "home" is hardly ever straightforward.

"Home" could furthermore be understood in contrast to what is by many considered as its antithesis: Naivasha. Survey respondents often did not immediately understand me when I used the word *nyumbani* when asking which language respondents spoke in their Naivasha households. As Kunas stated in the title of her unpublished thesis, many migrants consider Naivasha to be "just a place to work".[2] I heard migrant workers use the same expression, yet I found that this classification did not necessarily imply a negative qualification. In other words, I found that "home" is not unambiguously positive, nor do residents consider Naivasha only negatively.

Although life in Naivasha is difficult—described by inhabitants with the English terms a "struggle" or a "hustle"—it still can be easier than life "at home". For instance, although the strict control and the working rhythm within the farms are resented, the work itself is considered to be less demanding and extracting than practising small-scale agriculture. When I asked Lucy whether the work in the greenhouse could be compared to cultivating the *shamba* she and her husband own in western Kenya, she started to laugh and said that cultivation is much harder (*kazi ngumu*). Such statements show that the common wish of migrant workers to ultimately leave Naivasha should not be taken as a sign of unbearable circumstances or as proof that they never feel at home there. The qualification of Naivasha as a place of work does not preclude feelings of attachment to the place or keep migrants from attempting to make their house there homely.

In fact, not everyone has a home to return to, even when not being at home in Naivasha either. This was the case for Juliet, a resident of Kasarani who had led a troubled life. She separated from her husband in Bungoma and subsequently one of her children had fallen ill. It was suspected he had been bewitched, and Juliet's sister, who lived in the settlement KCC, advised her to move to Naivasha.[3] Juliet followed this advice and moved to Kasarani in 2005. Her child recovered, but she struggled to make a living. She worked on a temporary contract in one of the vegetable farms for some time. When she gave birth to twins while being single, she did no longer manage to make it to work in the morning and she had to give it up. She then turned towards the cooking and selling of *chang'aa* in her home, which she could not engage in continuously due to occasional police raids. Juliet did not manage to make ends meet, despite some support from her sister and the possibility to buy on credit at the shop in Kasarani where she always did her groceries. Figure 6.1 depicts her fairly small network. Remarkably, her region of origin Bungoma was no longer included in this network, as the family members she mentioned all lived somewhere else. Even though Kasarani was not Juliet's home, it was hard to assess which place would be.

Thus, even when trying to define "home" by describing what it is *not*—namely, the place where one works temporarily—this definition still has its ambiguities. Moreover, even in those cases where it is relatively clear what "home" means, the question remains what would be the proper time to move there, and who should move exactly (for instance, the whole family or only one of the spouses). These decisions are shaped by the relative success or failure of the diverse strategies for the future employed by migrant workers residing in Naivasha.

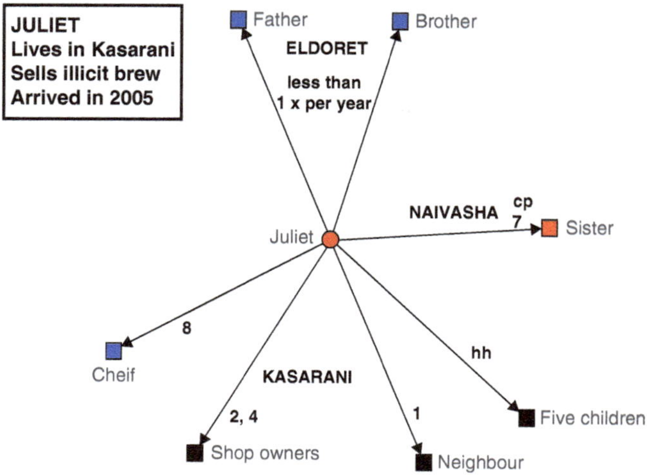

Fig. 6.1 The network of Juliet, based on her answers in the ego-centred network analysis. Developed using UCINET for Windows (Borgatti et al., 2002)

6.2 Strategies for the Future: Constructing a "Home"

Settlement residents prepare for their future outside Naivasha, whether "at home" or elsewhere, in several ways. In what follows, I discuss investing in social networks, investing in a plot of land "at home", and taking precautions for one's funeral. After that, a description of several individual cases will show that factors such as gender, ethnic background, age, household composition, employment, and financial possibilities not only shape definitions of "home" but also influence which strategies for the future someone chooses to employ. The discussion includes both those who were still fully engaged in life and work in Naivasha and those who had immediate plans to move away. It also includes workers such as Glory who felt "stuck" in Naivasha and who had little hope for a future outside the farms and the settlements. To throw these images further into relief, the hopes and plans of migrant workers are compared to those of a resident who owned land in Naivasha and had no plans to move away at all.

6.2.1 Investing in Networks: Visits and Remittances

A first strategy for the future is to maintain contacts by visiting "home" and by sending remittances to relatives residing there. As argued by Ferguson (1999, p. 134) for the case of Zambian miners, in addition to the economic means, a migrant worker also certainly needs cultural and social resources to build up a life in the rural area, after having lived in an urban area for so long. "The decision of *where* people would go was largely about *to whom* they *could* go, and what treatment they could expect when they got there" (Ferguson, 1999, p. 134, emphasis in original). Consequently, migrant workers invest in existing and perhaps even new relations in the place or places they consider to be home while staying in Naivasha.

The frequency of visiting "home" varies greatly, depending on the financial possibilities and the time period a worker can take off from work. It also depends on the relations at "home" and on who is actually living there. For instance, 14 of the 22 respondents in the ego-centred network analysis had a parent or both parents living in their "home region", for which they felt a (financial) responsibility. Respondents would try to visit their parents once a year during their annual leave. Some would try to find additional possibilities for one or several short visits throughout the year, especially seven of the respondents whose one or more children lived "at home". All respondents had a sibling or siblings, yet only three of the respondents who had migrated to Naivasha were the only ones in their family who were not staying "at home" at the time of the interview. The others all had at least one sibling who had moved away as well, and eight of them even had one or more siblings who also had moved to Naivasha (either before or after them). Respondents who had siblings living elsewhere would often only meet them if there would be a "function" such as a funeral or a wedding "at home". This home thus remained a meeting place for the family.

Next to visiting, sending remittances is another way of investing in a social network "at home". It is a common practice in Kenya (Oucho, 1996, p. 17), and 72.2% of the survey respondents said that they regularly sent financial support to someone outside the Naivasha household. The support would mostly go to parents or to a spouse or child living elsewhere. The other way around, only 16.5% of the respondents said that they regularly received financial support from someone outside the household. Again, they mostly received such support from relatives or a spouse residing elsewhere. Although the respondents did not regularly receive financial support from their rural homes, it can be expected that they received support in other ways, such as foodstuffs. Owuor (2003) found that many households in nearby Nakuru, especially those with a migratory background, depended on food produced on their *mashamba* in a rural area. The same applied to at least some of the residents of the settlements in Naivasha, either structurally or occasionally. When Flora and I went to visit her parents in Narok, her mother gave us kilos of potatoes and vegetables, freshly harvested from her *shamba* to take with us to Naivasha. Notably, there was no significant difference between male and female respondents with regard to giving and receiving financial support. I also did not find a correlation between the type of occupation and remittance behaviour.

In sum, many migrants continue to invest in their connections in the region of origin, such as their parents and other relatives. They do so with an eye to the future, as they plan to return there one day. Another reason to stay connected to the region of origin is that migrants remember they were nurtured there in the past. However, in the case of owning a plot of land or livestock "at home", regular contact is also important for economic survival in the present.

6.2.2 *Investing in Assets: Plots and Livestock*

Material investments in the region of origin or—less frequently—elsewhere (outside Naivasha) are another way to prepare for a future after wage labour. Table 5.2 in the previous chapter showed that a substantial minority of the settlement residents, and especially flower farm workers, own land and livestock.

Some migrant workers inherit or are allocated land located in their region of origin. For instance, Flora received a one-acre plot of land from her father (who had retained part of his land himself), on which her brother cultivated on her behalf. Others purchased a plot themselves. I met several employees during visits to Karibu Farm—some originating from other parts of Kenya—who owned a plot in Kasarani. There were furthermore two flower farms that had assisted their employees with purchasing a plot in Naivasha by giving out loans financed by Fairtrade Premium Committees. Yet, with steeply increasing land prices, acquiring a plot in Naivasha has become almost impossible in recent years. Furthermore, most migrant workers are "translocal" and prefer to move away from Naivasha again at some point in time. Thus, they mostly have access to land outside Naivasha.

A quarter of the survey respondents owned livestock, which was usually also kept outside Naivasha, with the exception of chicken. There is simply no space in the densely populated settlements for larger livestock such as cattle, sheep, or goats. Moreover, as residents of Sharma Farm's compound explained, it was forbidden to keep (large) animals in *kambi*. Furthermore, livestock—like plots—is sometimes a family asset and not individually owned. Respondents in the ego-centred network analysis who owned livestock "at home" explained that either they had a family member (sometimes even the spouse) to take care of it or they had hired a casual labourer to do so.

The first purpose of migrants who acquired a plot was to construct a house for themselves there for the future and to have a "home" where they eventually can be buried. Additionally, they could for the time being also involve family members in keeping livestock there or in cultivating the land, thus generating some additional income. Although urban households have higher incomes than rural households, the cost of living is also much higher. Furthermore, there is little space in Naivasha for small-scale agriculture. Except for growing some vegetables in a corner of the plot one lives on, there is no space for "urban farming". Subsistence or commercial agriculture on a *shamba* "at home" therefore not only reduces the need to send cash remittances to family members who remained there, but it can also assist in providing food for the household in the settlement, especially in cases where the *shamba* is located at a relatively small distance from Naivasha. These findings are comparable to the description of Owuor (2003) of rural activities supporting migrant households in Nakuru.

The uses of a plot "at home" can be exemplified by the network of Daniel (see Fig. 6.2). Daniel was clearly invested in both Naivasha and his region of origin. He worked on a flower farm in Naivasha, where he transported the flowers from the greenhouses to the packhouse. Simultaneously to his employment, he and his family cultivated maize, beans, and sugar cane on their *shamba* in Narok. He resided in Naivasha with his wife and his youngest child while his three elder children stayed "at home". Daniel's elaborate network makes clear that a strong connection to the region of origin does not necessarily imply weak ties to Naivasha. It also makes clear that such connections to a plot "at home" can already assist migrant workers and their translocal families while they still reside in Naivasha.

In addition to providing support in the present, such plots also provide a safety net for the future. This can be illustrated by the story of Gabriel, whom I already cited in Sect. 3.3 on his movements within Karagita since his arrival in 2011. Gabriel was born in the western part of Kenya in 1988

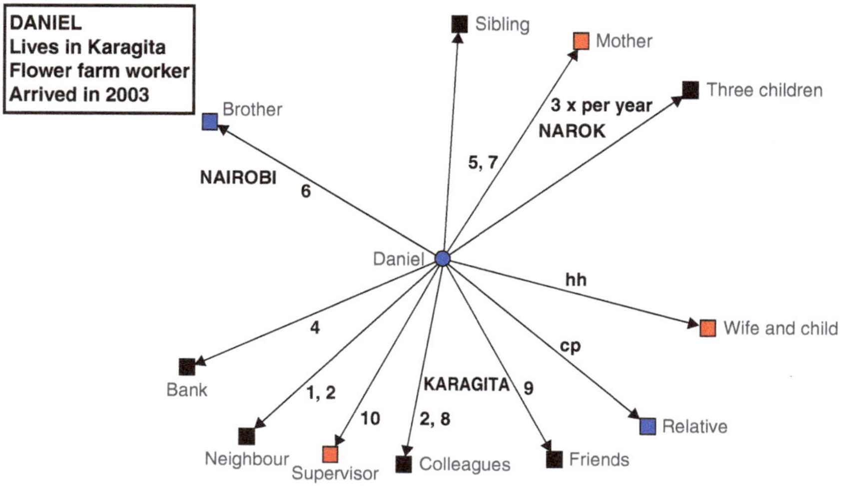

Fig. 6.2 The network of Daniel, based on his answers in the ego-centred network analysis. Developed using UCINET for Windows (Borgatti et al., 2002)

and married a woman originating from the same region in 2015. Despite this connection to "home", he did not regularly visit anymore. Ever since his grandmother, who had raised him, passed away, he had no close relatives anymore living in his region of origin. All his relatives had moved elsewhere for work, like him. Despite this lack of connections, Gabriel planned to move to Western Kenya in the future. He said he felt at home in Naivasha, yet the reason he gave for that is revealing: he found the cost of living to be relatively low when compared to bigger cities such as Nairobi. The lower cost of living enabled him to save money to invest in Western Kenya. Gabriel planned to work in Naivasha for some more years and was even thinking of opening up his own business there. However, he did not aim to settle there permanently. The reasons he gave for his wish to move back "home" were the relatively cold climate in Naivasha and the poor soils, which make it difficult to farm: "But there are those foods now, such as those we have been growing up with, there is food such as cassava and sweet potato, you know here they don't grow at all. But at home they grow."

Remarkably, and unlike most migrant labourers, Gabriel had access to a plot in Naivasha. A land-buying scheme of the Fairtrade Premium Committee of the flower farm where he was working enabled him to acquire a plot in a village in the hinterland of Lake Naivasha. However, he did not plan to go and live there. Instead, he planned to stay in his rental house in Karagita for some more years and then to sell his plot for a good price: "I know I can sell [it] at a good amount and then maybe now I can get a double portion [of land] back in Western. It's a calculation." Gabriel thus did not show a long-term interest in Karagita, even though he said to feel at home there. All he needed there was a decent and affordable one-room apartment to stay in with his family and an opportunity to earn money to invest "at home". As Oucho (1996, p. 20) found, acquiring a plot for the construction of a house or for cultivation is often a priority for migrant workers in Kenya. Assets such as plots of land and livestock not only assist the migrant workers while residing elsewhere but also provide a safety net for the future. A final important reason for acquiring a plot in the region of origin, also mentioned by Gabriel, is that it provides a proper space to be buried.

6.2.3 *Investing in Groups: Participation in Organizations*

A final strategy to prepare for the future is the participation in organizations in the settlements or *kambi* in Naivasha. Especially *vyama* and welfare groups do not only assist migrant workers in their daily lives in Naivasha but also make it possible to save money which can be used to send remittances or to invest in a plot of land.

Furthermore, some of the migrant workers continue to participate in a *chama* based in their region of origin while residing in Naivasha. This translocal participation has become more feasible with the introduction of mobile money (Kusimba, Chaggar, Gross, & Kunyu, 2013). These *vyama* "at home" can take the form of simple merry-go-rounds. Others are more elaborate self-help groups that finance economic activities and infrastructure such as schools and roads in the village of origin of the migrant workers (Oucho, 1996, pp. 123–140). Such voluntary organizations have been a common element among labour migrants across the African continent and have the double function of assisting newly arrived migrants in the urban areas and of maintaining connections to the region of origin (Ross & Weisner, 1977, p. 361). This type of ethnic self-help group of migrant workers also has a long history specifically in Kenya. For instance, the Luo Union—which also was active among Luo residing in Naivasha[4]—ran several businesses and an educational institute in Kisumu in colonial times. Exclusively ethnic organizations were banned by the government in the 1980s—not surprising when considering that these organizations also had political aspirations—yet groups of migrants originating from the same village continued to be active (Oucho, 1996). According to Cohen and Atieno Odhiambo (1989, p. 35), such organizations and associated clubs such as football team served political goals and enhanced the construction of a Luo nation during colonial times. These groups thus partly accounted for the enduring importance of ethnicity despite high levels of labour migration. Such *vyama* in which membership is based on ethnic affiliation are—as described in the previous chapter—also common in present-day Naivasha. Even if these groups usually do not have explicit political goals, they likewise contribute to the continuing relevance of ethnicity in the settlements and flower farm *kambi*.

A specific type of welfare group that is based in Naivasha but orientated towards "home" is the burial organization. It assists bereaved family members with meeting the costs of transporting the body of a deceased group participant to the region of origin to be buried there. Burial organizations have a particularly long history in Kenya and existed already in colonial times, despite the dislike of the colonial government for saving arrangements for Africans (Alila & Obado, 1990; Cohen & Atieno Odhiambo, 1989; Ross & Weisner, 1977). In addition to acquiring a plot or otherwise securing access to land, migrant workers also have to think of how to meet the high transport costs and costs for the funeral itself, hence the popularity of such burial organizations.

In addition, some flower farms assist in paying these costs in case an employee passes away. The Collective Bargaining Agreement (CBA) even includes an allowance of 24,000 KES to be paid to the family members of employees who pass away (AEA & KPAWU, 2011, sec. 22). This allowance is meant to cover the funeral costs, including the coffin and the transport of the body to the home area. This CBA provision shows that, unlike the international standards introduced in Sect. 4.6, some of the flower farms' policies are tailored to local circumstances and take the migration background of workers into account.

A consequence of these practices is that there are relatively few cemeteries in the settlements. Kasarani has a large public cemetery of five acres, which was established when the original Tarambete Farm was subdivided. However, there is still a lot of space, despite the growing population in this settlement. The caretaker told me that it is mainly used by people who have settled in the area a long time ago (mainly Kikuyu and Turkana) and that only Christians are buried there. Muslims have their own cemetery elsewhere in the area. Although sometimes a funeral mass is organized in

Kasarani for deceased migrant workers, their bodies are usually transported "home", except in case there is no one to pay for the transportation. Furthermore, my assistant Richard later told me that people owning their own plot of land are—when possible—buried there. Although he had attended funerals of family members in Kasarani, he had never been to this cemetery before. This preference among land-owning families in Naivasha to bury on their own plots of land also appears from a court case in which the land-buying cooperative Kihoto Farmers attempted to prohibit a widow from burying her late husband on their (disputed) plot in the settlement Kihoto (*Kihoto Farmers Co. Ltd. v Mary Wanjiku Ndichu*, 2003). The general dislike of cemeteries was confirmed by Flora, who said she would not like to be buried on a cemetery ("it is bad there") and would prefer to be buried on a family plot. Although Flora said it would be up to those who she leaves behind to decide where she would be buried, some migrant workers consciously prepare for a burial "at home" through their participation in a burial organization and the acquisition of a plot of land.

6.2.4 *Postponing the Future: Flora and James*

Investing in networks, assets, and groups are thus common strategies to prepare for the future. However, like definitions of "home", the choice of strategy varies. As becomes clear from Ferguson's description of ten retiring miners on the Copperbelt (1999, pp. 123–162), not all migrant workers in the same location have the same (financial and social) possibilities when returning to their respective regions of origin. For the Kenyan context, Nelson (1992) and Wurster and Ludwar-Ene (1994) have elaborated on the different ways in which women and men relate to their rural "home" and to "town". Some of these differences surfaced in the case of James and Flora. Factors such as gender, generation, and family situation played a decisive role in their decision not to move away from Naivasha (yet), despite several immediate pressures—such as a threat of renewed ethnic violence and a state of unemployment—to do so.

When I asked Flora whether she felt at home in Naivasha, she confirmed that she did. She liked to stay there because there are many possibilities to make a living. When I asked her whether there were any other places that she considered to be "home", she mentioned both her parents' village close to Narok and the village close to Kisumu where her parents-in-law live. This was a clearly gendered answer, as James would not mention

Narok as one of the places where he feels at home. To him, Kisumu is what he calls "home". He also did not seem to consider the option of moving to Narok, despite the fact that Flora has been allocated a plot of land of her own by her father and they thus also have access to land there.

I visited James' parents in Kisumu together with Flora. They reside in a spacious house on their own plot. This piece of land had formerly been part of James' grandfathers' plot, which had been divided between James' father and uncles. In their turn, James and his brothers are expected to divide their fathers' plot among themselves after his father's death. James already has built a two-room house with wattle and daub next to his fathers' brick house, which is a common practice among Luo men, as described by Cohen and Atieno Odhiambo (1989, p. 11). This house is the place James calls home and where he expects to retire to. Yet, from conversations with him, it became clear that he does not *feel* at home in his place of birth. Perhaps this is so because he hardly ever lived there, as his father was also a migrant worker. James' plans to move to the family plot in Kisumu are plans for the far future: he called it a place for *wazee*, "old people". He explained there are simply too little opportunities there to make a living, either in employment or in business.

After the production of Sharma Farm completely came to a standstill in the spring of 2016, both Flora and James were rendered jobless. With a second child born the year before, it was a difficult time for the family. When I saw them in June 2016, they were moreover already a bit fearful for the elections of 2017 and the possibility of renewed violence. Nevertheless, despite these harsh times, they still had no plans to move away from Naivasha. Even though both of them thought of Kisumu as their future home, they were not seriously considering moving there already. When I asked Flora where she would like to live, she replied:

> Live? Where work is available. Now I can't even say I will go and stay in Kisumu right now. I will stay and do what? Right now am I not still just looking for work?

James was still heavily investing in his football network in Naivasha, not letting go of his dream of making a career as a professional football coach. Flora was waiting to get her savings recovered, with which she had vague plans of opening a small-scale business in clothing or in milk produced on her parents' plot in Narok. In the end, it was James who started a small-scale business in trading fish, while Flora went to work for a friend who had a hairdressers' salon in Naivasha Town. Flora earned less there than she had earned as a supervisor within Sharma Farm. However, she was happy to have a steady job again, located much closer to her house in Kihoto than the farm had been.

Both Flora and James clearly hoped they would continue to live in Naivasha in the near future, and the major threat to their plans was not even their state of unemployment but the fear of renewed violence around the general elections in 2017. It was confronting to see that the political climate in Kenya threatened Flora and James' existence in the place where they had built networks across different ethnic groups and had started a family. Their wish to stay there was partly related to economic considerations, yet it also clearly came forth out of a sense of affection for cosmopolitan Naivasha. Flora and James did not feel "stuck" in Naivasha and had no wish to return "home" (wherever that was for this multi-ethnic family) in the nearby future. On the contrary, they were against all odds trying to stay established in Naivasha, at least for the time being.

6.2.5 A Woman's Future: Helen

Despite the common goal of staying in Naivasha, I was struck by how little Flora and James discussed their plans for the future together. It even seemed that I spoke more to each of them about this question than they did with each other. They did not seem to make plans as a couple. I encountered even more individuality in making decisions for the future in the case of Helen, the flower farm worker-cum-business woman whom I introduced in Sect. 3.4. After she had moved to Kasarani to look for work, she had met a man there and they had three children. Whenever he was in Kasarani, they resided in the same rental house. However, both of them had purchased an individual plot in different regions in Kenya and planned to retire independent of each other to these respective plots. In fact, the father of Helen's children had already lived on his own plot in Kitale in the western part of Kenya for several years and had been farming there, even though he had returned now to his job on a flower farm close to Kasarani. Helen herself did not consider this plot in Kitale to be hers and had no plans to move there in the future. Nor had she been able to inherit a plot or even a part of plot as James expects to, as women belonging to her ethnic group traditionally do not inherit land. However, she had invested the money she saved with her business and with Karibu Farm's Saving and Credit Co-operative (SACCO) in buying a plot of land of her own in Siaya, her region of origin. She had constructed a house there made of corrugated iron sheets. Helen visited her plot frequently and hoped to be able to retire there in just a few years' time, after her youngest child would have finished secondary school in Naivasha and there would be no need to pay school fees anymore. Having been born in 1966, she stated she was old.

Helen's lack of access to family land and her ability to purchase a plot of her own shows that income earned on the flower farms can help women to attain a more secure economic position. Moreover, gender relations in Naivasha once more prove to be more complicated than the trope of the "single working woman" suggests. Whereas Helen lived with a partner in Naivasha, she planned to live on her own in later life.

Furthermore, despite Helen's wish to move "home" in the nearby future, her answers to my questions showed the ambiguous feelings many migrant workers have towards Naivasha. Even Helen, who felt insecure there after she had fled during the post-election violence and had lost her business capital, expressed ambiguous feelings towards both "home" and Naivasha. When I asked her to compare the two places, she said she preferred living in Siaya, simply because life is cheaper there. In Naivasha, she needs to buy everything, while she could get firewood and water for free close to her rural plot and could cultivate her own vegetables there. Nevertheless, when I asked her whether she feels at home in Naivasha, she laughed and said: "I stayed here for a long time. I am more used to the people here than at home."

6.2.6 A Future in Naivasha: Moses

Apart from the many migrant workers who aspire to move to their own plot of land elsewhere at some point in time, there is also a minority among the settlement residents who consider Naivasha to be their home. Their plans and strategies for the future do not essentially differ from the plans of other inhabitants—except that they are already living in the place where they plan to live during old age and want to be buried. This group consists mostly of (the descendants of) those who had settled in Naivasha and who had acquired a small plot of land there before the flower industry was established, either as former workers or squatters on a ranch or as members of land-buying cooperatives. It seems that this feeling of being at home is largely related to their access to land there. The life story of Moses can illustrate the similarities in both employment and migration biographies and in aspirations for the future between those who settled in Naivasha and the migrant workers.

Moses was born in Nakuru, about 70 kilometres north of Naivasha, in 1973. He came to Karagita when he was only seven years old, together with his parents and eight siblings. His father used to work as a pastry cook in one of the high-end hotels along the lake and acquired a plot in Karagita. Moses' family was among the group of first inhabitants of this settlement. Moses himself was trained as a carpenter after finishing secondary school, and he had worked as such on short-term contracts. He had from time to time been employed by one of the flower farms around to work in the construction department. He got married in 1994 to someone whom he had met while working on a flower farm. They had a son together, but soon after they split up. Moses moved to Mombasa in 1995, following two cousins, and worked there as a carpenter. While visiting Karagita ten years later, in 2005, he reconciled with his wife and decided to move back. He has resided in Karagita since then, and he and his wife had two more children since. At the time I met Moses, his wife was still working on the same farm where they had met each other more than 20 years before. Moses remarked that although she was still a general worker, she received quite some benefits because of her long-term employment. Although they were still a couple, Moses and his wife were not living in the same house at that time. He was renting a room in a compound constructed with wattle and daub in the old centre of Karagita, where he had a small-scale business in selling fish. He was also still now and then employed by a flower farm on short-term contracts. Apart from these income-generating activities, Moses was also engaged in voluntary work in Karagita. He was a representative for the tenants in Karagita in the stakeholders' committee of the World Bank project Kenya Informal Settlements Improvement Project (KISIP). He also had volunteered for a long time as a community health worker, in which role he provided home-based care to patients with long-term diseases such as diabetes or HIV. Furthermore, he was an active church member and participated in a *chama* with a monthly contribution of 1200 KES. He was thus heavily invested in Karagita.

When I last visited Moses in June 2016, I found him in less favourable circumstances than when I had first met him. He had fallen ill, had been hospitalized for quite some time, and had visibly lost weight. He had left his rental house and had moved back to his family's plot a few hundred metres closer to the Moi Lake Road. The plot contained several houses, including the one-room apartment he grew up in, and he stayed there with his sister and her family and a tenant. Moses' parents both had passed away already and had been buried on another family plot in Mirera, further away from the lake. Apart from these family plots, Moses had also purchased his own plot in Mirera. He had constructed makeshift housing there to rent out. Nevertheless, he had plans to construct his own house on the plot and move there in the future. When I asked him whether he had plans to move out of the wider Naivasha area again, as he had done when he moved to Mombasa, he asked me in return where he should go: Karagita was his home.

Thus, as with migrant labourers who reside only temporarily in Naivasha, where Moses felt at home was related to access to land. But feeling "home" also is implicitly related to politicized ideas of where an individual with a certain ethnic identity can claim belonging. I noted when I visited Moses at his family's house that he and his relatives spoke Kikuyu to each other. They even joked that after learning Swahili, I should learn Kikuyu now. It was clearly comfortable for them to live in an area where they could freely speak their vernacular language. Notably, I took James along when I last visited Moses in June 2016, and they had animated discussions. Both, for instance, had been community representatives for KISIP for the respective settlements they lived in. Nevertheless, whereas Moses asserted that no renewed ethnic violence would occur during the 2017 general elections, James was much more apprehensive. Moses—a Kikuyu—could afford to feel secure and ultimately at home in Naivasha while James—a Luo—could not.

Despite the different geographical orientations, the strategies for building a future are similar: like migrant workers, also those who settled in Naivasha more permanently build their future through investing in (more) land and in extending their networks. The fact that Moses for some years had been a labour migrant himself furthermore shows that this type of long-term return migration is not specific for the flower industry.

6.3 Leaving Naivasha: Wage Labour Pasts?

Do all these future plans materialize? What happens when people decide to or are forced to leave wage labour in the flower industry? Do indeed most of them return "home"? And if so, how is their life at "home" influenced by their wage labour pasts? Responses to a question I asked in the ego-centred network analysis could provide a start of an answer here. Most of the respondents in the ego-centred network analysis already knew somebody in Naivasha when they moved there, usually a family member and in some cases a friend. Significantly, not all of these "contact persons" had remained in Naivasha. Ten of the respondents reported that their initial contacts to Naivasha were still staying there at the time of the interview. But the initial contacts of four respondents had moved elsewhere (mostly to Nairobi) for work while the "contact persons" of the other six had moved "back home".

Sometimes it is those who are unsuccessful in securing employment in Naivasha who move "on" to Nairobi or to another city. Another reason to move could be better job opportunities elsewhere. And as also asserted by Staelens, Desiere, Louche, and D'Haese (2018, pp. 1625–1626) for flower farm workers in Ethiopia, those with access to land in rural areas usually have the firm intention of moving there and leaving wage employment, even if they are satisfied with their job and the work conditions. It is furthermore not uncommon to move to Naivasha for some years, to leave, and to come back again. One of the employees of Karibu Farm told me she had to leave her previous employment in another flower farm in Naivasha when her parents went to Nairobi to pursue long-term treatment for her father who had fallen ill. The responsibility to take care of the house then fell on her and she temporarily had to move there. She only came back to Naivasha after her father had passed away. She then had to look for a new job and a new place to stay.

The question of when to leave Naivasha is—for those working on a flower farm—partly influenced by policies of the farms. An example is the gratuity, which is only paid to those who have worked on the same farm for at least five years. To gain more insights into reasons for leaving Naivasha and into prospects after employment on a flower farm, I interviewed two of the workers of Karibu Farm who had given notice of resignation in the weeks before and who were about to leave Kasarani: Lawrence and Dominic.[5]

Lawrence was born in Laikipia in 1972. His family had a long connection to Kasarani. His father had already been working on one of the ranches in the area decades ago. Lawrence himself grew up in Laikipia, had been a small-scale farmer and livestock-keeper there, and only came to stay in Kasarani to look for a job in 2006. Lawrence was not alone in Naivasha: two of his sisters were also staying in Kasarani at the time of the interview and were even working on the same farm. And even his mother had moved to her own plot, purchased for her by her children, in nearby Ndabibi, where she was cultivating land. Nevertheless, in 2015, almost ten years after he had started working in Kasarani, Lawrence decided it was time for him to move back to Laikipia to develop the plot of land that he owned there. At the time of the interview, he had already stopped working and was waiting for his service payment and for his savings from the SACCO. He planned to use this capital to start up small-scale cultivation on his plot and to start constructing a house there, even though he expected the payments would not suffice to complete the construction. He consequently also did not foreclose the possibility that he would enter into wage labour again. He stated: "There was nothing wrong with the work [on the farm]. Let me go home to rest now." This quote makes clear that, even though a large part of Lawrence's family was residing in Kasarani and his mother even owned land nearby, he still considered their village of origin in Laikipia as "home". Nevertheless, he and his family could be considered to be thoroughly translocal: they were grounded in (at least) two places and were always on the move (Brickell & Datta, 2011). Significantly, Lawrence did not consider his move to Laikipia as final.

This was different for Dominic, whom I interviewed a few weeks later during one of his last lunch breaks on the farm. Dominic also happened to originate from Laikipia and had started to work for Karibu Farm one year before Lawrence, in 2005. He had followed a brother, who had been working in a ranch close to Kasarani at the time, but who had, by the time of the interview, already moved back. Dominic worked as a sprayer and resided in a rental house in Kasarani with his wife and some of his children. His other children were staying in Laikipia with their grandparents. By 2015, Dominic had no other siblings or close relatives anymore who like him were residing outside Laikipia: all who had left previously had returned home. When I asked him why he now also had decided to resign, he said he had worked for Karibu Farm for a long time. It was now time to move ahead. Notably, Dominic used the Swahili word *kuendelea*, which means "to move on" or "to proceed". I would have expected him to use the word *kurudi*, "to return" or "to move back". His wording revealed that he considered moving to Laikipia as a step forward and not as a step back. He wanted to return to what he called "Maasailand", where he planned to engage in small-scale business and livestock keeping. When I asked him whether he was happy to go home, his face lit up and he said: *kabisa*, "entirely".

In addition to these two employees who were about to leave Naivasha, I interviewed several former workers who had already returned "home" some years previously. When Flora and I visited Kisumu, she arranged for us to meet with three of her former colleagues from Sharma Farm: Daisy, Evelyn, and Sam. On a different occasion, I interviewed John, a former colleague of Flora who had returned to his region of origin Narok. The four interviewees had held diverse positions within the farm and had had

Table 6.1 Main characteristics of four former flower farm workers who had left Naivasha

Name	*Year of birth*	*Year of arrival*	*Last position*	*Year of leaving*	*Reason for leaving*	*Current occupation*
Sam	1980	2002	Irrigation operator	2008	Post-election violence	Machine operator in a company that manufactures water tanks
Daisy	1972	2002	General worker (husband: maintenance)	2009	Husband fell terminally ill	Small-scale commercial farming (maize, beans, millet, peanuts) in her husbands' home village
Evelyn	1972	1997	Grader	2009	Contract terminated	Casual labourer in Kisumu City
John	1973	1997	Electrician (wife: none)	2012	Contract terminated	Self-employed electrician; farming (by his wife) and herding

diverse reasons to leave, which shaped their lives when they returned to their region of origin. Table 6.1 summarizes these positions and reasons.

The interviews provided insights into what these former migrant workers gained from their migration experience and their work on a flower farm. These include monetary gains but also relevant work experience and social experiences. When I asked Daisy and Evelyn how their employment in Sharma Farm had benefited them, they provided a similar answer. They replied that they had been able to save some money, with which Daisy (and her husband) had bought a rural plot and constructed a house, and with which Evelyn had paid for the school fees of her children in the past few years. Although both Evelyn and John had lost their jobs after the financial problems of Sharma Farm had started, they in hindsight had been fortunate: they, like Daisy, had come out of it with their service payments and savings from the SACCO, unlike those who lost their jobs at a later stage (such as Flora). These payments and savings together could be a considerable amount of money, even though John considered the service payments to be little: "Just a small thing. That is just a ticket to return home." Nevertheless, when taking a fictive example in which a worker contributes 1000 KES per month to the SACCO and works for a farm for eight years, it shows that he or she can save 96,000 KES. The gratuity, which according to the CBA consists of 22 days of basic pay for every year worked, would in such an example also amount up to several ten thousands of shillings (AEA & KPAWU, 2011, sec. 24(a)). Sam would probably have been happy to have been able to take such an amount with him, while he left Naivasha without receiving any monetary benefits. He had literally fled the area after the post-election violence erupted and the house that he rented in Naivasha Town was burned down. He had not dared to return to Naivasha to recover his service payments and, traumatized as he was, would never consider moving there again.

Fortunately, Sam had acquired a well-paying job in Kisumu City, partly thanks to the experience he had gained in his farm job and partly due to a diploma in machine operation. He had earned this diploma through self-study at an institute in Nairobi while being employed in Naivasha. John had already earned a diploma in electrical engineering even before he started working for Sharma Farm and therefore could continue with this work after returning home. The two female workers on the other hand had not learned a trade during their time in Naivasha and had no tertiary education, and their work experience therefore did little in terms of helping them to find a job back in Kisumu. However, although not providing any material gain, Evelyn stated explicitly that the flower farm work had given her the opportunity to learn how to work and live with people from different ethnic backgrounds. Even Sam had positive memories of the labour relations on the farm: he said he had learned there how to relate to people and had gained a bit of management experience as an assistant to the irrigation supervisor. All four were happy to see Flora and were eager to hear news about former colleagues and about the farm. Daisy even had several pictures hanging on the wall of her rural home from the time she worked for Sharma Farm, some taken in the greenhouses.

Whereas Sam, Daisy, and John all in some way or the other now had attained a secure (if modest) livelihood in their region of origin, Evelyn was struggling. But despite the low chances of finding employment as a low-skilled worker in Kisumu, she had decided not to stay in Naivasha because of the implicit threat of violence and the feeling of being unwelcome. She stated that "people" say that migrant workers from the western parts of Kenya steal their jobs. Evelyn's hesitance to move back to Naivasha thus shows the enduring impact of the post-election violence.

John also felt too insecure to apply for another position in Naivasha, but this related more to insecurity of employment than to ethnic tensions:

Didn't you consider asking for a job somewhere else in Naivasha?
I didn't like that very much.
Why not?
You know I thought if there things could change all of a sudden, it's not good.

John's decision to leave Naivasha concords with the finding of Staelens et al. (2018) among flower farm workers in Ethiopia that job security is an important determinant for job satisfaction. Although Sharma Farm's demise formed a blow for the reputation of the flower industry, the general increase in permanent jobs made the industry an attractive employer, even for those who planned to leave wage labour again in the future.

When comparing living conditions in Naivasha to those in the region of origin, Evelyn's situation in Kisumu City was actually not much different from her situation in Naivasha: she was renting a two-room apartment in an urban area. The contrasts were much bigger in the case of Daisy. While residing in Naivasha, she had stayed in a single room on the Sharma Farm compound, together with her husband and (eventually) seven children. When I asked her whether the living situation had not been very cramped, she said it had not been a problem as the children still were small. Nevertheless, the house they had constructed on their rural plot was much bigger. It contained several rooms, and her living room was even so exceptionally spacious that the *chama* she participated in had its meetings at her house.

Due to her precarious position in Kisumu, with no access to land nor permanent employment, Evelyn was the only one who vaguely seemed to consider becoming a migrant worker again. The others planned to stay where they were. These plans were informed by their economic security there but also by their biographies (Sam's encounter with violence in Naivasha) and by their stage in the life cycle (John and Daisy considered themselves to be too old to be a migrant worker). When I asked John about his plans for the rest of his life, he gave me the following answer:

> Open my own company and continue with my work. If I will be employed, it will be with the government. Perhaps the county government or maybe the Maasai Mara University, close to home. The years have gone by, I'm not fit to go very far away.

6.4 Conclusion: Securing the Future

Even though residents of the settlements around Lake Naivasha frequently stay for years or even decades, many of them are migrants for whom their migration is not a completed act. Their position in the settlements can be understood as "emplaced mobility" (McGarrigle & Ascensão, 2017). This chapter has described the different understandings of "home", which in their turn reflect different understandings of Naivasha as a place of work. The chapter furthermore discussed the different plans and strategies that develop out of this "emplaced mobility" or translocality. It showed the various ways in which residents of the settlements prepare themselves for the future and attempt to construct a "home", quite literally in the sense of securing access to land and building a house and more discursively in the sense of creating a social network that they can fall back on.

The chapter furthermore indicated that there are differences in the "cultural capacity to aspire" (Appadurai, 2013) and showed how individual plans relate to factors such as gender, generation, ethnic affiliation, and economic position (more specifically land ownership and occupation). These plans in turn influence how migrant workers position themselves within farms and other places of work and within the settlements and farm compounds in Naivasha. Such factors, for instance, impact on membership of organizations.

Finally, I discussed the varied ways in which planned futures materialize—or not. Some workers are forced to move back to their region of origin without attaining their goals, for instance, after being rendered jobless or because of threats of violence. These former workers are facing an insecure future, despite moving "home". Thus, as asserted by Ferguson (Ferguson, 1999), "home" is for migrant workers not necessarily a safety net to fall back on. Only those who succeed in Naivasha can feel secure when moving "home".

Notes

1. The exception was a small minority among the residents who considered the settlement to be their home, for instance, the owners of the plots in the original part of Karagita. I discuss the future plans of one of those residents, Moses, in Sect. 6.2.4.
2. In German: "*Dies ist nur ein Ort zum Arbeiten*".
3. Oucho (1996, p. 77) had 7 respondents in his survey among 417 migrants who said witchcraft had played a role in their decision to move. Few of my respondents in Naivasha referred to witchcraft when discussing their motives for past decisions and their future plans. I attribute this to my position as a foreigner and my distant relationship to most of the respondents. It should therefore not be taken as an indication that such considerations did not play a role in more cases than only in Juliet's case.

4. KNA, DC/Nais/1/1/1/52, AR Naivasha District 1958.
5. According to the CBA, workers who wanted to resign should give a notice 30–60 days (the exact amount of days depending on the total period of employment) prior to leaving the job (AEA & KPAWU, 2011, sec. 18).

References

AEA, & KPAWU. (2011). Collective Bargaining Agreement between the Agricultural Employers' Association and the Kenya Plantation and Agricultural Workers' Union 2011–2013. Retrieved from http://www.agriemp.co.ke/downloads/cbas/flower-growers-cba

Alila, P. O., & Obado, P. O. (1990). *Co-operative credit: The Kenyan SACCOs in a historical and development perspective* (Working Paper No. 474). Nairobi: Institute for Development Studies.

Appadurai, A. (2013). *The future as cultural fact: Essays on the global condition.* London: Verso.

Borgatti, S., Everett, M., & Freeman, L. (2002). *UCINET 6 for Windows: Software for social network analysis.* Harvard, MA: Analytic Technologies.

Brickell, K., & Datta, A. (2011). Introduction: Translocal geographies. In K. Brickell & A. Datta (Eds.), *Translocal geographies: Space, places, connections* (pp. 3–22). Farnham: Ashgate.

Cohen, D. W., & Atieno Odhiambo, E. S. (1989). *Siaya: The historical anthropology of an African landscape.* London: James Currey.

Coquery-Vidrovitch, C. (1997). *Women in Africa: A modern history.* Westview Press.

Ferguson, J. (1999). *Expectations of modernity: Myths and meanings of urban life on the Zambian Copperbelt.* Berkeley: University of California Press.

Kihoto Farmers Co. Ltd. v Mary Wanjiku Ndichu (High Court of Kenya at Nakuru) (2003). Retrieved from http://kenyalaw.org/caselaw/

Kusimba, S., Chaggar, H., Gross, E., & Kunyu, G. (2013). *Social networks of mobile money in Kenya* (Working Paper No. 1) (pp. 1–33). N.p.: Institute of Mobile Money, Technology and Financial Inclusion.

McGarrigle, J., & Ascensão, E. (2017). Emplaced mobilities: Lisbon as a translocality in the migration journeys of Punjabi Sikhs to Europe. *Journal of Ethnic and Migration Studies*, 1–20. https://doi.org/10.1080/1369183X.2017.1306436

Moore, H. L., & Vaughan, M. (1994). *Cutting down trees: Gender, nutrition, and agricultural change in the Northern Province of Zambia, 1890–1990.* Portsmouth, NH: Heinemann.

Nelson, N. (1992). The women who have left and those who have stayed behind: Rural-urban migration in central and western Kenya. In S. Chant (Ed.), *Gender and migration in developing countries* (pp. 109–138). London: Belhaven Press.

Oucho, J. O. (1996). *Urban migrants and rural development in Kenya*. Nairobi: Nairobi University Press.

Owuor, S. O. (2003). *Rural livelihood sources for urban households: A study of Nakuru Town, Kenya* (ASC Working Paper No. 51). Leiden: African Studies Centre.

Ross, M. H., & Weisner, T. S. (1977). The rural-urban migrant network in Kenya: Some general implications. *American Ethnologist, 4*(2), 359–375. https://doi.org/10.1525/ae.1977.4.2.02a00090

Staelens, L., Desiere, S., Louche, C., & D'Haese, M. (2018). Predicting job satisfaction and workers' intentions to leave at the bottom of the high value agricultural chain: Evidence from the Ethiopian cut flower industry. *The International Journal of Human Resource Management, 29*(9), 1609–1635. https://doi.org/10.1080/09585192.2016.1253032

Warouw, N. (2007). Industrial workers in transition: Women's experience of factory work in Tangerang. In M. Ford & L. Parker (Eds.), *Women and work in Indonesia* (pp. 104–119). New York: Routledge.

Wurster, G., & Ludwar-Ene, G. (1994). Commitment to urban versus rural life among professional women in African towns. In R. Mechtild & G. Ludwar-Ene (Eds.), *Gender and identity in Africa*. Münster: LIT.

CHAPTER 7

Conclusion

At the time I am finishing this book, Valentine's Day 2019 is approaching. The workers on the Naivasha cut flower farms have just made it through the busiest time of the year, and all red roses should have been packed for shipment by now. This time of the year, along with Christmas and Mother's Day, is traditionally also the peak season for critical media reports on the flower industry in the European consumer markets. Newspaper articles with titles such as 'Exploitation for Valentine's Day' (Endres, 2012) and 'The stinky truth about your beautiful Valentine's Day roses' (Finnigan, 2016) portray the flower farm workers as victims of a ruthless global agro-industry. In addition, the flower industry has over the past two decades been under intense scrutiny by NGOs. These NGOs—for example, Hivos (n.d.)—have developed campaigns targeting consumers of flowers, focussing on issues such as the potential health risks of pesticides used by the farms and the position of female workers.

The situation of labour within the flower farms in Naivasha is thus highly contested. With this book, I did not aim to produce yet another evaluation of the labour conditions in the industry, as provided by, for instance, Dolan, Opondo, and Smith (2003) and KHRC (2012). Instead, I have aimed to understand how labour arrangements and conditions within the Naivasha flower industry came into being and how these have changed over the years. I have furthermore attempted to move beyond a "workerist" approach that perceives of workers as full-time urbanized proletarians without any income-generating activities apart from wage labour (Moyo,

G. Kuiper, *Agro-industrial Labour in Kenya*,
https://doi.org/10.1007/978-3-030-18046-1_7

Rutherford, & Amanor-Wilks, 2000). I have aimed to assess the position of flower farm workers in a more holistic way instead. I understand the migrant workers to be "translocal": temporarily grounded in Naivasha but with networks stretching out to other places, and ultimately on the move (Brickell & Datta, 2011; Greiner & Sakdapolrak, 2013). I have explicitly addressed temporal dimensions of migration, as reflected in the chronological chapter outline. Migrant workers' pasts and their plans for the future shape their experiences of wage labour on the Naivasha flower farms.

Remarkably few researchers have investigated the experiences of translocal workers around Lake Naivasha, even though their situation has been the topic of intense public debate. Naivasha has been researched extensively, yet most studies have focussed on the lake's ecological characteristics. The flower industry's arrival has been portrayed as a sudden rupture with the past, which could even lead to the collapse of the lake's social-ecological system (Becht, Odada, & Higgins, 2005; Seal, 2011). Such accounts ignore that the flower industry established itself in an area with a long history of agricultural wage labour on ranches. Flower farms could take over large tracts of land that had fallen in private hands due to the colonial land tenure system. In addition, they could tap into an existing system of agricultural wage labour recruitment.

Global agro-industries are usually associated with land-grabbing and with the dispossession of African smallholders (Hall, Scoones, & Tsikata, 2017). But the flower industry was able to establish itself in Naivasha because of earlier transformations. In a paper presented at the conference *The Global South on the Move* (Cologne, June 7 to June 9, 2017), Mia Siscawati likewise described how palm oil companies in North Kalimantan, Indonesia, could make use of earlier "disturbances of the landscape" created by logging companies. The logging activities had literally provided the plantations with the open space they needed. Local histories thus prove to be crucial, both in the choice of production sites by global industries and in the way local people experience the arrival of such industries. I have argued in Chap. 2 that a representation of Naivasha as a natural paradise under threat by unsustainable agro-industry is based on a partial and elitist interpretation of Naivasha's history. It does not reflect the perspectives of small-scale landowners in the settlements or of migrant workers, for whom the arrival of the flower industry implied new economic opportunities.

Apart from offering a more diverse understanding of Naivasha as a place, this book is also meant to fill a theoretical void by providing a case study of agro-industrial labour on the African continent. Agro-industry is commonly understood to be a highly mechanized way of farming with a decreasing need for human labour (Barlett, 1989). Following Mintz (1985), I define agro-industry through its organization of labour, which is reminiscent of factory work, instead. Agro-industrial farms are—like factories—characterized by a high level of discipline, a segmented labour force, and a strict rhythm of the work. What is needed is "industry" in the sense of diligence, not in the sense of mechanization.

Regardless of how it is defined, agro-industrial labour rarely figures in detail in anthropological literature, especially when it comes to labour on African farms or plantations. This book has addressed this lacuna. Moreover, the case of the labour-intensive, highly disciplined Naivasha flower farms challenges the binary that associates "Africa" with "traditional" peasant agriculture and "the West" with "modern", large-scale, and industrialized agriculture (Piot, 1999).

The similarity to industrial production is most poignant with regard to work rhythm. Thompson (1967) argued that industrial labour is characterized by an adherence to "clock-time", which replaced "task-time". Flower farm work shows signs of both. The fixed working hours for most employees, stipulated in the increasingly important Collective Bargaining Agreement (CBA) and in labour legislation, indicate the use of clock-time. Yet the organization of the work within these fixed hours, for instance, the varying amount of time spent on harvesting flowers, implies the use of task-time. In line with Mintz (1985), I argue that the rhythm of work within the farms is not characterized by an orientation either towards the clock or towards the execution of certain tasks but by a high level of compulsion and discipline. Employees are expected to be flexible yet punctual and to work at high speed. Notably, this is an aspect of the work that is particularly resented.

However, agro-industry is not simply industry. The product is "natural" and therefore inherently instable. The crop is sensitive to changing weather conditions and to pests and diseases, and the end products, the cut flowers, are highly perishable. Following Besky's (2014) approach in studying labour relations on tea plantations, I have examined the Naivasha rose's "social ecology". The industry's move to Naivasha in the first place was partly due to conducive climatic conditions. In addition, flower production is labour-intensive yet requires relatively little space, thus allowing for a coexistence with other economic sectors such as tourism, and even with wildlife and environmental conservation activities. This accounts for a much more varied landscape in Naivasha than the landscape dominated by sugar cane described by Mintz (1985, p. xviii).

Moreover, apart from these spatial dimensions, ecological characteristics of the crop also influence the organization and conditions of labour. With the shift from the production of seasonal flowers to year-round rose production, farms could afford to hire permanent labour (Gibbon & Riisgaard, 2014). The flower farms even have an interest in retaining their workers, as the vulnerability and perishability of the cut flowers require a workforce that can work meticulously yet on a fast pace.

This need for stability contrasts to the situation in global factories, as indicated by the following quote. "Highly monotonous, repetitive operations, accelerated work rhythms, lack of promotions and inadequate working conditions combine to prevent long-term employment. It is not in the interest of the maquiladora industry to maintain a stable and permanently employed work force, especially in an environment where assembly operators may be easily replaced" (Fernández-Kelly, 1983, p. 68). In contrast, the Naivasha flower farm worker has *not* become an "interchangeable part" in the production process (Braverman, 1998). The *agricultural* and therewith perishable nature of cut flowers requires an *industrial* way of organizing production within the farms. Yet the resulting levels of responsibility placed on individual workers in the flower industry are much higher than levels of responsibility in many other global industries, such as along industrial assembly lines. The work on the flower farms is rigorously monitored, and individual workers can be held accountable for any mistakes or sloppiness (Gibbon & Riisgaard, 2014).

Why do the workers agree to work on these highly disciplined farms where most of them stay at the bottom of the hierarchy for the whole period of employment? Why do many stay around for years or even decades? How do the farms "manufacture" consent (Burawoy, 1979), despite wage levels that do not represent a "living wage" (Anker & Anker, 2014)? As discussed in Chap. 4, labour conditions are geared towards retaining labour. Examples are yearly salary increments and the payment of gratuity after at least five years of employment. Moreover, despite all criticism on labour conditions in the Kenyan flower industry, they compare favourably to conditions in other economic sectors in Naivasha, especially since the increasing adherence by flower farms to the CBA. Vegetable farms in Naivasha, for instance, pay lower wages and work primarily with temporary contracts.

Moreover, flower farms' conditions also compare favourably to the conditions in other global (agro-)industries. With its move towards more permanent contracts, the flower industry is a remarkable exception in a world of increasing precarity and "flexibilization": "the substitution of permanent workers with occasional workers; the loosening of job demarcation; the reorganization of work from individual to team work" (Ortiz, 2002, p. 400). For instance, workers on Southern African commercial horticultural, wine, and tobacco farms, and especially migrant workers, only saw labour conditions deteriorating with the shift from a paternalistic system of labour control to more hybrid and formalized systems (Addison, 2014; Bolt, 2016; Du Toit, 1993; Rutherford, 2001). "Across all forms of commercial agriculture there has been a trend towards less permanent salaried work, except in management positions, and towards a greater reliance on casual, temporary work" (Hall et al., 2017, p. 526). This temporary labour is moreover increasingly recruited via "brokers" or intermediaries. The risk of such a brokerage system is that moral and legal considerations are bypassed, as the workers become dependent on their intermediaries for their jobs (Meagher, Mann, & Bolt, 2016). In contrast, the Naivasha flower farm workers experience higher levels of job security than before, and recruitment processes have been formalized in recent years (Gibbon & Riisgaard, 2014).

Some other global (agro-)industries furthermore make use of a segmentation of the workforce as a tool in labour control, and provide different types of jobs and different labour conditions—such as either permanent or temporary contracts—on the basis of ethnic distinctions (Addison, 2014; Bolt, 2013; Thomas, 1985). Moreover, in many global factories, the division of labour is highly gendered. It is especially women who are confronted with low payments and insecurity of employment. Indeed, such industries deliberately recruit young, single women, as they are perceived to be docile, cheap, and easy to dispose of (Lee, 1998; Ong, 1987; Salzinger, 2003; Wright, 2006). In contrast, the Naivasha flower farms primarily make use of migrant workers' networks in recruiting new labour. They do not officially make use of ethnicity in recruitment processes and in fact consciously attempt to evade accusations of "tribalism". And whereas the farms have a gendered division of labour, women do not work under notably worse conditions than men, nor do they only work in subordinate positions. The flower farms have received much scrutiny for the issue of sexual harassment and for the existence of a "sexual economy" in the settlements (Dolan et al., 2003; Jacobs, Brahic, & Olaiya, 2015; Lowthers, 2018). Yet women's economic position and their bargaining power in conjugal and other sexual relations only seems to improve rather than deteriorate through employment by the flower industry (see Friedemann-Sánchez (2009) on the Colombian flower industry).

The Naivasha flower industry thus shows developments that are very dissimilar to trends in other global industries, which is partly due to its agro-industrial nature and partly due to local histories and contingencies. On the other hand, certain developments characteristic of neoliberal industries can also be observed in this case. An example is the increasing role of private parties, and especially NGOs, in governance (Little, 2014). Chapter 5 has discussed the settlements where the majority of the migrant workers live, in the absence of a workers' compound on most farms. Even though the settlements largely owe their existence to the industry, the farms have generally denied responsibility for the provision of infrastructure there. Farm managers blame the government for a lack of investment in the settlements, while government officials hold the farms accountable for the provision of services to the scores of people they had attracted to the area. Moreover, both government officials and farm managers lament the residents for not taking interest in their living environment. However, a discussion of the problem of solid waste in the settlements indicated that residents are simply not always able to organize the necessary infrastructure, despite organizing themselves in self-help groups. The lack of investment has resulted in dense, seemingly disorderly settlements, which stand in stark contrast to the order within the farms. Yet, following Cooper (1983, p. 25), I have argued that the settlements form an integral part of labour arrangements within the industry, as they indicate limits to the responsibility that farms are willing to shoulder for their workers. The installation of infrastructure and the creation of some "order" in the settlements have thus largely been left to international NGOs and to industry funds channelled through certification schemes.

Another example of a neoliberal trend discernible in the flower industry is the "responsibilization" of both workers, who are increasingly held accountable for their work, and consumers, who are made responsible for labour conditions through the choice they now have to either buy conventional flowers or certified flowers (Dolan, 2007; Gibbon & Riisgaard, 2014). Thus, although the flower industry was not a conscious neoliberal project and rather provides an example of "accidental neoliberalism" instead (Bolt, 2016), certain dynamics usually associated to neoliberalism are also at play in this case.

Global linkages have shaped the definition of Naivasha's flower farm workers (Meagher et al., 2016). They generally are perceived of as poor urban dwellers in need of stable employment and development projects. The aspirations of African workers to own land and livestock, which would make them less dependent on wage labour, are usually not acknowledged in such "workerist" and "welfarist" approaches (Moyo et al., 2000). Chapter 6 discussed that the migrant workers in Naivasha usually aspire for a future as a landowner instead of as a tenant, and as a small-scale businessman, farmer, or livestock-keeper instead of as a wage labourer. However, most of them lack access to land in Naivasha because of both increasing land prices and political ideas on ethnic territories, rooted in colonial histories. These factors induce migrants to remain closely connected to their (supposed) region of origin and inhibit them from making Naivasha their permanent home. They plan to move "home" and make material and immaterial investments in such a "home", partly enabled by the salaries earned on the flower farms and the savings they have with SACCOs associated to the farms.

Most migrant workers "struggle" during their time in Naivasha to find money to invest in such a future or even to make it through another day without going hungry. Nevertheless, other migrant workers achieve their goals. Some even already start constructing a house or engage in small-scale farming while they continue to work in Naivasha. Thus, I have aimed to show in this book that although migrant workers' lives in Naivasha are heavily shaped by their work (or the lack thereof) on the agro-industrial flower farms, they are not defined by it.

References

Addison, L. (2014). Delegated despotism: Frontiers of agrarian labour on a South African border farm. *Journal of Agrarian Change, 14*(2), 286–304. https://doi.org/10.1111/joac.12062

Anker, R., & Anker, M. (2014). *Living wage for Kenya with focus on fresh flower farm area near Lake Naivasha*. Retrieved from http://www.fairtrade.net/fileadmin/user_upload/content/2009/resources/LivingWageReport_Kenya.pdf

Barlett, P. F. (1989). Industrial agriculture. In S. Plattner (Ed.), *Economic anthropology* (pp. 253–291). Stanford, CA: Stanford University Press.

Becht, R., Odada, E. O., & Higgins, S. (2005). *Lake Naivasha. Experience and lessons learned brief.* Kosatsu: International Lake Environment Committee Foundation. Retrieved from https://worldlakes.org/uploads/17_Lake_Naivasha_27February2006.pdf

Besky, S. (2014). *The Darjeeling distinction: Labor and justice on fair trade tea plantations in India*. Berkeley: University of California Press.

Bolt, M. (2013). Producing permanence: Employment, domesticity and the flexible future on a South African border farm. *Economy and Society, 42*(2), 197–225. https://doi.org/10.1080/03085147.2012.733606

Bolt, M. (2016). Accidental neoliberalism and the performance of management: Hierarchies in export agriculture on the Zimbabwean-South African border. *The Journal of Development Studies, 52*(4), 561–575. https://doi.org/10.1080/00220388.2015.1126252

Braverman, H. (1998). *Labor and monopoly capital: The degradation of work in the twentieth century* (25th Anniversary ed.). New York: Monthly Review Press.

Brickell, K., & Datta, A. (2011). Introduction: Translocal geographies. In K. Brickell & A. Datta (Eds.), *Translocal geographies: Space, places, connections* (pp. 3–22). Farnham: Ashgate.

Burawoy, M. (1979). *Manufacturing consent: Changes in the labor process under monopoly capitalism*. Chicago: University of Chicago Press.

Cooper, F. (1983). Introduction: Urban space, industrial time, and wage labor in Africa. In *Struggle for the city: Migrant labor, capital, and the state in urban Africa* (pp. 7–50). London: SAGE.

Dolan, C. S. (2007). Market affections: Moral encounters with Kenyan fairtrade flowers. *Ethnos, 72*(2), 239–261. https://doi.org/10.1080/00141840701396573

Dolan, C. S., Opondo, M., & Smith, S. (2003). *Gender, rights and participation in the Kenya cut flower industry* (NRI Report No. 2768). Chatham, UK: NRI.

Du Toit, A. (1993). The micro-politics of paternalism: The discourses of management and resistance on South African fruit and wine farms. *Journal of Southern African Studies, 19*(2), 314–336.

Endres, A. (2012, February 13). Blumenindustrie: Ausbeutung für den Valentinstag [Flower industry: Exploitation for Valentine's Day]. *Zeit Online*. Retrieved from http://www.zeit.de/wirtschaft/2012-02/blumen-ausbeutung-valentinstag

Fernández-Kelly, M. (1983). *For we are sold, I and my people: Women and industry in Mexico's frontier*. Albany: State University of New York Press.

Finnigan, L. (2016, February 12). The stinky truth about your beautiful Valentine's Day roses. *The Telegraph*. Retrieved from https://www.telegraph.co.uk/women/life/the-stinky-truth-about-your-beautiful-valentines-day-roses/.

Friedemann-Sánchez, G. (2009). *Assembling flowers and cultivating homes: Labor and gender in Colombia* (1st Paperback ed.). Lanham, MD: Lexington Books.

Gibbon, P., & Riisgaard, L. (2014). A new system of labour management in African large-scale agriculture? *Journal of Agrarian Change, 14*(1), 94–128. https://doi.org/10.1111/joac.12043

Greiner, C., & Sakdapolrak, P. (2013). Translocality: Concepts, applications and emerging research perspectives. *Geography Compass, 7*(5), 373–384. https://doi.org/10.1111/gec3.12048

Hall, R., Scoones, I., & Tsikata, D. (2017). Plantations, outgrowers and commercial farming in Africa: Agricultural commercialisation and implications for agrarian change. *The Journal of Peasant Studies, 44*(3), 515–537. https://doi.org/10.1080/03066150.2016.1263187

Hivos. (n.d.). Power of the fair trade flower. Retrieved January 24, 2014, from http://www.powerofthefairtradeflower.nl/

Jacobs, S., Brahic, B., & Olaiya, M. M. (2015). Sexual harassment in an East African agribusiness supply chain. *The Economic and Labour Relations Review, 26*(3), 393–410.

KHRC. (2012). *Wilting in bloom: The irony of women labour rights in the cut-flower sector in Kenya*. Nairobi: KHRC.

Lee, C. K. (1998). *Gender and the South China miracle: Two worlds of factory women*. Berkeley: University of California Press.

Little, P. D. (2014). *Economic and political reform in Africa: Anthropological perspectives*. Bloomington: Indiana University Press.

Lowthers, M. (2018). On institutionalized sexual economies: Employment sex, transactional sex, and sex work in Kenya's cut flower industry. *Signs: Journal of Women in Culture and Society, 43*(2), 449–472. https://doi.org/10.1086/693767

Meagher, K., Mann, L., & Bolt, M. (2016). Introduction: Global economic inclusion and African workers. *The Journal of Development Studies, 52*(4), 471–482. https://doi.org/10.1080/00220388.2015.1126256

Mintz, S. W. (1985). *Sweetness and power: The place of sugar in modern history*. New York: Viking.

Moyo, S., Rutherford, B., & Amanor-Wilks, D. (2000). Land reform & changing social relations for farm workers in Zimbabwe. *Review of African Political Economy, 27*(84), 181–202.

Ong, A. (1987). *Spirits of resistance and capitalist discipline: Factory women in Malaysia*. Albany: State University of New York Press.

Ortiz, S. (2002). Laboring in the factories and in the fields. *Annual Review of Anthropology, 31*(1), 395–417. https://doi.org/10.1146/annurev.anthro.31.031902.161108

Piot, C. (1999). *Remotely global: Village modernity in West Africa*. Chicago: The University of Chicago Press.

Rutherford, B. (2001). *Working on the margins: Black workers, white farmers in postcolonial Zimbabwe*. London: Zed Books.

Salzinger, L. (2003). *Genders in production: Making workers in Mexico's global factories*. Berkeley: University of California Press.

Seal, M. (2011). *Wildflower: The extraordinary life and mysterious murder of Joan Root* (Paperback ed.). London: Orion Books Ltd.

Thomas, R. J. (1985). *Citizenship, gender, and work: Social organization of industrial agriculture*. Berkeley: University of California Press.

Thompson, E. P. (1967). Time, work-discipline, and industrial capitalism. *Past & Present, 38*, 56–97.

Wright, M. W. (2006). *Disposable women and other myths of global capitalism*. New York: Routledge.

Glossary

Boda boda (pl. boda boda) Motorcycle taxi
Chama (pl. vyama) Private saving group
Chang'aa Illicit brew
Chief Government official in charge of a location, the smallest administrative unit in Kenya
Cold store Storage area with a controlled climate where flowers are kept before grading and transport
Fairtrade Most well-known standard within the Kenya flower industry
Fairtrade Premium A percentage of the price of Fairtrade-certified flowers to be used for projects assisting the flower farm workers
General worker Flower farm employee without a specific job description at the bottom of the farm hierarchy
Grading The task of preparing the cut flowers for shipment
Hoteli (pl. hoteli) Small restaurant serving local, affordable food
Kambi (pl. kambi) Workers' compound provided by a farm or ranch
Maquila Short for maquiladoras
Maquiladoras Assembly-line manufacturing plants located on the Mexican-US border
Matatu (pl. matatu) Minibus that functions as a public transport vehicle
Mzungu (pl. wazungu) White person
Nyumbani Home

G. Kuiper, *Agro-industrial Labour in Kenya*,
https://doi.org/10.1007/978-3-030-18046-1

Packhouse Building, containing cooled storage rooms and a grading hall, where the cut flowers are prepared for shipment
Scout Flower farm worker who monitors crop diseases and deficiencies
Shamba (pl. mashamba) Plot of land, used for cultivation
Shop steward On-farm representative of the union, elected by fellow workers
Sizing The task of measuring and piling flowers
Sprayer Flower farm worker who sprays the pesticides
Squatter Resident labourer on a ranch in the colonial period
Standard A document attached to a certification scheme governing labour-related and environmental practices within participating farms

Index[1]

[1] Note: Page numbers followed by 'n' refer to notes.

G. Kuiper, *Agro-industrial Labour in Kenya*,
https://doi.org/10.1007/978-3-030-18046-1

I

K

L

FSC
www.fsc.org
MIX
Papier | Fördert
gute Waldnutzung
FSC® C083411

Kolibri 360 GmbH
Ferdinand-Jühlke-Straße 7
99095 Erfurt, Deutschland
produktsicherheit@kolibri360.de